Damming the Reservation

NEW DIRECTIONS IN NATIVE AMERICAN STUDIES
Liza Black and Colin G. Calloway, General Editors

Damming the Reservation

Tribal Sovereignty and Activism at Fort Berthold

ANGELA K. PARKER

UNIVERSITY OF OKLAHOMA PRESS : NORMAN

Publication of this book is made possible in part through the generosity of Edith Kinney Gaylord.

Library of Congress Cataloging-in-Publication Data

Names: Parker, Angela Kay, 1976– author.
Title: Damming the reservation : tribal sovereignty and activism at Fort Berthold / Angela K. Parker.
Description: Norman : University of Oklahoma Press, 2024. | Series: New directions in Native American studies series ; vol. 23 | Includes bibliographical references and index. | Summary: "A historian who grew up on the Fort Berthold Indian Reservation in North Dakota tells how the Mandan, Hidatsa, and Arikara communities on the reservation fought and lost the battle against the inundation of a third of their land by federal construction of the Garrison Dam but, in the process, found ways to preserve and rebuild their culture, their shared history, their stories, their sense of place, and their sovereignty"—Provided by publisher.
Identifiers: LCCN 2024007584 | ISBN 978-0-8061-9461-5 (hardcover)
Subjects: LCSH: Indians of North America—Relocation—North Dakota. | Indians, Treatment of—North Dakota. | Indian land transfers—Missouri River Valley. | Missouri River Valley—Race relations. | Indians of North America—Government relations—1934– | Sovereignty. | Three Affiliated Tribes of the Fort Berthold Reservation, North Dakota—History. | Garrison Dam (N.D.)—Social aspects. | Fort Berthold Indian Reservation (N.D.)—Politics and government. | BISAC: HISTORY / Indigenous Peoples in the Americas | HISTORY / United States / 20th Century
Classification: LCC E78.N75 P375 2024 | DDC 978.4004/97—dc23/eng/20240501
LC record available at https://lccn.loc.gov/2024007584

Damming the Reservation: Tribal Sovereignty and Activism at Fort Berthold is Volume 23 in the New Directions in Native American Studies series.

The paper in this book meets the guidelines for permanence and durability of the Committee on Production Guidelines for Book Longevity of the Council on Library Resources, Inc. ∞

Copyright © 2024 the University of Oklahoma Press, Norman, Publishing Division of the University. Manufactured in the U.S.A.

All rights reserved. No part of this publication may be reproduced, stored in a retrieval system, or transmitted, in any form or by any means, electronic, mechanical, photocopying, recording, or otherwise—except as permitted under Section 107 or 108 of the United States Copyright Act—without the prior written permission of the University of Oklahoma Press. To request permission to reproduce selections from this book, write to Permissions, University of Oklahoma Press, 2800 Venture Drive, Norman OK 73069, or email rights.oupress@ou.edu.

For the coming generations of Mandan, Hidatsa, and Arikara leaders

Contents

Acknowledgments | ix

Introduction | 1

1. Sovereign Territoriality during the Reservation Era | 12
2. Reorganizations, 1934–1941 | 42
3. Indigenous Citizenship, 1940–1945 | 74
4. The Deluge, 1945–1952 | 106
5. Relocations, 1952–1960 | 141

Conclusion | 173

Epilogue | 180

Notes | 213

Bibliography | 239

Index | 255

Acknowledgments

This project spanned decades of my life, and in those years, I generated many debts. My largest gratitude is for my family who sustained, housed, funded, and encouraged me throughout the writing and revision of this project: my parents, Larry and Karol Parker; my aunts, Tillie Walker, Elizabeth Morsette, and Patricia Baker-Benally; my sisters, Myra Parker, Sara Parker, and Leslie Morsette—all of them put up with my smart mouth and crazy ways with love and tolerance. Thank you to my cousin/daughter Leah Ann Walker, who always brings me along for a wild ride and shows up for me without question. My kids—Tolaska Hunts Along, Katt LaSarte, and Xaxi Ogemahgeshig—gave me the joy and hope I needed to keep writing. A special thanks to my partner, Ty Ogemahgeshig, who unfailingly encourages, supports, and believes in me.

Another debt I will never repay goes to the oral historians and interviewees who agreed to share their insight, memories, and histories with me: Alameda Baker, Fred Baker, Gail Baker, Patricia Baker-Benally, Lyda Bearstail, Edwin Benson, Charles Cambridge, Bruce Davies, Mary Elk, Dreke Irwin, Rosemarie Mandan, Karol Parker, Reba Walker, and Tillie Walker. Too many of the interviewees from Fort Berthold are now gone, but I keep their phone numbers in my cell phone to trick myself into thinking that I can still call them up and pester them. Thank you for teaching me about the most important things in life.

My friends and colleagues from the University of Michigan–Ann Arbor have scattered across the globe, and their work and commitment continue to inspire and educate me. Thank you, Rabia Belt, Heather Brink, , Franklin Dollar, Kelly Fayard, Federico Helfgott, Daniel Hershenzon, Paul D. Irwin, Tandi Moyo, Regev Nathansohn, Patrick Parker, Nicol Partida, Veronica Pasfield, Melynda Price, Isa Quintana, Esteban Rozo, Kiri Sailiata, Guillermo Salas, Keisha Simmons, Alice Weinreb, Mira Yusef, and Kathy Zarur. Thank you also to my academic mentors Fernando Coronil, Phil Deloria, Greg Dowd, Stuart

Kirsch, Tiya Miles, Michele Mitchell, and Maria Montoya. I was so lucky to be in your orbits and benefit from your brilliance if only for a few years.

Several people sustained me when I was a new mother during my first faculty position: thank you, Kate Beane, Hinhan Cetanhotanka, the late and brilliant Makoquah Jones, Vera Palmer, Hilary Abe and Aza Erdrich, and Rena Mosteirin and Jed Dobson. Daniel Cobb and John Troutman read an earlier version of this manuscript during these years and gave generous and kind feedback to a very junior scholar: thank you for your advice on this project and for the histories you write. Mishuana Goeman deserves my biggest thanks, because she taught and supported me to expect better for myself. Mishuana, you kept me moving forward, and this project would never have moved to publication without you.

When I stepped away from academia, friends and colleagues helped me regroup and heal by reminding me of all the beauty and love in Native communities. Much love to Cara Wallace and Charles Peele, Laurie Williams, Dena Starr, Victoria Lucyk, and Danica Miller.

I have supportive, thoughtful, committed colleagues at the University of Denver: thank you, Ramona Beltran, Elizabeth Campbell, Sophia Cisneros, Kate Crowe, Viki Eagle, Liz Escobedo, Carol Helstosky, Rafael Ioris, Kimberly Jones, the late and much missed Jodie Kreider, Stevie Lee, Dan Melleno, Chris Nelson, Trish Patel, Bill Philpot, Tom Romero, Susan Schulten, Jonathan Sciarcon, Hillary Smith, and Ingrid Tague. Friends like Anna Tsouhlarakis and Daron Carreiro, and Kelly Fayard and Rob Quintana have brightened my family's life in Colorado with debate, laughter, and encouragement.

I am never so grateful as I am toward people who daily do excellent work in jobs I cannot do. Thank you to Alessandra Tamulevich, acquisitions editor at the University of Oklahoma Press—she made moving this project toward publication seem eminently possible. Another debt of gratitude belongs to Steven Baker, the managing editor at OU Press, who provided calm and thoughtful direction to a first-time author. Amy Hernandez in the marketing department and my copyeditor, Kelly Parker, were both thankfully patient and rigorous in their work. I adore the maps produced by Erin Greb, and deeply appreciate the indexing accomplished by another scholar of dams, Varsha Venkatasubramanian. My sincere gratitude as well to the two anonymous reviewers who provided such thoughtful and necessary comments.

This project benefited from the expertise and professionalism of the archivists at the National Archives and Records Administration (NARA) in Kansas City, the National Anthropological Archives, the University of Chicago Archives, and the North Dakota State Historical Society (NDSHS) Archives. I want to particularly recognize Stephen Spence and Wade Popp at the Kansas City NARA and Sarah Walker and Lori Nohner at NDSHS for their speedy and good-humored assistance in tracking down both documents and images for this book.

Last and most, maacigidaac to my home community, the Fort Berthold Indian Reservation.

Introduction

The Fort Berthold Indian Reservation holds many origin stories. Located near the geographic center of North America, Fort Berthold sits in the northwest corner of North Dakota. Under an inescapable and all-seeing sky, the flatness of the Great Plains begins to rumple into rolling hills the closer you get to the Missouri River, forming badlands or what people call "the breaks," where prairie lands crumble into the erosive force of the river. Fort Berthold contains not only prairie but badlands and of course the Missouri River itself.

The three tribes at Fort Berthold—Mandan, Hidatsa, and Arikara—possess different origin stories, but even within the same tribe conflicting narratives exist. Hidatsa stories reflect the various histories of three allied bands; in one story, people came from the sky; in another, they came from under the ground or from beneath a large lake to the east and lived on the plains until they found and settled in the Missouri River valley. Mandan origin stories identify the Missouri River as the remnant of an original water around which First Creator and the first human, Lone Man, created land, plants, and animals. Yet the Mandans also recognize a history of migration from near the Gulf of Mexico during which their people moved up the Mississippi and the Missouri Rivers as part of a religious imperative. Arikara origin stories also speak of moving from under the earth to its surface, with the help of a deity called Corn Mother. Their journey out of the earth and through or over physical obstacles, such as a large body of water, a large cliff, and a forest, also explains the creation of animal life. All these stories hint at a diverse and complex history of migration and convergence—possibly one we will never completely unravel. But, in all these origin stories, Awáati, the Missouri River, is a landmark, a center, a source of life.

The story in this book explains what happened to the Three Tribes at Fort Berthold when that river swelled and rose behind the Garrison Dam and inundated the heart of the reservation landscape. Built between 1947 and 1953, this massive earth-filled dam at the edge of Fort Berthold flooded every major settled community on the reservation and more than 150,000 acres of prime grazing and agricultural land. Six other reservations along the Upper Missouri eventually also became the unwilling hosts of massive, main-stem dams, but none lost as much land or as many communities as Fort Berthold. The federal government forced nearly 90 percent of Fort Berthold residents to relocate to escape the rising waters as they lost the river valley lands that had been their tribal home for a millennium or more. "The people fought it like beavers," tribal member Anna Dawson told anthropologist Robert Merrill in 1950, as community members sought to stave off the actual physical flooding. She explained that the US government had broken faith with the tribe: "At Fort Laramie there had been a big council—a solemn agreement. Then came the dam."[1]

Anna Dawson referenced the Fort Laramie Treaty of 1851, nearly one hundred years after it had taken place, because the supposed inviolability of the treaty terms underscored the injustice of the eminent domain taking and flooding of a beautiful and beloved homeland. At Fort Laramie, Mandan, Hidatsa, and Arikara leaders, along with five other indigenous groups, had signed a treaty with the US government recognizing their claims to traditional tribal territories. As the first major treaty between the Three Tribes and the United States, the Fort Laramie Treaty serves as a foundation for every subsequent assertion of tribal sovereignty. Dawson and other tribal members drew upon the nascent rhetoric of tribal sovereignty enshrined by the treaty to assert and affirm self-determination.

George Gillette, the tribal chairman strong-armed by the US government into signing away the tribes' beloved river valley, told newspaper reporters in 1949, "The truth is, as everyone knows, our Treaty of Fort Laramie, made in 1851, and our tribal constitution are being torn into shreds by this contract."[2] Why did Gillette reference the tribal constitution? Tribal leaders debated and wrote the tribal constitution during the Indian reorganization era—covered in chapter 2 of this book—and their work asserted and bolstered tribal self-determination. Such references to the 1851 Fort Laramie Treaty and the tribal constitution signal what we now term tribal sovereignty at Fort Berthold.

Anna Dawson and George Gillette alluded to what tribal members have always known, and what historians of Native America track: that modern tribal sovereignty developed in reservation spaces just as much as it developed in white judges' words written in Supreme Court decisions. This sovereignty was always, irrevocably, rooted in cherished landscapes. It was inextricable from the stories and bones of our beloved relatives born on and buried in our lands. Those stories and histories allowed Native communities to theorize, narrate, and mark place, space, and territory. From these indigenous territories and their personal and collective histories, tribal sovereignty and US sovereignty grow. And we cannot fully understand Native or US sovereignty unless we confront how indigenous land claims and identities have been recognized or silenced to promote or destroy a national identity.

Tribal sovereignty survived, revitalized in the twentieth century because tribal communities formulated and practiced our own concepts of citizenship and territorial self-determination. Community practices of tribal citizenship, political autonomy, and activism undergird the formation of modern conceptions of tribal sovereignty. We battled for our lands both to preserve our cultures and communities and to pursue a viable future. Fort Berthold's experiences with the Garrison Dam illustrate the paramount importance of land. Territory—land and water—does not only concern life in the past or the present. Land constitutes continuity for the *future*. And the endangerment of land through takings or environmental degradation not only endangers the past and memory but also narrows the pathway to a viable future. The loss of land within the Missouri River valley—tied to tribal members' conceptualizations and narratives of their lived environment—changed political and community identity.

While Fort Berthold is unique, the challenges it faced were not. The federal government and state entities attempted to gut tribal sovereignty in many Indian communities across the United States during the twentieth century. Communities used whatever nooks and crannies they could find in the structures of a dominating sovereignty to assert their own—their own right to self-rule, to manage and defend their territories, to control their resources, or to define their identities. The history told in these pages is an origin story about tribal sovereignty.

Sovereignty

Religious wars were tearing Europe apart when French philosopher Jean Bodin and English philosopher Thomas Hobbes elaborated their notions of sovereignty to conceptualize appropriate, legitimate authority within a territory. The search for a legitimate authority to counter the disorder of these thinkers' political, religious, and social contexts shaped their theorization of sovereignty as a legitimizing logic for power, even if their notions of sovereignty never truly existed in their chaotic context. Similarly, contemporary governments invoke sovereignty to explain international rights of the nation-state—for example the right to self-governance, or the right to enter agreements with other nations (treaties). But governments invoke and assert such rights in reaction to a disorderly reality. Michel Foucault considered European expansion into the Americas one of the events that guided the development the modern nation-state and its apparatuses of power. Just as the sovereignty of American nation-states evolved in dialogue with European sovereignties (and vice versa), South and North American national sovereignties also evolved in dialogue with indigenous sovereignties. The continued presence of indigenous peoples required—and *continues* to require—these nations to contend with indigenous authority, land claims, populations, citizens, and narratives of the past, present, and hopes for the future.[3]

Many indigenous scholars question whether Native North America should adopt the historical and structural weight of sovereignty as a supporting concept of indigenous authority given its imbrications with colonial and imperial structures—mostly because settler colonial sovereignty is structurally oppositional to indigenous land rights. Sometimes I am one of them. But I believe we must continue to engage conceptually because in the United States, Native communities use and will continue to use the principles of tribal sovereignty as developed in federal Indian law to fight for our cultural, territorial, and social rights.[4]

Several concepts recur as part of a constellation of ideas that, together, constitute sovereign power, and I track these elements in my history of Fort Berthold. First, legitimacy as linked to authority. Sovereignty requires a populace to agree that the person or structure exerting power holds a legitimate authority. In the trajectory of John Locke and as interpreted by Foucault, effective management of a populace and a territory buttresses legitimate authority, while sovereign mismanagement can result in revolution. The next two crucial concepts in the constellation that comprises modern understandings of sovereign power are territory/land and populace/citizenry. Sovereign authority is meaningless without a citizenry and, similarly, requires a territorial base within which to act. When postcolonial states asserted political and economic rights in the twentieth century, international organizations increasingly elaborated the rights of a sovereign power to exert control over its own territorial boundaries, holdings, and natural resources. And as the historiography of twentieth century US immigration illustrates, the definition and practice of citizenship—the liberal embodiment of "the people" subject to sovereign authority—remains one of the most important powers of a sovereign authority.[5]

Finally, the temporal narration of legitimate power forms a crucial aspect of sovereignty's conceptual constellation. Sovereignty requires an origin story. It tells us what constitutes legitimate authority, the best way to govern a population, and how to define and delineate between who and what lands are subject to sovereign authority. But it also narrates legitimate authority into the past. Postcolonial theorists link history and other academic disciplines to the narrative legitimization of the nation-state, and temporal narration is one of the key strategies of the structures that support a sovereign authority. These power structures use narratives of the past—histories—as powerful tools to bolster notions of legitimate authority in the present.[6]

Structures of power also perform this narrative work to extend sovereign authority into the future. The authorities claiming sovereignty may use the past to legitimize authority, but they also use it to extend a constituted sovereignty indefinitely into the future. This temporal narration is important for tribal sovereignty. Many times, tribal communities sought self-determination, a recognition of their own legitimate authority within their territorial boundaries, because they saw it as the only way to continue to exist as a community. Territory—land, water, or other natural resources—allows a polity to continue to exist not only in the present but in the future. When territory is jeopardized, the physical jeopardy endangers a polity or community's viable future.[7]

Each tribal community, as it sought to challenge the authority of the US nation-state—or claimed lands, or practiced its own version of citizenship or identity, or remembered and told its own histories and hopes for the future—built tribal sovereignty. Structures such as the nation-state or the machinations of capital define sovereignty, but Native communities also generate, practice, and contest it. When land claims entered the US court system, or when tribal leaders resisted territorial annexation, assimilation, or the loss of community authority to practice self-determination, they forced the structures of the US nation-state to explain or defend themselves, to silence their critics, to admit wrong, or to admit defeat. This book tells one such story of creative defiance, to illustrate that the earthy foundations of modern tribal sovereignty rest in those beloved landscapes—territories, places, and spaces narrated by our origin stories, populated by our peoples, and transformed through our physical and mental work.

Collecting and Telling Histories

Historians of twentieth-century Native America possess an embarrassment of riches in terms of sources. The legendary invasiveness of the Bureau of Indian

Affairs during the early and mid-twentieth century produced endless documentation of landholdings, finances, genealogies, and personal lives of individual Indian people. Tribal members can find out how many cows and chickens their great-grandparents owned, if they know where to look. Additionally, graduate advisors dispatched legions of anthropologists, musicologists, and folklorists to cut their academic teeth by researching reservation communities. Their monographs and field notes remain valuable sources for the historian of twentieth-century Native America. Finally, the temporal proximity of the period allows historians to talk to the people who lived through the era, providing us a wealth of extant oral histories and the potential to collect one's own.

This book draws from Bureau of Indian Affairs documents in the National Archives, field notes and ephemera collected and produced by students of anthropologist Sol Tax at the University of Chicago, and oral history interviews other researchers and I conducted with Mandan, Hidatsa, and Arikara elders. The voluminous sources from the federal archives are a godsend, but the assumptions and prejudices of BIA employees color them all, and exclusive use of federal archives can produce a narrative shaped by the bureaucracy. This book tells a community story, not one about Indian agents, mid-level managers, or federal commissioners. It reflects a fascination with the tribal context—stemming from the belief that we must understand even the most private, domestic spaces and choices to reveal the larger story of the development of tribal sovereignty and the elaboration of a tribal identity.[8]

Anthropological field notes revealed community dynamics and the roles individuals played in tribal politics, and the personal details recorded brought midcentury Fort Berthold vibrantly alive. But such sources also brought challenges. Field notes, as records of an anthropologist's experience, are not meant for publication, and at times contain what amounts to sixty-year-old gossip about community members. As a member of the tribe I study, I struggled over whether to include important but sensitive information about individual tribal members from the time, knowing that the cost might be borne by current community members who hold them dear.

The oral history sources in this book come from those I collected for this or other projects, and those conducted and archived by other researchers. National Park Service employee Eric Wolf collected a valuable cache of nearly thirty oral history interviews in the 1990s. The bulk of my oral history sources come from those he gathered. Aside from two interviews conducted for regional television broadcasts and Wolf's, I gathered the remaining oral history interviews.

Collection and analysis of oral histories generates ethical and methodological issues. Gathering other people's stories forces researchers to confront questions of memory, compensation, and the ownership of narrative. Serious ethical dangers result from refusing to confront these questions. Facile assertions regarding the power of narrative to create bonds of understanding and empathy, or the failure to examine the social, political, and economic power structures affecting any oral history research, could easily allow a researcher to slide into "the misuse of sentiment as a research tool."[9]

Yet oral histories represent a crucial tool for the historian of twentieth-century Native America, because they allow for the inclusion of Native voices in the historical narrative, and because they transmit cultural values. Most importantly for this project, they document indigenous historical analysis.[10] My oral history practice rejects the idea that "the distant knower . . . has perspective and, by virtue of less or different stakes in the interpretation, the possibility of objectivity."[11] I attempted to follow Fort Berthold community best practices in the selection of narrators. Community standards regarding who holds expertise and authority to give information on tribal history may not be readily apparent even to members of younger generations of tribal members.[12] For academic work based in small, local communities in which community members know intimate family and personal histories, researchers approach the "community experts"— the people whom other community members consider as holding important cultural or historical expertise—rather than just anyone who will talk to them.

I also tried to respect and become familiar with local standards of asking and compensating for information and knowledge shared.[13] As a tribal member entering her own community and engaging with respected community elders, I attempted to understand what constituted not just *adequate* compensation, but culturally appropriate compensation. In addition to a monetary gift, I also brought either a blanket (Pendleton or star quilt) or food to the interviews— some combination of corn soup, bread, fruit, a dessert, and tea or coffee. I always left the interviews feeling that the small things I gave to interviewees in a gesture of reciprocity did not adequately compensate them for the time they spent sharing their insight and analysis.

In a methodological departure from standard academic oral history practice, I consider all interviewees fellow historians. I believe they are experts in their personal history and tribal history; thus, I accord them the same intellectual respect as I would any established historian. During interview collection, I shared interview questions before the interview and asked respondents specific questions about their analysis or interpretation of historical events. Antonio Gramsci theorized organic intellectuals as scholars who not only develop strong roots in their community but also cultivate involvement in local issues and controversies experienced and debated within the community. Additionally, these intellectuals use their analysis of societal structures to influence other community members to develop a consciousness of their own identities that allow for similar structural critiques and analysis. I regard the community elders and experts represented in this book as organic intellectuals—and specifically, as organic historians.[14]

During analysis, I treated each interview as a separate historical analysis, rather than as a data point. I chose not to position myself as a researcher who could discern subtext by analyzing word patterns and pauses, or by guessing at what was left unsaid. My work did not involve, for example, listening to the moral language and self-evaluative statements of the narrators, identifying the "meta-statements" in which the narrators comment about their own thoughts or something they just said, or attempting to parse and analyze the internal logic of the oral history narrative.[15] Instead, I subjected each interview to the same mixture of credence and critical analysis that my training expects me to apply to the work of an academic historian. I avoided being gullible but accorded respect to the experience and analytical skills of the organic historians who took the time to teach me. I discussed the intellectual and practical aims of my project and interview questions with them. And most importantly, I trusted their expertise to express themselves in the manner they intended.[16]

While academic knowledge production creates and maintains power structures that historically colonized and dominated indigenous communities, I do not retreat to *either* a historical relativism *or* an indigenous-based fundamentalism. This project's formulation of oral history interviewees as organic historians, rather than as informants, means that it treats the narratives and information shared by historians both academic and organic with an intellectual respect that includes a deep engagement, including critique.[17]

Organization of This Book

A 1907 map created by Mandan tribal member Sitting Rabbit provides the narrative frame for the first chapter, "Sovereign Territoriality during the Reservation Era," and helps us explore the construction of the Fort Berthold Indian Reservation as a place, space, and territory. The Sitting Rabbit map provides a visual doorway to analyze how the Three Affiliated Tribes negotiated place, space, and territory with neighboring Plains tribes and the federal government. The physical environment and history of the Mandans, Hidatsas, and Arikaras before 1934 show a growing territoriality as a land-greedy federal government forced the Three Tribes to defend their remaining territories—a concept this project calls "sovereign territoriality."

Chapter 2, "Reorganizations," covers the years from the Indian Reorganization Act (IRA) to US entry into World War II and documents how New Deal programs and legislation contributed to the reorganization of legitimate authority at Fort Berthold. Shifts in political authority, tribal territories, and the definition of tribal membership constituted important changes as the tribal council reconstituted sovereign power. Tribal leadership rearranged the boundaries and roles of tribal territoriality and membership to protect tribal lands. This new politicization led tribal members to claim and exercise an indigenous citizenship rooted in tribal culture, committed to claiming the rights of US citizenship, and protective of treaty and land rights. This indigenous citizenship strategically mobilized US citizenship and tribal self-rule to realize a viable community future. Chapter 2 argues that the dynamics of intratribal factions, and the exercise and contestation of tribal authority, contributed to the development of modern conceptions of tribal sovereignty.

The third chapter, "Indigenous Citizenship," considers the meaning of military service, US and tribal citizenship, and patriotism during World War II. Oral histories describing community gatherings, flag songs, and honor songs lead to an interrogation of how this labor constructs place. On Fort Berthold during the Second World War, tribal members mobilized jingoistic state narratives of military service, production, and consumption; but community *practice* maintained a tribally centric, nonstate version. These practices developed and maintained a uniquely indigenous patriotism and citizenship.

"The Deluge," chapter 4, documents the narratives used by tribal members as they fought the Garrison Dam. As two sovereignties—that of the United States and that of the Three Affiliated Tribes—clashed over the notion of the public good, tribal members mobilized concepts from their arsenals of indigenous citizenship and defense of tribal territories. Community members asserted individual and community rights based on a history of treaties and a recently developed government-to-government relationship institutionalized by the Indian Reorganization Act to formulate an indigenous citizenship praxis to protect the tribal land base.

Chapter 5, "Relocations," covers the years 1950–1960 and draws upon oral histories, field notes produced by anthropologists, and government photographs to discuss how community members dealt with intense emotional, political, economic, and spatial turmoil. The turmoil allowed the BIA to usurp vast authority over land management, and the tribal authority structure dwindled due to infighting over financial control of the federal compensation for the inundated tribal lands. Tribal members said goodbye to their river valley, and their move to the prairie became defined by what was lost. They also, however, sought to build a viable future for their families and the community. Tribal members mobilized the tools they developed through the early twentieth century—sovereign territoriality, indigenous citizenship, and the struggle to exert legitimate political authority both inside and outside the community—both to fight the Garrison Dam and to rebuild after the federal government took our lands.

The conclusion to this book provides a brief overview of political and economic developments at Fort Berthold after the flooding of our river valley, and connects them to a broader history of the dialogic construction of nation-state sovereignties. Finally, the epilogue tracks the life and work of Tillie Walker, an activist from Fort Berthold whose life shows us how tribal members across the United States saw the need to bolster the intellectual arsenal of tribal rights to protect their territories and communities. Walker and other Native activists began to build coalitions across tribal and racial lines locally and nationally, and their individual and collective work indicates that the dialogic nature of repression and resistance undermines the simple story of decline so often used to frame indigenous histories.

Endings

This book's narrative could easily devolve into one of loss and tragedy as it tracked the vast changes Fort Berthold traversed in the mid-twentieth century. For too long, these declension narratives structured histories of Native America, perhaps because indigenous peoples weathered the irrevocable and violent impact of non-Native value systems and structures of power since colonization. For example, anthropologist Gilbert Wilson interpreted the Hidatsa agriculturalist Maaxiiriwiash (Buffalo Bird Woman) in a widely reproduced and disseminated summary of change and loss for the Hidatsas:

> I am an old woman now. The buffalos and black-tail deer are gone, and our Indian ways are almost gone. Sometimes I find it hard to believe that

I ever lived them.... We no longer live in an earth lodge, but in a house with chimneys; and my son's wife cooks by a stove. But for me, I cannot forget our old ways. Often in summer I rise at daybreak and steal out to the cornfields; and as I hoe the corn I sing to it, as we did when I was young. No one cares for our corn songs now.

Sometimes at evening I sit, looking out on the big Missouri. The sun sets, and dusk steals over the water. In the shadows I seem again to see our Indian village, with smoke curling upward from the earth lodges; and in the river's roar I hear the yells of the warriors, the laughter of little children as of old. It is but an old woman's dream. Again I see but shadows and hear only the roar of the river; and tears come into my eyes. Our Indian life, I know, is gone forever.[18]

Maaxiiriwiash and her communities experienced much loss, but there is a reason her story of endings is so widely reproduced, whereas her stories of origins or of agricultural practice—literally creating and tending life in a beloved landscape—do not often appear in anthologies of Native oral tradition, or on websites. The stories of origins and persistence, of course, are more complicated, less easily digestible by non-Hidatsas—and require much more time "sitting" with them—than the evocative story of loss Wilson translated. The "loss" story of Native America, the declension narrative, is also a powerful trope used to structure the story of American exceptionalism—a story soaked in imperialist nostalgia, one that explains why Indians are "gone" and white people are "here" through a shallow and performative regret.[19]

And while the history on the following pages contains loss, tragedy, and sorrow—a reflection of the experience of Fort Berthold tribal members—it is also an origin story. It tells a part of the story of tribal sovereignty in the twentieth century, by examining what happens to an indigenous community and its expression of self-determination when its land base is gutted.

Chapter 1

Sovereign Territoriality during the Reservation Era

In 1907 a Mandan named Sitting Rabbit—also called Little Owl, as many adult men at Fort Berthold carried several names based on their life accomplishments—drew a unique map of the Missouri River. His map covers twenty-three feet of canvas and represents the Missouri River from the North Dakota–South Dakota boundary line to the Montana border. Because that portion of the Missouri twists and turns in its course so much it could not fit on a linear stretch of cloth, Sitting Rabbit drew and narrated the Missouri in pieces.[1]

The then-forty-three-year-old Sitting Rabbit had grown up in Like-a-Fishhook Village, born in 1864 to a Mandan community still rebuilding from the devastation of the 1837 smallpox epidemic in which Mandan communities totaling more than three thousand residents perished to fewer than two hundred people. Alongside other men of his generation, he protected the village from relentless Lakota violence, sundanced to pray for his family and community, and rode horseback hundreds of miles across the plains eating cornballs and pemmican his aunties or sisters made to hunt eagles, bison, and elk. Sitting Rabbit likely spoke not only Mandan, but also Hidatsa and some Arikara, and grew up hearing the multiple creation stories of both his tribe and those that lived with him in Like-a-Fishhook—Nuxxbaaga, or Our People, in the Hidatsa language; Nueti in the Mandan; or Sahnish in Arikara. He knew the sweet smell of cooling prairie grass after it baked in the sun all day, and the biting cold of the January winds during a blue and pink sunrise over gentle, snowy hills. This man knew the Missouri River, its valleys, and the lands surrounding it as a *place*.[2]

"Place" refers to the lived understandings humans create within and attached to the landscapes they inhabit. Per Keith Basso and Edward Casey, place as a theoretical tool connects our consciousness, our bodies, and the

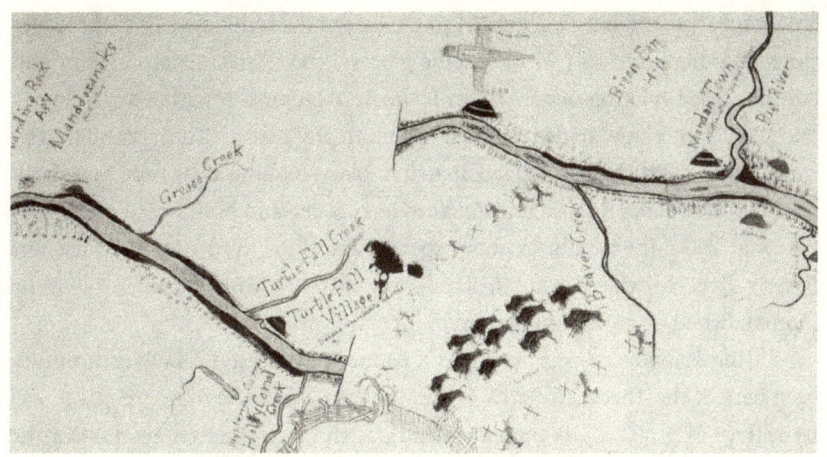

Figure 1.1. Sitting Rabbit Map—detail of Turtle Fall Creek. North Dakota State Historical Society.

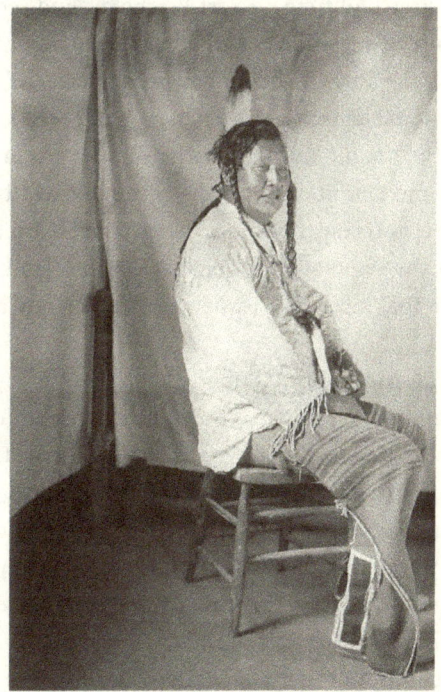

Figure 1.2. Portrait of Sitting Rabbit, ca. 1910. North Dakota State Historical Society.

landscapes we inhabit. It allows us to consider how individual or community story and memory—as tied to specific *places*—create and sustain history and culture. Place-making occurs in an intimate relationship with a landscape—and I use "landscape" to denote the nonhuman physical environment altered by human labor. Sitting Rabbit participated in place-making as he rode horseback through Mandan, Hidatsa, and Arikara territories, and both heard and retold personal and cultural stories about specific locations in or near the Missouri River valley. He helped create the landscape of the Three Affiliated Tribes as he hunted, fished, rode, or built homes in it.[3]

Sitting Rabbit's map provides us a frame to understand how community members of the Three Affiliated Tribes thought about the Missouri River and its valleys as a place. His map also leads us through their co-creation of the vibrant communities on the Fort Berthold Indian Reservation, in the last years of what historians of Native America call the reservation era—the decades after the implementation of the last major treaties that recognized reserved land status for tribal communities in the 1870s, but before the legislative changes in the federal-tribal relationship embedded in the Indian Reorganization Act of 1934. During this stretch of time on Fort Berthold—and every other reservation across the country, regardless of whether the communities were on historic tribal land like the Three Tribes or had been relocated from their original homes—the heavy hand of an intrusive federal bureaucratic apparatus forced tribes to redefine their communities' relationships to the landscape. Notions of place, the ideas and definitions humans fasten to their lived environment, shifted as the federal government labored to curtail tribal autonomy.[4] To track this shift shows us the symbiotic relationship between land, community, and self—a relationship that must adjust when a people's landscape transforms or degrades.

This chapter considers Sitting Rabbit's map as an entry point to understanding how community place-making evolved into an elaborated sovereign territoriality before and during the reservation era. The negotiation of treaties and need to mitigate federal land takings challenged tribes' control and use of their landscapes and required tribal leaders and members to think differently about their landscape. "Territoriality"—a group-produced definition of space regardless of whether that social group is federal, regional, or tribal—preexisted Euro-American presence on the plains due to intertribal disagreements over hunting rights and landownership. But it sharpened into a sovereign territoriality when the United States exerted military, economic, and juridical control. Indian-federal relations, and the specific history of land cessions forced on the Three Affiliated Tribes by the federal government, turned the land from a place into a territory for Mandan, Hidatsa, and Arikara tribal members. Sitting Rabbit's map reflects and serves as a guide for this evolution.

Using Sitting Rabbit's map as a touchstone, this chapter marks and identifies the evolution of sovereign territoriality at Fort Berthold and clarifies the essential connection between land, identity, and self-determination, or what would later be identified as sovereignty. Individual tribal members worked to build society and culture as they built homes, bore and raised children, cared for and buried elders, and circulated ideas about their collective past and potential collective future.

Growing Place

Turtle Fall Creek sits near the end of the map's very first segment, which details the stretch of river from the boundary between North and South Dakota to a bit past what is today called the Little Beaver Creek. Sitting Rabbit used many of his visual conventions in this section, starting with the pictograph of a Native man, Water Chief. A pictograph of an earth lodge labeled "Mandan Town" follows, then "Wood-dividing creek," and another pictograph of "High Eagle." In quick succession the Standing Rock Agency, identified both in English and Hidatsa, leads to an outcropping, then "Grease Creek." A creek flowing into the Missouri from the west ends this segment of the map, labeled by the mapmakers as "Náakaka aruwiríhkita arure:š," which can be translated from Hidatsa as "the turtle's going into the water" or "where the turtle went into the water." The person who wrote the English labels, Congregationalist minister Charles Hall, labeled it "Turtle Fall Creek."

Turtle Fall Creek. The word used for turtle in the Hidatsa—*náakaka*—means snapping turtle, and the creek commemorates the place where one of the four turtles Lone Man made, as he and First Creator created and shaped the lands, flora, and fauna west and east of the Missouri River, slipped away from him, into the river, and continues to support the dry land to prevent it from sinking. For both the Mandans and Hidatsas, the Missouri River flows through the center of their origin and creation stories, a remnant of the waters before humans, plants, or animals existed. Turtle Fall Creek both represents a snapping turtle slipping back into the waters of creation and reminds us of the creation story, of that fourth turtle who still supports the dry land for human habitation.[5]

In a landlocked state like North Dakota, it can be easy to forget that landscape includes not just *awa* (land in Hidatsa), but also *miri* (water, also in Hidatsa). Turtle Fall Creek and its story of the fourth turtle reminds us of the inextricability of land and water in creating place. Creation stories like this resulted from long and deep imaginings and retellings and illustrate the most profound ideas about the landscape and waterscape in which tribal members lived.[6] The map itself centers on Awáati, the Missouri River, and tribal narratives use Awáati and its tributaries as reference points for key stories embedded in the landscape. Sitting Rabbit's inclusion of Turtle Fall Creek reminds us how the land and the river—together—laid the foundation for culture, place, and history for the Fort Berthold community. Tribal communities constructed place, history, culture, and memory using both awa and Awáati as the concrete elements of the landscape that signified the remembered.[7]

Geology is another story we tell about the landscape. Geological explanations tell how waves of huge glaciers and the rise of the Rocky Mountain chain shaped the land, producing differing effects on the east and west sides of the Missouri. East of the river lie rolling hills formed by glacial drift left behind on what had previously been a flat plain, largely unmarked by erosion. The lakes dotting Awáati's eastern side, eventually proliferating into the woodlands of northern Minnesota, contrast with drainage patterns on the western side. Erosion and drainage shaped Awáati's western side, where the rise of the Rockies tilted an old seafloor, and mountain drainage carved badlands that reveal the banded, sedimentary rock underneath the grasslands of the plains.[8]

Although the dry, eroded badlands surrounding the streams and rivers that feed into the Missouri look stark, they usually border valleys containing greater plant and animal diversity fed by proximity to water and the nutrient-rich floodplain. Heavy timber growth populates the valley floors—willows, cottonwoods, cedars, elms, boxelders—as well as diverse animal, bird, and riverine life. The surrounding top lands, on the other hand, gain their sustaining water not from the rivers and streams but from rainfall. Prairie plants such as grasses, sage, and small brush evolved complex root networks, or sod, to capitalize on moisture from the rainfall that the Rocky Mountain rain shadow minimized. These resilient prairie plants allowed large grazers—bison, elk, and deer—to develop migration patterns that stretched from northern Canada to the southern United States.[9]

The Great Plains contains three grassland biomes: tallgrass, mixed grass, and shortgrass. Polar and gulf fronts shape biome boundaries, and the long durée trends of these fronts control temperature, rainfall, and the length of seasons. Most of present-day North Dakota falls within the mixed grass biome, populated both by tallgrass species that spread in the area after the retreat of melting glaciers during the Pleistocene Era and by shortgrass species that came from the high plains of the desert southwest at the tail end of the Pleistocene.[10] When you walk through these grasses, the short grass species crunch underfoot while you avoid short cacti and huge anthills, and the long grass species tickle your legs and the tips of your fingers.

The known archeological record—archeology representing another story we tell to imagine space and place—reveals that the presence of large grazers spurred human habitation of the Great Plains during and after the retreat of the last massive glacier. Ancient indigenous communities feasted on and processed the nomadic herds as the foundation of their food sources. Some groups maintained a nomadic lifestyle, while others lived in villages, pueblos, or larger cities and developed farming techniques that allowed the three sisters of Native American agriculture—corn, beans, and squash—to flourish and provide sustenance in arid environments with a wide range of growing seasons. The short growing season of the northern plains required the Mandans and Hidatsas to develop corn, bean, squash, and sunflower species that matured in sixty to seventy days.[11]

Large grazers such as bison drew human communities into the prairie landscape, but the river allowed us to live in this semiarid landscape receiving only fifteen to seventeen inches of rain per year. Awáati allowed the Plains Village cultures—or the "proto" Mandans, Hidatsas, Arikaras, Pawnees, and Wichitas—to flourish agriculturally between 1000 to 1500 CE in an extreme environment. Bitingly cold winters in which minus-ten degrees Fahrenheit with a windchill of minus-thirty can last for weeks at a time, and hot, dry summers in which the temperature ranges between eighty and a hundred degrees create enough of an agricultural challenge even without considering the sixty- to seventy-day growing season.[12]

From its headwaters near the present-day town of Three Forks in the Rocky Mountains of southwestern Montana, Awáati flows east through Montana before turning south in North Dakota. From its turn south, the river runs through South Dakota, Nebraska, Iowa, and Kansas before merging with the Mississippi near St. Louis, Missouri. At the end of this 2,341-mile sinuous journey, the light tan color caused by high silt content from the Upper Missouri states makes Awáati's union with the darker waters of the Mississippi visible from the air, before that silt then pushes and pulls even more soil from the riverbanks of its journey all the way down to the Gulf of Mexico.[13] More than twenty-eight Native tribes used the Missouri before Euro-Americans came, drawn not only to the flowing water in an arid steppe climate but also to the river valley environment as a source of timber, diverse animal and plant species, and fertile lands for agriculture. The give and take of the river and its nutrient-rich silt allowed gardens and fields and plant and animal species near the river valley to flourish.[14]

Tribal stories and histories are as diverse as the ecosystem, but all center on the river as a marker of place. For example, both Mandan and Hidatsa accounts agree on how the two tribes grew to be neighbors and allies. One day a group of Hidatsa hunters coming from the east encountered a Mandan village. Although separated by the river, the Mandans shot arrows with corn tied to them over to the Hidatsas and communicated that they should eat it. The Hidatsa hunting party returned to their original village and told of their discovery, and the community moved west to settle near the Mandan village—but in their own separate town where they learned to cultivate gardens from the Mandans.[15]

The Three Tribes agree that a combination of Lakota aggression and decimation due to smallpox forced the Arikaras upstream into Mandan and Hidatsa territory. Hidatsas claim that the Arikaras were left pitiful from the Lakota attacks when a Hidatsa chief "approached the Ree [Arikara] chief, and invited him to bring his people across the River to join the [Hidatsas], offering them the protection of the [Hidatsas] and suggesting that by combining forces they might both become more powerful." The Arikara chief refused, "saying they had buried their medicine deep in the ground. By this . . . they meant that they had come to feel at one with the place, and attached to the place, and felt that they couldn't take themselves away from it to go and live across the River." Myra Snow (Mandan, Hidatsa) told a similar narrative in the 1980s, recounting,

> The first time they came, there was a large band of Arikaras came, and they said—this my mother told me—they got kind of high, kind of like they were better than the Mandan, and they said, no, we're alright, they said, we have powerful medicines and oh, they were just much better than our tribes. So they went away and then they come back and there was just a few. They were getting slaughtered by the Sioux.

Regardless of the reasons behind the Arikara decision to join the Mandans and Hidatsas, the river valley landscape tied all Three Tribes near each other. As the Arikara chief related, "they had their medicine buried deep into the ground."[16]

Between 1000 and 1500, the Central Plains Village culture—the communities that grew into the Mandans, Hidatsas, Arikaras, Pawnees, and Wichitas—lived in the grasslands river valleys in large earth lodge villages, gardening, trading, and hunting to maintain their communities. After 1500, Mandan and Hidatsa communities consisted of earth lodge dwellings clustered in a fortified village around a central plaza that also served as the center of social and religious gatherings—and of course, they always built these communities along the Missouri River. Women constructed the circular earth lodges with help from clan members: men erected the four large center poles connected by crossbeams to support the roof, and set eleven to fifteen smaller poles in a circle around the center posts. They covered the entire structure by rafters at the top and ringed it with smaller willow posts around the edges before insulating it first with a layer of grass and then a layer of earth and clay. Each earth lodge contained an average of ten family members, and each village contained between forty to a hundred lodges, so a village could consist of anywhere from four hundred to one thousand people.[17]

The organization of the village and its earth lodges testify to the relationship between Mandan, Hidatsa, and Arikara communities and their river valley environment, for the communities built their villages on the bluffs above the Missouri River valley—both for defensive purposes and to make use of the fertile valley lands for crop production. Tribal members could not have built their earth lodge villages without easy access to the diverse timber resources of the valley, the grass of the prairie, and the mud and clay of the river.[18]

Agriculture centered on the cultivation of corn, beans, squash, and sunflowers; each family cultivated three to five acres, and gardens exemplified polyculture based on the companion planting of corn, beans, and squash. Corn provided a structure for the beans to climb as they grew, the beans helped to fix nitrogen into the soil for the other plants, and the squash spread along the ground not utilized by the corn or the beans, helping to prevent weeds and to retain soil moisture. Sunflowers often bordered the main garden plots to help deter pests, birds, and grazing wildlife. The relatively sheltered bottomlands of Awáati made all this agricultural activity possible and allowed the tribes to remain loyal to their gardens despite the difficult ecology of the northern plains. Gardening, hunting, and preserving food allowed Mandan and Hidatsa villages to maintain prosperity well into the nineteenth century, and to serve as a nexus of a transcontinental trade network.[19]

Contrary to the oversimplified characterizations of tribal groups by early European explorers and Euro-American government agents, an intricate set of intertribal relations enfolded the Three Tribes. These relationships used but did not completely center around the Missouri. Although rivers functioned as transportation lines and connection points, on the northern plains rivers were not the only moving aspect of the landscape. Once horses spanned the continent, the movement of buffalo herds became as important as the movement of the water of the Missouri, and so trade networks extended north, south, and west regardless of the direction of the river. Additionally, the extension of mobility due to the introduction of the horse changed not only hunting patterns but also military and intertribal conflict patterns.[20]

European arrival in the Americas introduced new social and environmental change catalysts. Smallpox, measles, cholera, and the bubonic plague swept across the continent with a pitiless thirty-year regularity.[21] Later, the prevalence of a horse-based hunting economy set the foundations for the growth of cattle economies throughout the plains. Northern European settlement and population growth—accompanied by violence and dispossession—displaced and pressured eastern indigenous communities to expand west, setting off a chain reaction of migration that reached the plains.[22] By the time of the French fur trade and exploration, ethnic groups under the following contemporary names made the northern plains their homes: Arikaras, Assiniboines, Arapahos, Blackfeet, Cheyennes, some Cree and Ojibwe bands, Crows, Gros Ventres, Hidatsas, various bands of Lakotas, and Mandans.

After the horse reached the northern plains, most of these groups assimilated to an almost entirely nomadic lifestyle that focused on the horse and the buffalo to sustain communities. Only the Mandans, Hidatsas, and Arikaras instead maintained a permanent village life on the northern plains. Thus, when non-Native people arrived, indigenous groups had already experienced the northern plains as a contested place and space. Lakota conceptualizations of the Black Hills as sacred overlapped with Mandan accounts of the Black Hills as past territories; Lakota spatial practice of nomadic hunting at times intruded on Hidatsa hunting and agriculture, and Hidatsa agricultural goods served as a resource—via trade or theft—for other Northern Plains tribes. Each held their own spatial constructions, their own territories, and their own stories about the land that marked place.[23]

Generations of Mandans, Hidatsas, and Arikaras transformed lands in the northern Great Plains through agriculture, settlement, transportation, storytelling, and history-telling. Their work in this landscape and the stories they told about it, from memories of warfare to those of childbirth, claimed specific portions of the land. This naming and claiming happened within a complex intertribal world that the next group to arrive on the plains—Euro-Americans—attempted to understand, exploit, and at times destroy. Sitting Rabbit's map narrates this complicated history from a Mandan understanding of the place that grew along the Missouri River, starting—as the Mandan world started—near Turtle Fall Creek.

Spaces of Change

Turtle Fall Creek indicates indigenous place-making, but several conventions of Sitting Rabbit's map reference a coterminous federal definition of the Upper Missouri as a *space*. In this book, *space* is used as a shorthand to refer to what Henri Lefebvre called "social space," or how society constructs the physical environment by the ascription of meanings and assignment of values to certain spaces, in ways that produce and shape human practices and perceptions. Unlike place, space implies the influence of large institutions and structures in shaping the landscape. These concepts of space and place allow us to describe the overlap and conflicts more accurately between local and distant narrations, meanings, and use of a landscape.[24]

For example, Sitting Rabbit's map starts near the North Dakota–South Dakota border, and follows the curves of the Missouri River until it hits the mouth of the Yellowstone River near the North Dakota–Montana border.

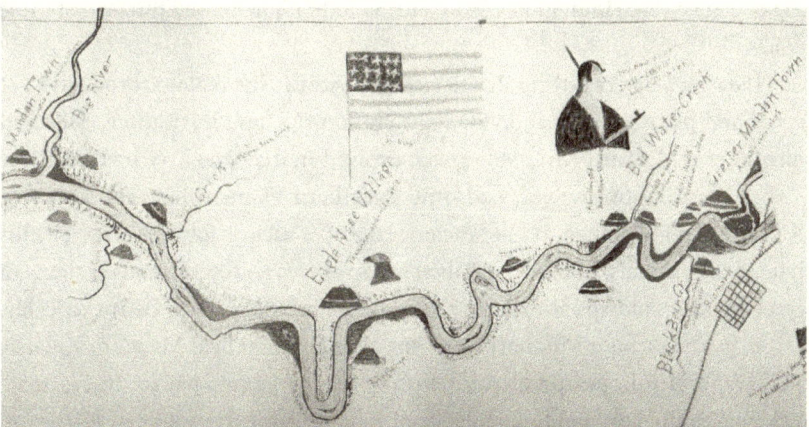

Figure 1.3. Sitting Rabbit's Map—detail of Eagle Nose Village. North Dakota State Historical Society.

His map shows Hidatsa and Mandan historical and mythical markers, but also the locations of Euro-American settlements along the Missouri, usually marked with a grid pattern to represent towns. The Great Northern Railroad crosses map sections like a scar, stretching across the canvas with little to anchor its path. Pictographs of earth lodges represent current or past villages, and log or frame houses mark Euro-American trading posts or Indian agencies. At one portion of the map Sitting Rabbit drew a large US flag.

Illustrations of Euro-American settlements, landmarks, and the US flag indicate an historical and physical narrative enmeshed with the history of US and non-Native presence in the region. Because Sitting Rabbit took as his model and template a survey map created by the federal government, his map also represents its spatial constructions.[25] He based his map and its detailed and curiously segmented Awáati on one provided him by North Dakota Historical Society secretary Orin G. Libby. Libby mostly likely provided Sitting Rabbit the 1892–95 Missouri River Commission (MRC) Survey map, as the segments represented in the Sitting Rabbit map align exactly with sectional maps produced by the MRC.

In 1884, when Sitting Rabbit was a young man of twenty, Congress created the War Department's five-member Missouri River Commission to survey the entire length of Awáati in anticipation of commercial transportation development. Mapping as a practice both reveals and constructs space. The federal government wished to represent the ever-changing course of the Missouri River to prepare for the *future* discipline of the river.[26] Before the commission disbanded in 1902, it produced a map of the entire length of the Missouri River consisting of eighty-three individual plates. Sitting Rabbit's map used thirteen of these plates.[27]

The genealogy of Sitting Rabbit's map illustrates the dialogic production of space and place between individuals, communities, and institutions. His map illustrates a Missouri River valley that evolved in dialogue between the Three Tribes, the US government, and other Northern Plains tribes. The Missouri River Commission map did not include concepts such as fourth turtles or hills named for animals, but Sitting Rabbit's map shows us coterminous systems of place-making and space-making so closely intertwined as to be inextricable. His map represents a Missouri River environment that held Mandan, Hidatsa, Arikara, and European-American history in an organic whole. In his map, Lakota accounts of Mandan, Hidatsa, or Arikara land as a potential extraction point of stored agricultural goods overlap with the US government's view of those same lands as a space ideal for a trading fort to extract furs, which overlap with the understandings of place developed by the Three Tribes as they tended gardens and hunted to produce furs for trade.

Space develops when groups of humans imagine, delineate, classify, create purpose for, and bound their landscapes and places. Prior to Euro-American contact, Native communities employed space-making activities when they mapped and defended community lands or engaged in diplomacy in their region. When Euro-Americans entered the plains, however, they not only carried supplies, guns, ammunition, and disease—they also brought the priorities conceptualized and solidified by distant institutions and governments.[28]

The first white explorers came by river and used Awáati as a bloodline of exchange and exploration. They ventured into a set of tribal spatial practices and conceptions that defined and enforced tribal territorial boundaries through trade, warfare, and kinship. French and Spanish Euro-Americans explored the Missouri River in the eighteenth century to extend colonial claims against other European nations in tribally controlled territories. Similarly, after the Louisiana Purchase, the United States engaged in the same process when the Lewis and Clark Expedition traveled west, using Spanish and English maps and local Native knowledge to find a route to the Pacific. These explorers aimed to gather knowledge to help the United States strategize for territorial control, and along the way they wintered at a Mandan village where they enlisted the help of Cagáagawia (Sacagawea) to lead them farther west. Tribal versions of Cagáagawia's life attest to complicated tribal spatial practices and understandings: for the Shoshone and many academic historians, she was a Hidatsa community member who began her life as Shoshone before the Hidatsa captured and adopted her, after which she married and bore the child of a French trader. Hidatsa tribal histories, however, identify her as ethnically Hidatsa.[29]

Sometimes Awáati transported unimaginable change. In the summer of 1837, an American Fur Company steamboat traveled up the Missouri from St. Louis, and the smallpox carried by the passengers and traders infected the Mandan, Hidatsa, and Arikara villages along the Upper Missouri. Smallpox had swept the villages at least twice before. During a four-week period in 1781, smallpox killed nearly 80 percent of the Mandans and Hidatsas living in villages along the Missouri, and the resulting depopulation forced the Mandans to abandon On-a-Slant Village, where they had lived for over three centuries, and combine forces with the Hidatsas at the Knife River Village farther upriver. The

1837 smallpox epidemic nearly destroyed the communities. The virus traveled in Euro-Americans from St. Louis up Awáati at the height of the summer in mid-July; this particularly infectious and lethal variant could kill victims within hours of its initial symptoms. Infected relatives died so quickly that their families, likely also infected, had neither the time nor ability to bury them. The villages filled not only with the sounds of mourning but also with the remains and odors of rotting human bodies. Over 90 percent of those in the Mandan villages perished; an estimated 70 percent of the Hidatsa villages died. The devastation shook the Three Tribes. It must have seemed like the end of the world.[30]

To understand the magnitude of the loss, start by envisioning a family of ten people—a grandmother and grandfather, a mother, a father, and six children. Then imagine all of them dying except for two of the eldest children. Next, see in your mind's eye this happening not only in one family, but in an entire town—and in the next town over. In fact, picture that within a collection of five small towns, with only one or two people from each family surviving a terrible, frightening epidemic. Entire families ended.

Rosemarie Mandan (Mandan, Hidatsa) gave a detailed accounting of her ancestors, concluding, "and that's where the record ends, because of the smallpox... [emotional pause] no records." Emmarine Chase (Mandan, Hidatsa) recalled her grandmother's story, who survived the last major smallpox epidemic as a small child:

> [After smallpox] she said they just left everything. All our winter food, she said, we didn't even take time to try to carry anything cause we all traveled on foot and there was very few that had dogs, you know. Even dogs were just dying off. It was really pitiful, she said. There was women that had their little babies in bundles that got that smallpox, and she said they were crying, and they took those babies and tied them up as high as they could on trees, strapped them so that no animal would eat them. And the babies were just crying, but they, the whole village was just, nothing but *wailing*, you could *hear* it, it was *terrible*.... And she actually went through that.

Chase's sister, Myra Snow, also related a story from her grandmother's experiences in which Awáati played a central role in survival.

> My grandmother used to tell that—my mother told me this—she was so, just burning up with fever when they had this smallpox, they'll break

out with sores and they had a high fever, she was just about dead. And she decided, well, I'm not gonna lay here and just, I'm gonna go down to the river and take a bath and clean up, maybe I'll feel better she said. So she made her way down to the river and she got in that cold water and took a good bath and everything, boy, it just brought her fever down and she felt real good, so she come back up and told the others . . . she said, go down and take a bath, you're gonna feel good, she said, so different ones went down there and they took baths and they come up slow but I guess it must have brought their fever down or something, that cold water.

European Americans also documented tragic stories. One trader noted that after one Native man became ill, he killed himself, and his wife, certain of death, "killed her two children, one a fine boy of eight, and the other six, and to complete the affair, she hung herself."[31]

Smallpox forced both tribes to reevaluate themselves and their communities. Mandan and Hidatsa smallpox survivors left their village at Knife River and banded together in 1845 to create a unified village called Like-a-Fishhook Village. Itinerant tribes—especially the Lakotas—harassed and attacked both Mandan and Hidatsa villages throughout the eighteenth and nineteenth centuries. Lakota aggressions increased on the northern plains in order to provoke the Mandans and Hidatsas—who maintained friendly relations with the US government—into rebellion over the United States' inability to protect them from Lakota incursions. Epidemics and Lakota aggression had troubled the communities in the past, but their combination forced both tribes, historically separate, into the same village. As the Mandans and Hidatsas consolidated their communities, the Arikaras moved into their abandoned villages and took possession of the cornfields left untended.[32]

After the smallpox epidemic, the Mandans divided into three groups— the largest lived with the Hidatsas, a few stayed with a group of Arikaras, and yet a third group established a separate village on the river above Fort Clark. The third group held a special relationship with the Yanktons, affording them some protection against the attacks of Lakota bands. The Hidatsas also spread between several villages, and one group even went to live with the Crows and never rejoined the tribe. Thus, none of the tribes that would eventually live at Fort Berthold held a unified political front during the majority of the nineteenth century; the unity was cultural, and any political unity was cooperative rather than regimented. Further, alliances could shift. Historian Roy Meyer described an incident in 1838 when the Arikaras warned the Hidatsas of an impending Lakota attack, allowing the Hidatsas and Mandans to defeat the attackers. After this, the Arikaras held a victory dance for the Hidatsas and Mandans in honor of their bravery.

When the Mandans moved to Like-a-Fishhook, they laid out their own section of the village with their traditional plaza centered around a sacred cedar representing one of the Mandan creators, Lone Man. Too few Mandans remained to "complete the circle of lodges around the plaza," so some Hidatsas joined their circle of earth lodges and began to participate in Mandan ceremonies. At the same time the tribes established Like-a-Fishhook Village, Pierre Chouteau, Jr. and Company—previously the American Fur Company—built Fort Berthold just above the village. These changes presaged a move toward the political unification of the Mandans, Hidatsas, and Arikaras into a unit eventually termed the Three Affiliated Tribes, or Three Tribes. As smallpox, cholera, and measles continued to cycle through the communities with devastating regularity, and as community members maintained gardens together and invested in mutual protection strategies against Lakota bands, Like-a-Fishhook Village accrued important histories and stories that unified the tribes under a common history in later years.[33]

Contact with Fort Berthold traders produced more changes. During the years at Like-a-Fishhook, from 1845 until 1885 when the government successfully pushed for its destruction, Mandan and Hidatsa life shifted in form and content, even though the Missouri River valley remained our home. Community members less often built and lived in earth lodges. When Sitting Rabbit was born in 1864, most community members still lived in earth lodges and only a few log cabins existed in Like-a-Fishhook. They had weathered a storm of disease, but at high cost—from a population of over twenty-five thousand several decades earlier, they had been reduced to fewer than a thousand people. Six years later, at the height of Lakota aggression, and when Sitting Rabbit must have been an active six-year-old running around playing with other boys, log cabins outnumbered earth lodges. Twenty years later, when Sitting Rabbit was a young man, most community members lived in log cabins. The implications go beyond household organization. In both Mandan and Hidatsa communities, women supervised the construction of earth lodges and owned them—young women had to buy the right to build and practice the ceremonies surrounding construction from older women.

The shift to log cabins may have changed the gendered power structure of the tribes.[34]

Land use also changed. More and more men worked in the fields each year, and instead of women breaking ground using metal hoes or older implements made of buffalo or elk shoulder blades, families increased the amount of land used for gardens by hiring traders to plow their land in the spring. The 1870s saw a decisive shift in this direction, accompanied by increased federal government presence in the community. By 1876, families still used the land west of Like-a-Fishhook for the older gardening, but to the east the local Indian agent broke and fenced the land to convert it into a large field controlled by the agency. Food grown in the gardens changed—root vegetables such as potatoes and turnips supplemented corn, beans, squash, and sunflowers. Such shifts toward mechanized labor and crops changed the way both men and women interacted with the landscape, sustained their bodies, and organized their families.[35]

Sitting Rabbit's map signals these shifts in the organization and sustenance of everyday life. For example, Like-a-Fishhook Village sits near the middle of his map, right before the last cluster of heavy settlement represented by Elbowoods. Sitting Rabbit used a pictograph of a large earth lodge to mark Like-a-Fishhook, across from a tributary to the Missouri, Dancing Bear Creek. Three labels mark the site: Fort Berthold, Bua-idutskupe hisa atis, and Fish-hook house. (In Hidatsa, *bua* or *mua* means fish, *idutskupe* refers to something bent like a hook, *hisa* means like or similar to, and *ati* is the word for house or village.) The village's location, placement, and labeling tells a story not just of Mandan- or Hidatsa-centered place-making through the earth lodge pictograph placed across from a well-known tributary, but of the influence of capital and the US space-making (the trading fort). The priorities of capital and the state would become the engine behind massive land loss that in turn created a new way of understanding territorial boundaries.[36]

Sovereign Territoriality

Orin G. Libby, the first director of the North Dakota State Historical Society, commissioned Sitting Rabbit's map. Libby wanted Sitting Rabbit to produce a map that detailed all extant knowledge about old village sites of the Mandans and Hidatsas; in return, Libby would pay Sitting Rabbit. When Sitting Rabbit produced the map, he did so at Libby's request, using tools—the canvas and MRC maps—provided by Libby. Libby asked him to "draw the banks and islands of the river just as they used to be. Be sure and put the names of the villages on the map out at one side so as not to cover up any part of the map." He added, "Make the map a very long one so as to show all the curves, with the creeks, buttes, and woods just as they used to be." But Sitting Rabbit also culled indigenous historical knowledge of old village sites, creation stories, and historical narratives of indigenous leaders and events. Reverend Hall wrote to Libby that Sitting Rabbit believed that "there was more work on these last than on the first pictures he made for you. So he thinks he should have $25.00 dollars."[37]

Libby grew upset when he received the initial version of the Sitting Rabbit map—he felt Sitting Rabbit had not used enough accrued community historical and territorial knowledge, so Libby refused to pay. He wrote to Sitting Rabbit, lapsing into stereotyped "Indian-speak" that he may have imagined would allow him to better communicate with Sitting Rabbit:

> Now my friend I want you to be very careful and get this all right.... The map of the Missouri River is not good. I know many more villages than you have put down. You have not put down any on the east side of the river, south of Bismarck, and I know many are there, for I have seen them.... Did you talk to Bad Gun and Poor Wolf about this map? You did not put down the little Mandan village of 15 lodges, where the Mandans went after the small pox of 1837.... Now my friend Sitting Rabbit you must make this map right, so that all the head men of your tribe, when they see it, will say, "It is good" and be glad that you made it so well.... But these pictures you send me now are no good to go in the book, and you must do them better.[38]

Libby may not have recognized it, but the map holds histories and stories of place. Sitting Rabbit embedded villages, leaders, physical landmarks, and references to tribal histories in his map. It is not a complete representation, but neither is any history, any map, any archive. The conflict over the ownership of and payment for the intellectual material produced by Sitting Rabbit not only reveals aspects of its creation but also reminds us that landscape and ideas of ownership combine to produce ideas of *territory*.

Territory—seen in agreements between parties that use the lines of rivers or mountain ranges (or sometimes entirely imagined lines) to delineate between "us" and "them," between "our lands" and "theirs"—emerges from the soil of both place and space. Yet the true conceptual crux of territory is ownership. Humans imagine ownership just as they do place and space: as a product of negotiation, contestation, and changes based on the interactions between multiple groups of people. These imaginings and contestations require the imagination of an "us" and a "them," people within and outside of a community identity.

Tribes practiced territoriality before Europeans set foot in the Americas—we defined ourselves against outsiders and marked and enforced notions of territory and use. But Europeans, and later Euro-Americans, carried new technologies of ownership and associated rights—specific legal forms of title to land, methods of measuring and marking land, and codified practices to transfer title or sell these parcels of land. They narrated and demarcated territories through these systems of ownership and the rights that ownership entailed, especially regarding natural resources. Euro-American notions of territory assumed that all resources, all lands, all territories, were quantifiable and interchangeable.[39]

Euro-American societies forced Indigenous communities to grapple with the notion that land—*every* parcel of land—and the resources upon it could be assessed, quantified, and ultimately either paid for or exchanged for another parcel of land. Setting aside simplistic and essentialist discussions of indigenous ties to land—"the land cannot be sold" narratives, for example—it is imperative to note that the practice of creating *place*—a local, lived knowledge of a landscape—entails a different understanding of ownership and interchangeability of land than the practice of making *space* or organizing *territory*. When stories, origins, histories, and relationships populate a landscape, ownership carries a different weight and meaning.

The first Fort Laramie Treaty in 1851 provides an early example of these competing ideas of place, space, and territoriality on the northern plains. In the treaty, the US government attempted to define the traditional territorial claims of eight Northern Plains tribes, including the Mandans, Hidatsas, and Arikaras—in other words, to use Euro-American legal technology to define space and territory along the Upper Missouri. At this multi-tribal gathering of more than twelve thousand people the federal government sought to define these territories to promote the safety of Oregon Trail migrants; in return, the government offered tribes annual payments to allow the migrants to pass through. But because the government and its representatives possessed no lived experience of the spaces they hoped to one day administer—and likely did not intend to honor the financial promises in the treaty—they eventually largely disregarded the terms of the treaty. Lakota bands also had no intention of adhering to the territorial claims negotiated at the first Fort Laramie Treaty; they proved to be the bane of Mandan and Hidatsa existence as they continually harassed and attacked tribal members, and at times burned Like-a-Fishhook Village. Later, the federal government legislated the boundaries of the Fort Berthold Reservation in 1870 with little reference to the 1851 treaty.[40]

Lakota aggression hit a high point during the mid-1860s, and the Mandans and Hidatsas grew disgruntled with the federal government—one of the intended aims of Lakota violence—as they adhered to the territorial agreements negotiated by the US government yet received little attention, while the Lakotas constantly breached the agreements and received more attention and treaty goods because of the continual rounds of peace negotiations. During a negotiation with the Lakotas brokered by the federal government in 1870, Arikara leader White Shield asserted, "When we listen to the whites we have to sit in our villages, listen to [Lakota] insults, and have our young men killed and our horses stolen, within sight of our lodges." Lakota depredations included not only stolen horses and food but also rape and murder. White Shield's analysis illuminates the atmosphere of violence created by Lakota attempts to instigate conflict in response to US hypocrisy in its dealings with Lakota bands—an atmosphere that created traumatic outcomes for Mandan, Hidatsa, and Arikara families who experienced the violence. In the same year as this peace agreement between the Lakotas and the residents of Like-a-Fishhook, the Interior Department and Indian Bureau approved and advocated for the creation of the Fort Berthold Indian Reservation via executive order.[41]

Notions of place and space also clashed when, during the early 1870s, the Indian agent at Fort Berthold pushed the Three Tribes to move to Indian Territory in present-day Oklahoma. The federal government made this suggestion to nearly all Plains tribes as it attempted to perfect its post–Civil War expansionist imperialism. Mandan and Hidatsa leaders from Like-a-Fishhook declined. "Although they found the country attractive, they feared that the climate was too warm for them and thought the long journey might be too much for their aged, infants, and infirm. Above all, they were deeply attached to their homeland, where they preferred to remain and 'work harder and have less.'" The symbiosis of the water and landscape combined with community histories and stories to make such a move unthinkable.[42]

Regimes of place and space also shifted after the 1870 executive order establishing the Fort Berthold Reservation reduced tribal territories from the first Fort Laramie Treaty. The US government quickly worked to implement yet another territorial reduction, this time to grant a right-of-way to the Northern Pacific Railroad through the center of the Fort Berthold Reservation. With nobody to advocate for the people of Fort Berthold in Washington, DC—and given the ballooning power of the railroads—the railroad-driven executive order in 1880 reduced the original Fort Berthold landholdings of 1851 by 90 percent.[43] When the federal government ceded the southern portion of the reservation to the Northern Pacific Railroad, the Mandans, Hidatsas, and Arikaras lost more than valuable land; they lost land with important historic and cultural ties, including all former village sites from the mouth of the Knife River down the Missouri. Sixteen-year-old Sitting Rabbit was old enough at least to understand the upset and consternation of his elders when this land grab occurred—and he perhaps remembered this when he included the Northern Pacific Railroad line like an unhealed incision across sections of his map. These massive shifts in place, space, and territory happened not over the easy distance of the historian recounting decades but over the course of individual life spans. Often, individuals too young to comprehend or participate in such land negotiations would spend their remaining lives grappling with the excisions forced upon their elders.

Five years later in 1885, when Sitting Rabbit was a young man of twenty-one, the local Indian agent forced the abandonment of Like-a-Fishhook Village, to undermine the communal lifestyles that impeded assimilation. The agent bribed first Arikara and then Mandan and Hidatsa families to relocate to smaller communities or to Elbowoods and destroyed the earth lodges and log cabins as the families vacated. By 1888 only a few elderly Mandan families continued to live in the earth lodges. The last resident of Like-a-Fishhook was a Mandan man named Red Roan Cow who had attended the negotiations at Fort Laramie in 1851. He lived alone in his earth lodge, tied irrevocably to the place. Susan Webb Hall, wife of Congregationalist minister Rev. Harold Case, remembered the emotional attachments tribal members associated with Like-a-Fishhook:

> One of the most pathetic pictures of the passing away of the old was the visit to the old village of one of our old Indian women, who had moved forty miles away. She came twenty miles on horse back. It was after all the old lodges had disappeared. I went with her to the old village. It was touching to watch her go over the old places and try to identify this spot and that. After going about awhile she made me understand

that she was going to the graves of her loved ones and wanted to go alone, so I watched her go, leading her horse after her and crying as she went.[44]

Maaxiiriwiash, Buffalo Bird Woman, who worked with anthropologist Gilbert Wilson to document Hidatsa agricultural knowledge, also conveyed a deep loss, telling Wilson, "I cannot forget our old ways." She continued,

> Sometimes at evening I sit, looking out on the big Missouri. The sun sets, and dusk steals over the water. In the shadows I seem again to see our Indian village, with smoke curling upward from the earth lodges; and in the river's roar I hear the yells of the warriors, the laughter of little children of old. It is but an old woman's dream. Again I see but shadows and hear only the roar of the river; and tears come into my eyes. Our Indian life, I know, is gone forever.[45]

Maaxiiriwiash, Sitting Rabbit, and other tribal members turned Like-a-Fishhook into a place—an area deeply loved, known through intimate daily use, and defined by the community and family and individual stories they told about it. When the Indian agent cleared Like-a-Fishhook, community members scattered on both sides of the Missouri within the boundaries of the reservation, mostly in family groups—almost a return to the tribally specific communities along the Missouri from before the village's existence.[46]

Such disruption helped strong-arm members to agree to sell two-thirds of the reservation and allot the remainder, in return for annuities and money to support Euro-American education and housing for tribal members. Ratified in 1891, the agreement authorized surveyors to measure and mark the remaining land, after which tribal members selected allotments that mostly clustered close to the Missouri on the most productive lands on the reservation. Sitting Rabbit, twenty-seven years old at the time, may have felt this land loss more keenly because he was now an adult and had likely hunted and traveled the entire landscape ceded. The local Indian Agency sought to lease land to white ranchers for cattle grazing as soon as the bureaucrats accomplished allotment—in large part to regulate ongoing abuse by Euro-American ranchers of Fort Berthold territorial boundaries. It took several decades for Indian ranchers to accumulate enough capital to ranch their own lands.

These cessions, sales, allotments, and leases shifted how tribal members understood and imagined their territories. The forced railroad cession, removal from Like-a-Fishhook, and allotment and sale of reservation lands—all of which older, traditionalist tribal members opposed—meant tribal members reconceptualized their lands not only as something that could be sold but as something that could be wrongfully taken from them and exploited. Tribal land became finite—a territory—and the federal government alienated far too much of it while the frequent incursions of local settler populations required constant vigilance. Hidatsa community member Wolf Chief—a somewhat larger-than-life personality during the first decades of the twentieth century—complained about the agreements his fellow tribal members made with local white ranchers to hold their cattle on reservations lands. Wolf Chief's complaint letter to the commissioner of Indian affairs spurred Indian agent Thomas Richards to investigate. He wrote to the commissioner that a group of tribal members and the assistant clerk rode the reservation boundary and found that "nearly all the surveyors mounds had disappeared." The group reconstructed the mounds to clearly indicate the reservation boundaries to the local white population, and even allowed one rancher to keep his cattle on reservations lands because it was almost winter and to move his cattle "would cause him great trouble and hardship." Economic concerns also required territorial enforcement—before 1910, almost half the total income at Fort Berthold came from beef sales to the federal government and larger markets.[47]

Territory and territoriality involve marking and controlling an area of space to control its human and natural resources.[48] The Three Tribes exhibited territorialism throughout their history—for example, in reaction to Lakota incursions—but the imposition of US land jurisdiction on the Great Plains during the second half of the nineteenth century intensified the need to protect the land base. Disagreements over land sales and use during first decades of the twentieth century illustrate this shift. In 1902, when Sitting Rabbit was thirty-eight years old, a government agent arrived at Fort Berthold to propose the sale of another 315,000 acres, only to be told by the Arikara leader Sitting Bear, "Away back in the olden times we did not know how to make treaties with the Government, but now we begin to know the value of our land." The Hidatsa leader Good Bear asked the government agent, James McLaughlin, to define the boundaries of the reservation only to correct his (inadequate) accounting before adding, "Congress makes laws and then breaks them, but we keep our pledges and live up to our agreements." Continual violation of tribal territory by Euro-American ranchers, the federal government, and the railroad solidified a new practice of sovereign territoriality in which communal tribal ownership of the land base required its defense against further alienation or legal encroachment.

Tribal leadership protected the land base even though leaders must have realized they were in the middle of a demographic nadir. By 1899, the tribal rolls only held 1,118 members. The Arikaras constituted a bit over one-third or 37 percent of that number; Hidatsa tribal members represented two-fifths or 41 percent; and Mandans comprised a little over one-fifth or 22 percent of the tribal population.[49] Tribal leaders also exhibited a protective stance toward their youngest members—their children. That same year, local Indian agent Thomas Richards sent a letter to the commissioner of Indian affairs relating the local response to the commissioner's search for children to attend the off-reservation Pierre Indian School. "The Indians with whom I talked," wrote Richards, "criticized the Department in severe terms for making such a request. . . . The feelings of the Indians are so strong against transferring their children to non-reservation schools that I think it unwise to make any further attempt to do so." The local arm of the federal government was threatening both their territories and their children—symbols of a viable and sustainable future as a community.

The government forced the tribes to cede more land in 1910, and tribal members experienced their reservation shrink yet again to include only their settlements along the Missouri. Three tribal leaders, Red Bear, Enemy Hawk, and Alfred John Hawk, wrote to the commissioner of Indian affairs after the 1910 cession, "They have got us now to our homes. That is the only thing we have now to protect. The land has been taken away and we have only to defend our homes."[50] Their statement reveals the tribal leaders defending notions of place ("homes") and space ("the land has been taken away") to elaborate the notion of sovereign territory. During this last cession, Sitting Rabbit was forty-six and a member of the tribal leadership. His two sons were fifteen and three years old, and his last surviving child, a daughter, would be born three years later in 1913. His map of Awáati and its surrounding landscapes, completed three years prior, already resided with Orin Libby, who likely still believed it contained little of value.

In the waning years of the reservation era (1880s to 1934), Fort Berthold community members acted on several fronts: they advocated for reparations for land seizures under the executive orders of 1870 and 1880; they worked to stem the exploitation of their lands from overgrazing by Euro-American leasers; and they attempted to counter Office of Indian Affairs

Figure 1.4. Sitting Rabbit (Little Owl), Assiniboine Woman, and baby, ca. 1910.
North Dakota State Historical Society.

cultural prohibitions, such as a ban on all dancing at community gatherings. Some might characterize this period—including the formation of the tribal business committee in 1910—as one of assimilation to Euro-American norms regarding education, religion, land use, and political structure, but their evidence does not consider continued tribal activism and cultural participation.[51]

After the 1910 cession, the legal boundaries of the reservation coincided with the current boundaries of the Fort Berthold Reservation. Leasing land to non-Native ranchers became a major source of revenue for the tribes, aided by the fencing of the reservation boundary. Leased land for farming and ranching, land sales, and the persistence of subsistence gardening created enough economic stability such that Fort Berthold tribal members no longer needed government rations. Despite the dire poverty on most reservations, by 1920, the local Indian agent proudly reported that he had not needed to distribute rations to Fort Berthold families for five years.[52]

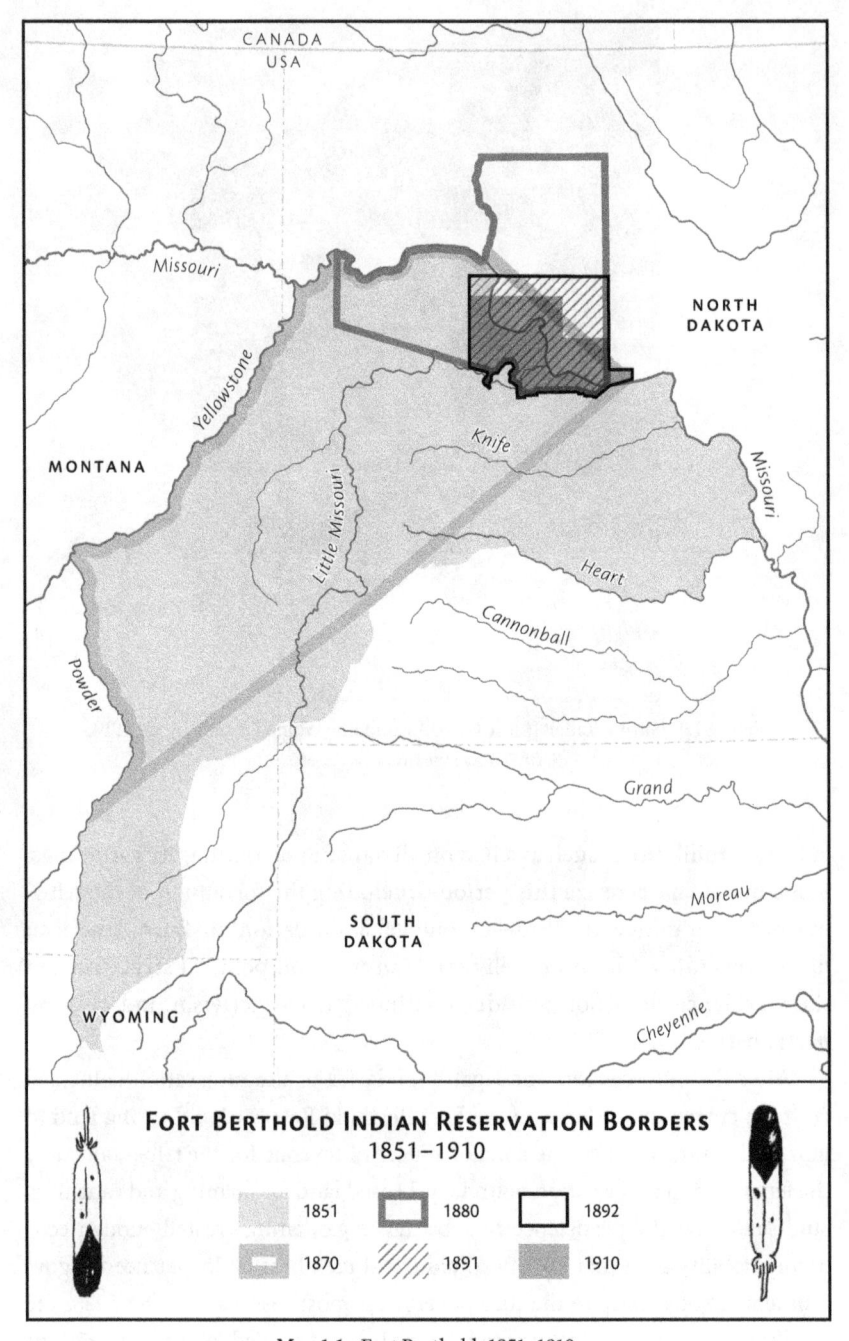

Map 1.1. Fort Berthold, 1851–1910.

In the last decade of the reservation era—a period noted for the heightened surveillance and discipline by the Office of Indian Affairs—Fort Berthold leadership achieved government reparations regarding a claims case based on the land cessions legislated in the 1870 and 1880 executive orders. Between 1898 and 1920, Fort Berthold tribal leaders pushed the government to recognize their claims, and finally in 1920 Congress passed legislation allowing them to file a case in the Court of Claims. Council for the Fort Berthold tribes filed the case in 1924, and by 1929 the Court of Claims ruled in favor of the Three Affiliated Tribes. The government distributed the money on a per capita basis starting in 1931, and the preponderance of the funds went toward housing, cattle, farm machinery, and other large purchases. These per capita payments provided an important insulation against the worst effects of the combined drought that sapped the northern plains in the 1930s and the Great Depression.[53]

The drought affected Fort Berthold, but because most did not farm on a large scale—and instead leased land to their Euro-American neighbors who did so—the drought resulted less in their own crop failure and more in their lessees' failure to meet lease terms when their crops failed. Subsistence gardening and the ability to mitigate the effects of drought on smaller garden plots allowed tribal members to weather the agricultural crisis. Further, gardens planted in the bottomlands of Awáati remained rich and irrigated from below due to the water table that sat inches beneath the soil. Tribal ranchers did experience the negative impacts of the drought, which forced them to liquidate large portions of their herds lest their cattle starve in the parched fields. But the Great Depression affected everyone—especially in the loss of leasing revenue—and some families experienced financial hardship that encouraged them to send their children to government or religious boarding schools to help make ends meet. Nevertheless, per capita payments combined with a tribal history of subsistence hunting and agriculture allowed the people of Fort Berthold to survive better than many in the United States at the time.[54]

Eight communities evolved along the Missouri after the destruction of Like-a-Fishhook Village—from north to south (with the tribal affiliation of the majority of residents noted in parentheses) were Shell Creek (Hidatsa), Independence (Mandan, Hidatsa), Lucky Mound (Hidatsa), Charging Eagle (Mandan), Elbowoods (all three tribes), Red Butte (Mandan), Nishu (Arikara), and Beaver Creek (Arikara)—and were insulated against the worst effects of the dual agricultural and economic crisis of the 1930s.

These communities became places—associated with home and family, tribal history, and cultural stories—and all who lived in them remembered them with nostalgia and affection. Dreke Irwin (Mandan, Hidatsa), a well-known announcer for community gatherings, remembered a place that sustained community members in all seasons: "All the places were kind of pretty, you know: timber, creeks, rivers, nice; hills, fields. Lot of shelter for livestock in the wintertime. In tough winters, some of them cattle, set them down in the timber and fed them, they kind of foraged around." Rosemarie Mandan, who grew up in Lucky Mound, remembered the easy connections forged between family members of all generations:

> We were *always* going to go see our grandparents [she and her cousin Philip]. We'd say, "Let's go to the river, *Awáati da*," which meant let's go to [the river]. Poor grandma had all those kids [laughs], now that I think about it.... My mother would say, "Your grandma probably needs her pots and pans washed," because she would cook and the pots and pans would gather. So I would walk over there and do her dishes, her pots and pans.

Such trips accomplished more than clean pots and pans; they solidified camaraderie between Rosemarie Mandan and her cousin Philip, enriched the relationship between Rosemarie and her grandmother, and provided both children with an emotional and mental map of the community that shaped their family and emotional relationships with the landscape and the river.[55]

The agricultural traditions of the Three Tribes—who, altogether, developed nine varieties of corn, four varieties of beans, and several types of squash—literally fed community survival. As Emmarine Chase (Mandan, Hidatsa) remembered of her childhood in the "teens and twenties," "We're corn people. Anytime we eat something it's always got corn in it. They fooled with that corn all the time." Many tribal elders remembered their parents' and grandparents' labor in their gardens. Cecelia Brown (Arikara) recounted,

> Oh yes, we had gardens. We had *nice* gardens. Even when we moved up we had nice gardens. Anything that was eatable we planted. And then they make us pull weeds [and tell us], "If you don't clean the garden, then we're not going to a certain celebration." ... And then we'd harvest that after in the fall, and we'd have all that to live on in the wintertime. Dry

our corn, I used to help my mother dry corn, even squash, and beans. We'd thrash the beans.

Brown watched her grandmother make cornballs, using a homemade mortar and pestle to crack the corn before she parched it. The crushed corn combined with dried juneberries, dried meat, and suet to make a nutritious and energy-rich treat. Chase also remembered her grandmother making cornballs for her as a child, noting, "That was our delicacy. We went to school, and . . . when we'd get back from school, why, we'd all sit down on a bench in a row and grandma used to pass cornballs and we'd eat that and then we'd go out and play before the real meal."[56]

Tribal members adopted things like day schools, churches, and playgrounds during the height of government intrusion typical of the reservation era, but maintained practices such as traditional dancing, indigenous languages, food preparation and storage, and traditional religious beliefs. For example, although each community housed a western church staffed by Native deacons and lay pastors, community members also maintained both the Hidatsa Nuxpike shrine and the Mandan Lone Man shrine that once stood in the central plaza of Like-a-Fishhook Village (and before that in the center of each of the Mandan villages along the Missouri before the move to Like-a-Fishhook). Some tribal members adopted Christianity wholesale, others honored both Christian and indigenous religious tradition, and still others maintained a commitment solely to their indigenous beliefs. But by and large, tribal members accommodated both systems.[57]

Successful accommodation of non-Native influence did not erase the need to defend tribal lands. The roots of tribal sovereign territorialism grew from the regional boundaries and behaviors that predated Euro-American intrusion onto the northern plains. But it flowered in reaction to a land-greedy US government to ensure the survival of the Three Tribes as social, cultural, and political community.

Sitting Rabbit's conversion to Christianity pleased Rev. Harold Case (his proxy in the correspondence with Libby), and Sitting Rabbit worked as an officer for the Nueta Mission Congregationalist Church, providing leadership for a congregation busy with "basket socials, selling of ponies, moccasins, dancing paraphernalia, making of quilts, giving of dinners and scraping together all the extra pennies and dollars possible" to build a church.[58] His conversion and church participation, however, did not erase his memories of journeying to the Yellowstone to hunt eagles with other young men of his generation, the loss of his parents and so many others to smallpox, and the need to defend his village against the Lakotas. By the time he drew his map, he had spent a lifetime riding across the top lands and through the valleys of Awáati. He had absorbed and continued to exist in a tribal-centric world that persisted in marking, mapping, and respecting the place where Lone Man's fourth turtle fell into the water and continues to support the dry land for human habitation.

The boundaries of Fort Berthold—both its lands and its people—should not be taken for granted. The Sitting Rabbit map, contextualized by the nineteenth-century and early twentieth-century history of the Three Affiliated Tribes, explains how the Three Tribes, neighboring Plains tribes, and the federal government negotiated conceptions of place, space, and territory. Smallpox, Lakota aggression, land cessions, and allotment threatened to shatter the lives of tribal

Figure 1.5. Sitting Rabbit (Little Owl), at age seventy-eight. North Dakota State Historical Society.

members and forced the Three Tribes to defend their remaining territories to protect their communities. Through this, the tribes developed a rhetoric and practice of a sovereign territoriality.

Sitting Rabbit, also known as Little Owl, a well-respected Mandan man of his generation, knew these things and mapped them. Orin G. Libby likely asked Sitting Rabbit to make his map because the community regarded him as a knowledgeable man, an expert who knew histories and stories and places. Some might call him a scholar of Mandan and Hidatsa places. He spent his life on horseback, riding through the landscapes he would one day depict on muslin. He also spent his life raising three surviving children with his wife, Assiniboine Woman, immersed in the language and history and culture of the tribes at Fort Berthold. Many places narrated by Sitting Rabbit in his 1907 map may be covered by the waters of the lakes ballooning behind the Oahe and Garrison dams, but his map allows us to remember them and the process of their construction.

Chapter 2

Reorganizations, 1934–1941

Two days before Franklin Delano Roosevelt signed the Indian Reorganization Act (IRA) in 1934, the Fort Berthold Indian Reservation gathered for a major event—larger and more important to the local community than the bill the president would sign into law in a few days. The Four Bears Bridge dedication drew more than eight thousand tribal members and visitors for three days to participate in "parades, rodeos, carnivals, races, games, Indian dancing, picnics, ceremonies and speeches." Amid one of the largest economic depressions ever experienced and a massive drought baking the Great Plains, Natives and non-Natives alike were thirsty for entertainment and celebration. In a warbonnet that marked his status as an important community leader, seventy-year-old Sitting Rabbit, now known as Little Owl, either because he had earned a new name or because he had honored someone else by giving them his name, led a delegation of Mandan leaders who crossed the bridge to Elbowoods with a group of singers and women dressed in their finest. He also spoke at the dedication ceremonies with other tribal leaders.[1]

Tribal protocol structured the dedication. Community leaders wore traditional clothing to parade across the bridge, and a beautiful young tribal member, Allison Grinnell, conducted the "ribbon cutting" ceremony in full traditional regalia. The tribes installed plaques with the names of important Mandan, Hidatsa, and Arikara chiefs on each end of the bridge—the names of men who had survived smallpox epidemics, signed treaties with the US government, served as Indian scouts, and protected the villages of each of the tribes against the Lakotas and other unfriendly tribes. Even before the dedication ceremonies, Mandan and Hidatsa community members petitioned the state highway commission to explicitly designate the "Elbowoods Bridge" as a memorial "to Charging Eagle and Four Bear[s], two great chiefs, for their labors among our people."[2]

Figure 2.1. Dressed in full regalia, Allison Grinnell (Mandan, Hidatsa) prepares to cut the ribbon at the Four Bears Bridge dedication, with Bears Arm (Hidatsa) standing in the foreground of a crowd of community members. Photograph by Leo D. Harris.
Courtesy of Reid Walker.

The Four Bears Bridge dedication celebrated Awáati and its landscape as central for tribal members even though federal resources altered the river valley. Mandan and Hidatsa systems of knowledge still defined the Missouri—traditional stories marked place and reminded tribal members of the correct way to behave. Before the bridge, when community members used boats and ferries to cross the Missouri, families prayed and offered cornballs to Grandfather Snake, a cultural hero who lived in the Missouri River, to ensure their safe passage over his waters. Children crossing the river to visit relatives in communities on the other side might still be instructed by their parents to feed their Grandfather as they crossed via ferry or boat to ensure a safe journey.

But the bridge dedication—and specifically the photograph above—also marks a moment when the priorities and projects of a national government and its local bureaucratic arm increasingly modified the Missouri and its surrounding tribal lands. The North Dakota State Highway Commission built the bridge using federal funds, and the Fort Berthold Reservation Civic Organization campaigned for its construction by combining forces with non-Native communities under the name of the Elbowoods Bridge Association, chaired by Fort Berthold's Congregationalist minister Rev. Harold Case. The campaign focused on the fact that the bridge would serve "two hundred thousand people" and that it was funded by "100 PERCENT FEDERAL AID [emphasis in original]." As such, this bridge dedication photograph commemorates a celebration of federal aid with local benefit. Native lands served as the catalyst for seeking federal monies for a local project even before the New Deal and the Indian Reorganization Act created official structures to bring federal money to rural North Dakota. And although many local communities benefited, Fort Berthold residents claimed the bridge as their marker of place.[3]

The Four Bears Bridge represents only the most visible manifestation of the changes wrought at Fort Berthold during the New Deal era between 1933 and 1940. The re-elaboration of space and place matched the reorganization of legitimate political authority on the reservation. The leaders whose names populated the dedication plaques—Poor Wolf, Crow Flies High, Old Dog, Black Hawk, Son of Star, White Shield, Charging Eagle, and Water Chief, among others—came to leadership during a time in which men laid their life on the line every time they left to hunt or protect the village. The legitimacy of their leadership rested in the bravery (and luck) of their efforts to protect and provide for their people, and the cost of leadership could be harsh. During the long years of the reservation era, that form of leadership evolved to fit new circumstances, and with the advent of the Indian Reorganization Act, leadership and legitimate authority would again change at Fort Berthold.

Shifts in governance indicate the vigor of self-determination or sovereignty. The exercise of sovereignty depends on legitimacy and authority—two points in a constellation of concepts that comprise the ability to maintain sovereign authority as a tribal nation or a nation-state. This conceptual constellation also includes territory, populace and definitions of membership, and temporal narratives that legitimize sovereign authority in the present by telling stories about the past—and the attempt to maintain that authority in the future. This Foucauldian formulation of sovereignty is itself a construction, but a useful one. It provides us a toolkit for understanding how these ideas become placed, understood, and mobilized in relation to each other.

When the IRA and other New Deal initiatives began to reorganize the space and political authority on Fort Berthold, they also rearranged the relationships and roles of tribal territoriality and membership. This process resulted in a grassroots evolution of ideas that would result in the flowering of tribal sovereignty claims later in the century. The IRA era re-imagination of tribal and federal citizenship ties directly to the shift in tribal members' intellectual construction and use of their land—the tribal territory that served as a basis for exerting Indian self-government. Fort Berthold—like many tribal communities during this time—strategically invested in the opportunity created by IRA legislation, to begin to build the local political infrastructure necessary to gain control of their political present and future. The Four Bears Bridge, a structure of metal and concrete funded by the federal government, was not the only bridge constructed the summer of 1934; the Indian Reorganization Act constituted another type of bridge to an uncertain political future.[4]

Reorganizing Citizenship

A folder of letters written in 1936 sits in the federal archives in Kansas City as part of the holdings from the Fort Berthold Indian Agency. The letters originated from Fort Berthold tribal members located all over the United States, including California, Maryland, West Virginia, Montana, Wisconsin, Kansas, Oklahoma, and Washington State. Some are typed on company letterhead, others are scrawled in pencil, and still others are carefully and beautifully written in cursive ink. Some ask the Indian agent for news of their family and relatives in North Dakota; others ask about leasing and land-management issues. One letter from a tribal member in Bucks County, Pennsylvania closes, "I remain one of your Indians from both sides of the Missouri River."[5]

These letters—sent to Indian agent William R. Beyer—confirmed that the senders had not "revoked" their tribal membership and wanted to participate in the upcoming tribal election to approve the new Indian Reorganization Act (IRA) constitution and bylaws. Tribal members wrote the letters because during this time the Indian Affairs bureaucracy hoped that Native people who lived apart from the tribal land base intended to abdicate their membership in the tribe of their birth—to assimilate into non-Native America. Tribal members still living within reservation boundaries did not need to submit such letters; only those who lived away from the reservation were required to. These letters exist because reservation era policies tied Native American identities as tribal members directly, concretely to land.

Not only did *tribal* membership remain tied to the tribal land base; the General Allotment Act of 1887 (the Dawes Act) explicitly tied US citizenship to the landownership status of tribal members. Historians often narrate US citizenship through the lens of "rights" and "obligations" that determine membership in a political community, as well as the political and legal struggles through which specific populations lobby for and achieve that membership. But for Native Americans, an earthier, physical reality rooted these abstract notions: the land.[6]

The Dawes Act of 1887 conferred US citizenship upon successfully allotted Indians; their allotment of land, divorced from the tribally held land base, became a symbol of detribalization, individualism, personal industry, and potential assimilation. Native land held in fee simple represented an individual's ability to hold the rights and fulfill the obligations of US citizenship. Charles Eastman, the famous Dakota physician, statesman, and Indian advocate—a man who helped identify and bury the bodies of Lakota tribal members killed at the massacre at Wounded Knee Creek—endorsed allotment, viewing it as a "major stepping stone to full citizenship."[7] The 1906 passage of the Burke Act eliminated the mandatory twenty-five-year waiting period required by the Dawes Act before individual Indians could sell their land—contingent upon allottees being determined "competent" to manage their own financial affairs. After Burke, the Office of Indian Affairs set up "competency commissions" to deem individuals legally "competent" and eligible for citizenship. Factors for competency included blood quantum, money management skills, self-sufficient income, and ability to speak English. Individuals classified as non-competent still received allotments, but the government held their land "in trust," and they could not sell it. Thus, the rights of citizenship remained closely tied to landownership status for Native Americans before the Indian Citizenship Act of 1924.[8]

Eastman's stance reflected what scholar Kevin Bruyneel terms an "ambivalent citizenship" of early twentieth-century Native America, one in which Native elites such as Eastman, Zitkala-Sa, and Carlos Montezuma often sought US citizenship to claim the social and political rights enjoyed by white Americans. These elites' arguments for full US citizenship, made to a national stage, recognized that preservation of Native lands would support tribal survival. At the same time, some local Native political leaders agitated to reject US citizenship—or at least remained suspicious of the status. More commonly, many Native community leaders and members appropriated the language of Americanism, citizenship, and patriotism to access the basic rights to practice their own culture, such as holding community dances and giveaways.[9]

The 1924 Indian Citizenship Act, signed by President Coolidge, extended US citizenship to the 42 percent of Native Americans who did not already hold citizenship through Dawes, previous agreement with the federal government, or wartime service. Although the act extended US citizenship it to all Native

Americans—whether it was wanted or not—Native people continue to toil to assert the social and economic rights of full citizenship. Some assert that the Indian Citizenship Act recognized "tribal citizenship" by disconnecting the conferral of US citizenship from the loss of tribal land rights, but at best the act opened the possibility for people to be both members of tribes and US citizens. After implementation, only *tribal* membership and the tribal land base remained linked for the federal government.[10]

Tribal communities possessed their own methods to determine tribal belonging. Tribal belonging did not hinge on landownership or tribal rolls. Rather, residence within the boundaries of the reservation, cultural practice, language, and most importantly kinship and clan relationships constituted a matrix of variables by which communities and community members determined belonging. The letters from tribal members confirming that they did not renounce tribal membership—and thus wished to vote in the IRA constitution election—indicate that tribal members living off-reservation measured their identity via tribal criteria; they saw no contradiction between living off-reservation and remaining an "Indian from both sides of the Missouri River."[11]

After the Indian Citizenship Act and before the Indian Reorganization Act, Native people *held* US citizenship status but *practiced* their tribal status. They possessed the political status of US citizen, like it or not. But because Native peoples' language, culture, phenotype, and kinship relations did not conform to the white, middle-class "American" cultural citizenship norm, the economic and political power structure continued to deny them the social and economic rights of citizenship. Native people could and were forced to imagine themselves as Americans, but could not *practice* that status due to racial harassment and discrimination. Most could not make large purchases without the approval of their local Indian agent, lending institutions rarely granted them access to loans, local governments denied voting rights in many state and federal elections, and all Native people faced racial harassment and violence from non-Native individuals and structures. But even while the social and economic rights of US citizenship remained barely tangible, Native people practiced—they lived—their tribal status. They did so by speaking their indigenous languages, learning and practicing familial and clan relationship expectations, attending community gatherings like powwows or dances, and working their lands in ways that merged historic tribal understandings and memories of the landscape with, for example, a modern version of cattle ranching for profit. They became experts in the "strategic deployment" of US cultural citizenship norms, emphasizing the "*rights* of citizenship when defending" their indigenous cultural priorities.[12]

The Indian Citizenship Act changed the relationship between tribal lands and US citizenship, but the Indian Reorganization Act shifted the way Native people understood themselves as community members. The IRA required tribal members across the country to organize for *or* against the imposition of the proposed new tribal political system. Also known as the Wheeler-Howard Act, the IRA grew as the brainchild of Roosevelt's commissioner of Indian affairs, John Collier. Collier based his legislation on more than a decade of activism against Office of Indian Affairs policies—particularly against the reduction of the Indian land base brought about by the Dawes Act and against Progressive Era policies that pushed Americanization or "detribalization." Historians classify the IRA as part of the set of community-focused New Deal initiatives alongside the Farm Security Administration (FSA), the Tennessee Valley Authority (TVA), the Civilian Conservation Corps (CCC), and the Federal Theatre, Writers and Arts projects. The act's main provisions set terms for tribal self-government, provided loans to tribal governments for education and small business, and ended allotment regulated by the Dawes Act. Collier's February 1934 press release called it the "bill of Indian rights" and emphasized "economic rehabilitation" and "self-government," while promising to stop the drain of Native American landholdings and resources due to allotment and to "curb the power" of the Office of Indian Affairs. Every tribe, excluding those in Oklahoma and Alaska, had to vote to adopt the reorganization measures. Two-thirds of the federally recognized tribes voted to accept the IRA (170 of the 258 total), but many did not. Historian Lawrence Kelly presents raw numbers on IRA adoption that make the legislation look unpopular—of approximately 97,000 eligible voters, only 38,000, or 39 percent, of Native Americans voted for the IRA; 24,000, or 25 percent, voted against it; and 35,000, or 36 percent, did not vote at all. These numbers may reflect Collier's failure to seek tribal input while structuring the bill, or his flaccid record of appointing Native Americans to top positions in the Bureau of Indian Affairs (BIA).[13]

In many ways, the IRA represented a change, not a reversal, in government policy. Intensified federal presence in individual Indian lives remained constant through the reservation era and into the IRA years. The late years of the reservation era saw this invasiveness at its peak as the government bureaucracy ballooned due to Progressive Era programming and regulations—as well as due to the effort necessary to continually push allotment land takings and the regulation needed to administer the leasing of tribal and individual allottees' lands. John Collier's IRA emerged from the tribally empowering activism of his early years—activism that advocated for tribal cultural, political, and economic self-determination—but it may also reflect the untenable workload for a bureaucracy whose attention to and attempt to control the intimate personal details of tribal members' lives peaked during the late reservation era. The IRA did not end the bureaucracy of Indian Affairs, even if it changed the tenor.[14]

Collier did not seek tribal input while crafting the IRA, but he organized a series of "Indian Congresses" throughout the country to answer questions from existing tribal leadership and Bureau of Indian Affairs staff about the legislation. Many concerns questioned the impact of the legislation on land issues, including allotment. The questions asked at a meeting in Elbowoods at Fort Berthold focused on land: the potential of white inheritance of Native land, transfer of title from individual Indian landowners, what the legislation would mean for the trust (tax-exempt) status of tribal and allotted lands, tribal jurisdiction over reservation lands, the nature of the proposed consolidation of scattered inherited landholdings, and the impact on landless Indians. One person asked, "As the white man is so crooked in getting our land away from us, how are we going to protect ourselves from losing our land in the future?" Another asked bluntly, "If we accept this bill, can we still sue the Government?"—a savvy question on the litigation of tribal land claims. Another queried whether the funds received to enact the provisions of the IRA at Fort Berthold would be considered as an offset to tribal claims in future litigation.[15]

Concerns over tribal land rights, the inheritance of land, the right to initiate litigation against the federal government, and whether the costs of implementing the IRA could be used to offset what the government might owe the tribe for a wrongful taking of land reflect, first and foremost, a tribal analysis of the half century of land loss due to implementation of the Dawes and Burke Acts. Between the 1887 passage of the Dawes Act and the 1934 passage of the IRA, ending Dawes, Native communities across the United States lost 63 percent of their total land base, or eighty-six million acres. Between 1880 and 1934, the US government took approximately 87 percent of the Fort Berthold land base, amounting to nearly seven million acres taken via executive order or allotment-related land openings. But the land-related concerns over the IRA also reflect the community's recognition that its land base served as a crucial foundation. Tribal concerns reflect a link between successfully defending tribal territories and ensuring a *future* for the tribal community.[16]

The IRA politicized the reservation in a new way. Tribal politics, of course, were hardly new. Dividing, uniting, and factionalizing, tribal politics remained rooted in family politics—who was related to whom and who they would support, which clan possessed and took care of which medicine bundle, and at Fort Berthold, which tribes held the majority. What anthropologists and other academics called "factions" existed long before the IRA (and continue to exist in local politics). But the IRA newly politicized the reservation as leadership rapidly held three elections, voting on whether to organize under the IRA, then whether to approve the constitution and bylaws, and finally whom to elect as the first tribal council under the IRA. After the circulation of an initial petition for incorporation—twelve pages of signatures and thumbprints still sit in the National Archives—the Three Affiliated Tribes voted on whether to organize under the IRA. On November 17, 1934, more than 93 percent of the reservation voted: 407, or 77 percent, for incorporation and 118 against.[17]

In October and November of 1935, the preexisting, ten-member tribal business committee along with five nonelected tribal members formed the constitutional committee to draft the tribal constitution and bylaws. The committee formed to ensure representation from all three tribes, the five largest communities, from both "Christian and Pagan forces," as well as those for and against incorporating under the IRA. For a period of a few weeks, the constitutional committee members traveled from across the reservation over dirt roads, "and were on the road early in the morning and late at night in severe weather." The work slowed and became more intricate due to the need to interpret every word of the constitution from English into three languages. The fieldworker reporting on the process described the committee as "a conglomerate and unwieldy committee made even more incoherent by personal antagonisms." Tribal and religious differences created distrust, and to top it off a South Dakota congressman and a Lakota tribal council member from the Standing Rock Reservation—both opposed to the IRA—also attended several of the meetings.[18]

From this difficult beginning, the work proceeded through the first half of November 1935. The fieldworker wrote to Collier that he felt great admiration for "these earnest and intelligent men," who refused to look at the models of other tribes' constitutions and bylaws until after they had crafted their own documents, "and then only for comparison, though later they came to desire revision in the light of what others had done, and, as a result, their constitution does not stand out as original as it really is." In its initial meetings, the committee spent a significant amount of time defining the territorial boundaries of the Three Tribes, and the "Land" section "required days of explanation." Tribal membership, on the other hand, "elicited little discussion," and the committee members agreed they did not want degree of Indian blood emphasized in determining membership. After the weeks of work, "Every item of their constitution and by-laws was accepted unanimously and every member went out to explain and defend it with every confidence that his work would be accepted."[19]

Thus did the constitutional committee lay the foundation to vote on the drafted constitution and bylaws. As the committee explained the constitution in four languages—English, Mandan, Hidatsa, and Arikara—tribal members continued to comment and suggest changes into January 1936. But the secretary of the interior approved the constitution to be put before Fort Berthold voters on March 11, 1936. The request for tribal affiliation for off-reservation members was sent soon after, and ballots were mailed in late April 1936. It was at this time that tribal members sent letters to Fort Berthold Indian agent William R. Beyer, confirming their continued tribal membership and claiming the right to vote in the constitutional election. Their act of claiming tribal suffrage despite physical distance from tribal territories illustrates a significant change. In the previous fifty years of federal Indian policy, the government not only would have ignored such claims to tribal membership and suffrage but would have never solicited them in the first place. As the senders of these letters reconfirmed their ties to the Three Affiliated Tribes and the Fort Berthold land base, as they asked for news of family members or land inheritance issues, they also show us that a new space opened in defining Indian identities. Tribal members could not only practice their cultural membership from afar; they could now practice their tribal *political* membership from West Virginia, Montana, or California.[20]

Immediately after the election approving reorganization for Fort Berthold and the development of the tribal constitution and bylaws, tribal leadership geared up for the next election: the approval of the constitution. The introduction to the constitution—crafted over long days of debate, translation, and negotiation in late 1935—reads, "We, the Arikara, Gros Ventres [Hidatsas], and Mandan Indians of the Fort Berthold Reservation, in North Dakota, eagerly embrace the opportunities for self-rule, and in order to enjoy the blessings of liberty and justice; to intelligently protect our vested rights under existing treaties and the Constitution of the United States; to guarantee to our posterity a more hopeful future; [and] to promote educational efficiency for the enhancement of good citizenship."[21] This constitution claimed a new citizenship identity for Three Affiliated tribal members, one of indigenous citizenship. It developed from complex tribal histories in reaction to the intricate forces of the federal government, the state of North Dakota, and the negotiation necessary to house three tribes in one juridical space.

This indigenous citizenship consisted of four components. First, it grew rooted in a lived, tribal cultural membership. Tribal identities, histories, and languages continued to be important to the communities, and served as the foundation—for example, the Three Affiliated Tribes' constitution begins by naming the tribes and the place. Second, while indigenous citizenship could at times be ambivalent and strategic, it also encompassed a deep commitment to the United States and citizenship within that polity. When the tribal constitution stated that it functioned to "intelligently protect our vested rights under . . . the Constitution of the United States" and "to promote educational efficiency for the enhancement of good citizenship," loyalty to the United States as an imagined space remained integral. Third, a dedication to indigenous land and resource rights balanced or perhaps outweighed this commitment to the United States and US citizenship. The "vested rights" mentioned did not only apply to rights under the US Constitution but also to rights retained "under existing treaties."[22]

Other scholars of the period and Native America alternately characterize indigenous citizenship claims in the first half of the twentieth century as "ambivalent," "hybrid," "strategic," or "differentiated." But ambivalence and hybridity as terms to describe indigenous citizenship actually indicate two mythos: first, what the white gaze is comfortable recognizing as indigenous; and second, what white America assumes is true about patriotism and US citizenship. Non-Natives imagine indigenous people as pre- (or anti-) modern—people and communities displaced or dominated by the modern nation—if they are thought about at all. Meanwhile, the nation-state—in this case, the US government—becomes part of modernity, and part of a liberal tradition of human rights. These become the two oppositional poles between which indigenous people supposedly feel ambivalence; they are the two traditions that supposedly combine to form a hybrid. But the modern nation-state and its accepted understandings of citizenship are not *owned* by the Euro-American tradition; they have been *built* over time as European nations enacted bloody expansion into the Americas, and thus built in dialogue with the everyday and exceptional resistance and persistence of indigenous communities. US citizenship, at least, has been shaped by and depends on its exclusions and exceptions as much as by the definitions of the so-called founding fathers in the US Constitution. Scholars of the sovereignty of the modern nation-state also mark European expansion into and resource extraction from the Americas as one of the seminal events that defined the evolution of modern state sovereignty. Thus, if citizenship and sovereignty are not *owned* by the Euro-American tradition—if they are also a product of indigenous action—how can there be a "hybrid" citizenship that understands indigeneity and the modern nation-state as conflicting traditions? "Hybrid," and "ambivalent" citizenship is, in fact, indigenous citizenship, a tradition that evolved and grew intertwined with Euro-American understandings of the nation, its citizenry, and its sovereignty.[23]

The characteristics of indigenous citizenship include, as summarized above, a steadfast commitment to tribal specificity and practices, a practical dedication to the nation-state as an imagined ideal, and a continuing pledge to asserting indigenous land and resource claims. These can all exist in the same place, at the same time, because they represent not a paradox but an integral struggle in the process of defining citizenship and sovereignty. The fourth and final characteristic of indigenous citizenship and sovereignty is seeing both as technologies for building a *future* for indigenous communities, embodied in the statement from the Three Affiliated Tribes' constitution that reorganization at least in part aimed "to guarantee to our posterity a more hopeful future."

Land provided the basis for this hopeful future. From the initial land-related concerns regarding the prospect of reorganization, to the long hours spent defining tribal territories within the constitution, to the fact that the largest portion of the constitution by far is the "Lands" section, which describes the administration of tribal lands, tribal leadership and community members saw the maintenance of the tribal land base as a key component to ensuring tribal survival and "a more hopeful future."[24]

The first article of the Three Affiliated Tribes' IRA constitution defined tribal territories. The Fort Berthold council decided on the following wording for their constitution—apparently the source of much discussion: "The jurisdiction of the Three Tribes of the Fort Berthold reservation to all lands now containing [sic] within the Fort Berthold reservation to such other lands within or without the present boundaries of the Fort Berthold reservation as may hereafter be added thereto under any law of the United States, excepting as otherwise provided by law." Historians characterize IRA constitutions as boilerplate documents, but the general truth of that accusation should not obscure the specific reality that tribal leaders drafted and worked to pass tribal constitutions. They debated and discussed each article because they knew their communities would hold them accountable. They also drafted constitutions that reflected concerns most dear to them and to their constituents.[25]

The transitional government submitted the constitution and bylaws to the reservation on March 11, 1936, followed by extensive community discussions and debates in which the constitutional committee explained, translated, and advocated for their constitution. In the election to ratify the constitution and bylaws, over 90 percent of the tribal electorate voted, and the majority endorsed the constitution by a vote of 366 in favor and 220 against—or 62 percent in approval of the constitution and bylaws.[26]

Fort Berthold communities varied in their reaction to the IRA—both in voter turnout and actual support for the constitution and bylaws—as shown by table 2.1.

The largely Hidatsa and Mandan communities of Elbowoods, Lucky Mound, Independence, and Beaver Creek all voted to endorse the IRA constitution and bylaws by 60 percent to 93 percent of their eligible voters. Meanwhile, the communities of Shell Creek and Little Missouri—largely Hidatsa communities—voted against the IRA constitution. But whereas Little Missouri possessed the lowest voter turnout with approximately 61 percent—indicating either a lack of investment in the election save by those who wanted to vote against the IRA constitution, or an overall lack of interest in the election—Shell Creek held one of the highest voter turnouts on the reservation at nearly 93 percent of their eligible voters casting a ballot. The approval vote was closely contested in Shell

Table 2.1
Reservation-Wide Vote on Acceptance of the Indian Reorganization Act

Community	Number yes votes	Yesses (%)	Number no votes	Nos (%)	Est. no. of eligible voters	Voter turnout (%)
Elbowoods	65	60.2	43	39.8	138	78.2
Lucky Mound	32	80	8	20	Unknown	Unknown
Shell Creek	53	44.9	65	55.1	127	92.9
Independence	80	93	6	7	111	77.5
Nishu	60	54.1	51	45.9	136	81.6
Little Missouri	22	37.3	37	62.7	97	60.8
Beaver Creek	28	82.4	6	17.6	32	At least 100
Absentee	26	86.7	4	13.3	Unknown	n/a
TOTALS	**366**	**62.5**	**220**	**37.5**		

Creek and the community with another high voter turnout, the largely Arikara settlement of Nishu, and both produced the smallest gap between the "no" and "yes" votes. In these two communities, residents likely experienced highly politicized months leading up to the election.[27]

After the approval of the constitution and bylaws, a third election immediately followed: the election for the first IRA-organized tribal council. The tribal business council, which previously held elections and meetings sporadically, could now exercise far more administrative authority than possible throughout the entire reservation era. These events altered the structure of elections, politics, and decision-making, and through the shift in authority and legitimacy, the nature of tribal sovereignty and citizenship also changed course.

The contest to define the impact and legacy of the IRA began shortly after Collier left office, when anthropologist H. Scudder Mekeel and Collier himself exchanged interpretations in a 1944 issue of *American Anthropologist*. During the 1970s and 1980s, scholars attempted to ascertain and measure the IRA legacy from a bird's-eye view of federal Indian policy and an emphasis on national (rather than tribal) politics. This approach sometimes lionized or demonized Collier as the lone change agent, and the BIA as the only source of political power impacting Native communities. Such analyses defined Collier and the BIA as the fulcrum and characterized political activism within Native communities as silent or reactive. Recent scholarship, however, illustrates that the question of whether the IRA succeeded or failed flattens and elides the importance of tribal politics and Native community activism. Regardless of whether tribal communities mounted successful political activism for or against implementation of IRA governments or stock reduction programs, or whether they participated in other New Deal programs, they all *used* the opening provided by the question of whether to organize under the IRA. Tribes used the IRA to argue over and agitate for a solution that fit the cultural, social, and community political needs of that specific community. Native communities retooled the priorities of the federal government via IRA legislation and used the debate over the legislation to express and realize longer-standing community concerns and needs.[28]

Fort Berthold communities also debated the success or failure of the IRA. Resistance to the IRA power structure, largely emanating from the community of Shell Creek, continued throughout the New Deal and World War II years. Those with authority within the IRA government, of course, saw the legislation as a success. In 1937 the Fort Berthold Tribal Business Council passed a resolution opposing its repeal as a message to North Dakota senator Lynn Frazier and in answer to the critics of the IRA nationwide. The resolution, dated March 18, 1937, read,

> Whereas: After the advent of the white man, the governing powers of the Indian were abrogated, their possessions in lands were given to other authority; they were driven onto Reservations created for them to live within the prescribed boundaries, agencies were established and Agents appointed to rule and take charge of all Indians and their affairs in their jurisdiction, and
>
> Whereas: The Indian has lost all power of self-government, and depends upon the Agent for all activities of business, as the Agent is empowered to set for him, and
>
> Whereas: The present Commissioner of Indian Affairs, the Hon. John Collier, has seen and recognized these injustices and is seeking to correct them and to restore to the Indian his self reliance and allow him to think for himself, . . .
>
> BE IT RESOLVED:
> That the Members of the Fort Berthold Tribal Council go on record as opposing the repealment of the said Wheeler-Howard Bill, and ask Senator Lynn Frazier to sustain and support the original bill.[29]

Whatever the failings of the IRA or internal power struggles due to the reorganization of political leadership on Fort Berthold, the community welcomed the change from ward of the federal government to state of self-governance.

The tribal business council minutes during this era show that the IRA-associated political shift toward self-government created the opportunity for community members to redefine citizenship and to defend and preserve their land base and its resources. Before the general tribal vote on the IRA constitution, a tribal elder and leader, Chief Bears Arm, told the tribal business council representatives,

> We older men are looking to you and have faith in your judgment to conduct our tribal affairs. I consider the Constitution and By Laws, which you have been discussing, a worthy accomplishment. It is an instrument of power which will enable you to properly pursue and accomplish the

happiness and contentment of our people. I favor the plan of submitting the document to each district for study, and of calling a general Council for approval and adoption by the three tribes. ... I wish to say one thing, and then I am through. That I have favored the Wheeler-Howard Act from its beginning and rejoice that our people have accepted the Act by a large majority and that I hope that when it becomes effective, you will be able to exercise larger powers as extended to you in its terms.[30]

Not even the BIA truly knew what would result from its own program, but Fort Berthold community members *hoped*. They hoped that reorganization would increase community and political autonomy. They hoped reorganization would secure the future of the lands and people of Fort Berthold.[31]

Exercising Authority: Land and Belonging

The new IRA government at Fort Berthold possessed larger powers. Reorganization required tribal leadership to define enrollment and tribal membership, create new leadership structures, build infrastructure, and redefine the relationship between tribal membership and land. Through this work, tribal leaders—and ultimately the population as a whole—redefined their narratives of space and belonging.

Before the IRA, the tribal business council (in existence since 1910) held ten members, one from each of the communities except Shell Creek and Nishu, which respectively sent two and three representatives to the pre-IRA council. While neither community stood as the largest on the reservation, Shell Creek contained the descendants of a community of dissenters, and Nishu held a largely Arikara population that often felt marginalized by the close cultural and family ties of their Mandan and Hidatsa neighbors. Each district also held a sub-tribal council, and these sub-councils elected representatives to the larger tribal council. The pre-IRA council possessed no constitution or bylaws and no regular meetings; it exercised its authority through tribal lease approval, enrollment decisions, and recommendations for local agency position vacancies. Traditional leaders possessed no formally enforced role, but communities continued to respect their opinions and afforded traditional leadership "every opportunity to voice their opinions in any official matters." When tribal business necessitated important representation, such as signing indigenous land claims papers, the pre-IRA council ensured that "the necessary papers were signed by hereditary chiefs."[32]

This snapshot of pre-IRA tribal authority falls in the middle of a spectrum on the northern plains, between tribes like the Crows and Blackfeet, who successfully advocated for a representative government reflective of traditional authority, and the situation on several Lakota reservations, in which Lakota cultural leaders fought an uphill battle against local Indian agents determined to strip traditional leadership of its authority. Though Fort Berthold was less contentious in its interactions with the local branch of the Indian Affairs bureaucracy, it did not have agents as racist and hateful as those at Standing Rock, Rosebud, or Pine Ridge. The relative lack of conflict allowed Fort Berthold, after a sweltering and dry summer, to elect the first IRA tribal council in a painless transition to an IRA government.[33]

The new tribal council structure granted less representation to Nishu and increased that of the Independence community; Shell Creek's delegates remained the same. Several members of the first IRA council had served as representatives in the previous iteration of the tribal business council, including the chair, Arthur Mandan from Lucky Mound district, and Peter Beauchamp from Nishu. Both men became elected to leadership roles within the new council, Mandan as tribal chair, and Beauchamp as secretary.[34]

The Fort Berthold IRA government threw itself into management, especially concerning land and its resources. The new tribal government worked to preserve resources to ensure sustainability. The new tribal business council hoped to reverse overgrazing damage, especially those in the "Big Lease"—the large communal grazing ground at the center of the reservation. Some might characterize this activity as acculturation and adjustment to the Euro-American economic system, but it also represents the protection of Fort Berthold land resources. Minutes from an early council meeting record, "[Tribal Chairman] Mr. Mandan called the attention of the committee to the distressing need of conserving the scanty pasture on all parts of the reservation. He stated that one way to bring about this change is to insist that all outside stock now running at large at present, in fact this trespassing of outside stock has for a long time been complained of by the Indians in all districts on the reservation." Reports of overgrazing or lax leasing practices resulted in immediate council enforcement of preservation-oriented regulations. The 1938 ballot for the second election, held after completing reorganization in 1936, included a measure to decide whether the tribal pastures would be an open or closed range. In an open range, Native-owned livestock could graze free of charge and farmers would be responsible for fencing their fields; a closed range would hold

Table 2.2
Fort Berthold Tribal Council Election Results, 1936
(winner's name in boldface)

Elbowoods (1)	**George Grinnell**	37
	J. B. Smith	22
	Joseph Packineau Jr.	21
	John Hunts Along	8
	Walter Stink Face	1
Shell Creek (2)	**Drags Wolf**	55
	Mark Mahto	40*
	Robert Dancing Bull	40*
	Leo Young Wolf	35
	Charles Fox	19
	Michael Mason	19
Independence (2)	**Ben Goodbird**	75
	Hans Walker Sr.	57
	James Baker	41
	Wolf Lies Down	13
Nishu (2)	**Peter Beauchamp**	62
	Clair Everett	50
	Albert Simpson	42
Beaver Creek (1)	**George Gillette**	26
	John W. Star	6
Lucky Mound (1)	**Arthur Mandan**	15
	Thomas Spotted Wolf	12
Little Missouri/Red Butte (1)	**Philip Atkins**	32
	Charles Huber	27
	Ben Benson	20

*Tie vote.

livestock owners liable for field damages, and Native ranchers would be responsible for herd management. The council also formed a land committee, charged with identifying reservation locations where pasture degradation required immediate action to reverse it. In these years of extreme drought, the council gave priority to such activities. The complicated status of lands within reservation boundaries—which, post-allotment, included "Indian-owned patent fee lands," "patent fee lands sold to aliens," "homestead lands on present reservation acquired by entry," "homestead lands on tract opened to entry," "homestead lands not filed on," "town sites," state lands, and government-owned pasture and sites—created urgency around the preservation of lands still held by the tribe.[35]

The council defended its territorial base in reaction to the long history of unwanted cessions and the depredations of local white cattlemen and farmers in overtaxing the grazing and agricultural lands of the reservation—some of the best pastureland in the Dakotas. The council's early decision to put together a reservation brand book, which listed all the brands of enrolled tribal members on the reservation, gathered necessary information for land management and preservation. Completed in 1936, the book lists cattle-owning tribal members alongside a hand-drawn representation of their brand. The book served an index necessary to discipline and control the cattle within reservation boundaries. The council also quickly invested in fencing the reservation boundaries—not only to exclude cattle from local ranchers, but to define and mark tribal territories. Finally, in a precursor of years to come, soon after the 1936 election, tribal leaders Peter Beauchamp and Arthur Mandan attended a conference at Devils Lake called by the Army Corps of Engineers, at which they "made a strong plea to not consider any project such as the Garrison dam site, that would drown out the Reservation bottom lands." Defense of the Fort Berthold territorial base required constant vigilance.[36]

The newly empowered tribal leadership regarded this moment as an opportunity to increase tribal territories and bolster self-government. The tribal council insisted on language in its IRA-organized constitution that planned for the conversion of purchased land to trust status; it prioritized capital accrual to fund new land claims litigation; and it carefully authorized infrastructure expenditures—only approving them in the form of schools, roads, and bridges for smaller communities such as Nishu and Red Butte. The Fort Berthold IRA government used its new powers to repair Dawes-related damage to tribal landholdings. It prioritized return of alienated lands, solidification of the land base, and even planned to buy lands allotted to elderly tribal members so sales to non-Natives would not alienate them from tribal holdings.[37]

Tribal leaders also worked to enact successful control of their lands and resources. The council created a game committee to manage reservation hunting and fishing and began to regulate the use and sale of natural resources such as coal and timber. It made strong distinctions between use by tribal members versus non-tribal members and prioritized Native access to land resources. Tribal leadership resolved to ensure that tribal resources benefited tribal members first and foremost.[38]

When the federal government expanded its structure, responsibilities, and interactions with its citizenry during the New Deal era, tribes also seized the opportunity to self-govern and expand their own authority. In the early years of reorganization, the tribal business council centered its practice of self-government around land and resource use. The previous fifty years of takings by the federal executive and legislative branches reinforced these priorities, but centuries of close ties with Missouri River valley lands and natural resources also played an important role.

The reorganized council also restructured tribal enrollment and membership because membership allowed access to land. The tribal council denied petitions for enrollment due to cloudy or denied parentage, or because a child lived with a non-Native parent. These enrollment denials illustrate a tribal council that viewed tribal status and enrollment as a protected resource. The council voted down one enrollment request despite the support by one council member:

1. Millie Anderson is a woman of good character and has raised this Sioux Indian child, who has become attached to her as her own.
2. Millie Anderson has no other living relatives and she has legally adopted this child.
3. Miss Anderson is raising the child properly and wishes it enrolled here. The child attends school here and probably will settle down here and marry into the tribe eventually.[39]

The next line in the meeting minutes states, "The vote was four for and five against," and so the council denied the child enrollment.

This represents a key change. Before the reservation era, the permeable boundaries of tribal belonging focused on culture and behavior rather than descent. Cagáagawia, or Bird Woman, variably spelled as "Sacagawea" or "Sakakawea" in English, represents the most famous example at Fort Berthold. Non-Hidatsa histories narrate Cagáagawia as a Shoshone girl captured by the Hidatsas as a child, who grew up in a Hidatsa village and in the early nineteenth century helped lead Lewis and Clark to the Pacific Coast. After the Lewis and Clark Expedition, she returned to the Hidatsa villages, despite opportunities to return to the Shoshones. During the reservation era, the federal government would likely have classified her descendants as "Hidatsa," had her son lived to also have children.[40]

During the reservation era, the federal government needed to quantify treaty-agreed financial obligations such as money, rations, or education, and so introduced a descent-based model of tribal membership via membership rolls. Tribal members and local Indian agents simplified tribal and cultural identities for membership rolls—and in some cases explicitly lied. But to this day, both tribes and the federal government treat the rolls as historical reality. When IRA-era tribal governments began to hold purview over enrollment and membership issues, they took on a high-stakes role. Enrollment, the legal acceptance of an individual as a member of a tribal community, represented more than personal ties and cultural affiliation. Had that been the entirety of the matter, it would be petty indeed to deny Millie Anderson's enrollment request for her adopted child. But enrollment and tribal membership rose in stakes due to Dawes-related allotment policies, the one-third increase in population between 1900 and the 1930s, and the per capita distribution of monetary settlements from successful land claims litigation. This context framed enrollment and membership so that it began to appear as a resource to be defended for future generations. And IRA-organized tribal councils that now held legal authority began to define their own membership criteria.[41]

The outcome of the split decision over Millie Anderson's petition for her adopted daughter shows that the council defined tribal membership in part via the descent or blood quantum system introduced by the federal government. The support for her request—four of the nine council members voted in favor of her petition—also indicates contestation of the imposed federal norm.[42]

Tribal leadership definitions of membership, enrollment, citizenship, and law—and that tribal communities debated, discussed, or accepted—evolved into a two-tiered indigenous citizenship. Tribal membership served as the first, local, immediate, and visceral tier. Community members interacted with each other daily—they spoke Hidatsa, Mandan, or Arikara to each other; told and retold local histories and traditional stories to each other in their homes; participated in the clan system and age societies and chose new religious and cultural leaders and participants each year; herded cattle together on the Big Lease or their family allotments; and helped each other process and dry corn and squash for the winter. Tribal members *lived* this membership—much in the same way they created place. Now for the first time since the reservation era began, the tribal council could define the legal status of that membership.

Tribal members also contended with a second citizenship tier that existed in constellation with tribal membership: US citizenship. The Indian Citizenship Act of 1924 created universal legal citizenship for all Native individuals, but the political, legal, and social benefits of that status remained far from realized.

Indian reorganization and federally recognized self-government, however, expanded the possibilities of the federal-tribal relationship. Even though Indian Bureau paternalism continued, local norms and assertions regarding the rights of US citizenship evolved. Communities could use reorganization to assert their competency via self-government, rather than individually prove their competency as wards of the federal government.

In the broader United States of the New Deal era (1932 to 1940), the behavior of the federal government shifted from a stance of minimal regulation of the worst excesses of capital to service provision and a naturalization of the federal regulatory role. The IRA, however, reversed this experience in tribal communities: the federal government ceased its tight control of reservation spaces, loosened direct regulation, and recognized the right of Native communities to define their own political power structures. This shift produced relief at Fort Berthold—remarkably similar to the relief felt in the general population regarding *increased* government services and regulation. It also produced a new understanding of US citizenship status; more than a set of economic and legal rights and responsibilities, it became a tool to claim political and social rights.[43]

Tribal leadership and self-governance at Fort Berthold included the draft and debate over the tribal constitution, the structure of the tribal council and internal committees, fundraisers to build a meeting hall for the tribal council, management and disbursement of tribal funds, and personnel actions toward Civilian Conservation Corps (CCC) managers deemed inefficient in their duties. These governance activities represent the assertion of US citizenship rights long denied to Indian tribes.

Long-standing tribal power and leadership structures grounded tribal self-government at Fort Berthold, despite the BIA's imposition of IRA structures. Early after reorganization, the tribal council built a central meeting hall large enough to accommodate not only the council but also community members who attended meetings to speak on behalf of petitions and issues. The council used tribal timber for the structure, but also fundraised using traditional techniques to defray the cost of the building. Families and individuals donated war bonnets—head coverings made of eagle feathers used as traditional symbols of leadership and authority—that the council sold to raise money for the new council hall. The donations emerged from Mandan and Hidatsa clan and family structure norms that predated the reservation era and represent male social connections and the work of men in making the war bonnets, and the social and cultural work of women. Women's social labor broadly enforced and enacted the clan structure and family relationships, just as a mother's clan determined her children's clan identity. This symbiotic gendered work of such a fundraising project required not only gendered reciprocity but also deep engagement with the sacred resources of the landscape in the form of eagle feathers and the purifying plants men used to work with the sacred objects. The local culture, traditions, stories, and practices, as well as the deep knowledge of the territories of the Three Affiliated Tribes, constructed both tribal membership and governance practice.[44]

Citizenship, and individuals' identities as tribal members and US citizens, deepened and solidified during the New Deal era because there was less of a perception of the two systems being at odds. Both tribal membership and US citizenship status took on new meanings with the organic interaction between the continuity of local meanings and constructions of place and identity and the opportunity to create new meanings as the IRA loosened the tight rein of federal paternalism within tribal territories.

Contesting Authority: Factionalism on Fort Berthold

Political efforts to undermine the IRA began even before implementation. Opponents rallied around the term reservation "factionalism." The IRA's political adversaries used the specter of intratribal disputes to criticize the legislation, and concerns over factionalism persist in analyses of its historical legacy. Scholars sometimes analyze factionalism as "a structural weakness" in reaction to colonialism, but the vibrancy of tribal communities despite long histories of factionalism requires a deeper interrogation.[45]

Intratribal struggles for control at Fort Berthold predate the IRA. Complaints about both the federal government and tribal leadership scatter the federal archives. Reservation life's highly local nature, in which everyone knew or held relationship ties with each other, easily led to personal resentments, particularly regarding law and order. The Fort Berthold community also contained economic divisions based on a confluence of race, access to Euro-American education, access to land and leasing, and profession. As early as 1910, the Office of Indian Affairs' (OIA; the official name of the BIA before Collier rebranded it) Forestry Division noted the consolidation of livestock ownership and the "monopolization" of access to common lands in the Big Lease as a potential problem. Often, larger stock operators built their herds by adopting "the ethics and management practices requisite to capital accumulation"—and moving away from Hidatsa, Mandan, or Arikara norms regarding the redistribution of resources. The IRA did not create these resentments or struggles for local political control, but it did create a new forum through which they could be voiced and fought.[46]

Immediately after the IRA election, a coalition of tribal members, dissatisfied with the election results and perhaps with the very idea of the IRA, circulated and submitted a petition calling for a reelection. Signed by forty-seven tribal members from most of the communities along the Missouri, the petition called for a reelection based on "irregularities" with the first tribal council election after reorganization. They charged that leadership failed to hold the election within thirty days after the adoption of the constitution and bylaws; that some candidates failed to file intent to run at least fifteen days before the election; that the newly elected tribal council did not meet within three days of the election; that one council member committed fraud by inducing another candidate in a different district to withdraw; and that one candidate lied by saying that yet another candidate withdrew, "thereby, strengthening falsely his position in the race."[47]

The greatest percentage of petition signatories came from Shell Creek—a community largely comprised of the descendants of tribal members who followed the Hidatsa leader Crow Flies High to live off-reservation in Montana from 1870 until 1894 (when an armed guard returned them to the reservation). During the IRA years, these community members—still known today as the Xo'shga—continued this pattern of dissent with the reservation power structure. Shell Creek provided over one-third of the overall names, and Shell Creek signers represented just over one-fifth of the eligible voters from that district. At the other extreme, Beaver Creek, one of the smallest communities on the reservation, contributed no names to the petition.[48]

Of the petition leadership from Shell Creek, tribal members Floyd Montclair, Philip Atkins, Frank Heart, and George Parshall persistently and vocally criticized the new IRA government. Soon after the circulation of the petition for a new election, the group created a resolution against the IRA government according to "the sentiments of the 260 [no] citizens"—the tribal members who voted "no" to organizing under the IRA. The resolution used US citizenship rights claims to push the group's anti-IRA agenda and invested in rhetoric of "civilization" and "citizenship": "[S]ince Congress passed a general law declaring all American Indians to be citizens of the United States, certainly we should now be recognized as citizens of the United States; treated as such and educated as such." The resolution centered around their opposition to "self-government

Table 2.3
Reelection Petition Signers by District

	% of eligible voters in the district represented by signers	% of total signers from the district
Elbowoods	6.5	12.2
Little Missouri/Red Butte	8.2	10.8
Shell Creek	21.3	36.5
Independence	11	16.2
Beaver Creek	0	0
Nishu	2.9	6.8
Lucky Mound, off-reservation, or unknown	n/a	14.9

rule," as the group did not want to "sacrifice their citizenship rights as granted to us on June 1924." The "resolved" section enumerated three suggestions to accompany the repeal of the IRA—apparently linked in the minds of the authors. The petitioners linked freedom from BIA-enforced guardian-ward status to their demand that social and law and order services to the reservation be administered by the state of North Dakota. A demand that "property and heirship confusion" be untangled accompanied the other requests.[49]

The petition sent to the Bureau of Indian Affairs illuminates the dissatisfaction some tribal members felt over the restructure of reservation authority. The new IRA government became a lightning rod for challenges to authority, and a spate of petitions immediately followed the election. Concerns became more personal, more fraught, and centered largely in the Shell Creek community. Shell Creek evolved into a hotbed of antagonism following the first IRA tribal council election. Tribal member Rufus Stevenson sent a detailed complaint to the Bureau of Indian Affairs in June 1936, claiming that the IRA created warring factions on the reservation, and that corruption plagued reservation policemen and a specific judge. Although the petition is not present in the federal archives, Fort Berthold superintendent William Beyer's response details and answers its claims. Beyer did "not think that 'warring' is applicable" and instead described the situation as a "difference of opinion amongst Shell Creek residents," one faction supporting Rufus Stevenson, and the other supporting Shell Creek tribal council representative Drags Wolf. Beyer characterized the factions as two cliques in a "very small community ... in constant disagreement on most any consideration." He described how before the dissidents circulated the petition, the daughter of tribal member George Parshall—also one of the signers of the previous petition—entered "an unladylike fight with another Indian lady over the outcome of the election on the Reorganization Bill." The police took Parshall's daughter to Indian Court, where she was sentenced to thirty days in the McClean County Jail. Beyer suggests that this incident led to the corruption accusations lodged against the local police and tribal judge. The accusations also criticized tribal judge Daniel Wolf as insufficiently educated to fill his post. Beyer's defense of Wolf reveals the intensely personal nature of reservation politics:

> Our Indian Judge receives only $15 per month for his services; this amount is inadequate when it is considered that being a judge on an Indian Reservation among ones relatives, friends, and tribesmen is not an easy position to fill. Judge Daniel Wolf may not have obtained a high degree of proficiency in his schooling, but long years of living among Indians as a member thereof, has instilled into his mind an experience of thoughtfulness, and all due consideration of angles that eventually reach a common point.... We do not think the signers of the petition who in some cases signed the same by a thumb-mark thereon, are in a position to offer a complaint against another as being "ignorant and uneducated." Obviously some of the signers needed the petition interpreted to them before understanding its contents.[50]

The attacks against the new authority structure continued. In September 1936 at the first meeting of the IRA-organized tribal council, Mark Mahto from Shell Creek, who consistently criticized the IRA, objected to his fellow Shell Creek representative Drags Wolf. Mahto alleged that Drags Wolf had circulated the claim that another Shell Creek candidate, Charles Fox, had withdrawn his candidacy. Drags Wolf clearly won the district, while Fox received the lowest votes, and Beyer insinuated that Mahto's objections arose from a desire for a bloc of council members from Shell Creek who agreed with his anti-IRA views.[51] That same month, tribal member Floyd Montclair sent a petition to both Collier and Secretary of the Interior Harold Ickes that stated, "Candidates for Tribal Business Council shall be able to speak the English language fluently," and that "candidates for Tribal Business Council shall be new members, and not any of the old councilmen." Other petitions called for an age limit to be set for council membership. When the BIA and federal government declined to intervene in Fort Berthold affairs—and when the new tribal council announced via the reservation newsletter, "These petitions were carefully considered by the Business Council and by a unanimous vote were found to be unwarranted of favorable consideration. Consequently, the requests contained in these petitions were not granted"—the attacks on the authority of the new tribal council ended.[52]

Dissident tribal members regrouped and focused their economic disgruntlement on attempts to undermine the IRA. Their discontent with the IRA continued through the 1940s and linked to national efforts to repeal the IRA. *Indian Truth*, an Indian Rights Association magazine critical of Collier and the IRA, published an anti-IRA article drawn from Fort Berthold tribal member experiences. The tribal council felt compelled to officially contest the claims in the article. After emphasizing the over 90 percent participation rate in each election and reiterating the affirmative votes on the adoption of the IRA, the constitution and bylaws, and the charter, the council's statement then debunked the accusations that federal representatives had threatened to send children away to school if parents did not vote for the IRA, that candidates bought votes in the IRA election, or that reservation authorities committed a tribal member to an insane asylum due to his opposition to the tribal constitution. They closed their letter:

> [The article] says that the Indians are coming to hate the whites because of the Wheeler-Howard Act, and coming to feel superior to the whites. That is not true either. There has always been good feeling on our reservation between Indians and whites and between full-bloods and mixed-bloods, and there still is. For instance, lately when times have been so bad and the white men who leased some of our Indian land could not pay, we modified our leases and put them on a crop-share basis instead. We knew they couldn't pay and it was all done with good neighborly feeling. We don't want any race feeling to start at Fort Berthold.[53]

In 1938 the dissidents organized a chapter of the Oklahoma-based American Indian Federation, an organization with three goals: repeal the IRA, remove Collier, and abolish the BIA. In 1940, the same American Indian Federation members began to organize dissent activities through the local American Legion post. These efforts bore little fruit, but they proved an effective and persistent distraction in the decade following reorganization.[54]

The economic criticisms of the dissidents, however, deserve further examination. They indicate the outlines of the Fort Berthold class structure and economic inequities. These issues intensified during the 1940s as the Three Affiliated Tribes organized against the construction of the Garrison Dam, and as the stress and pressure of organizing against what became the inevitable tide of the Garrison Dam played upon older fractures: class, blood quantum, and conflict over legitimate authority at Fort Berthold.

The dissidents criticized the use and distribution of tribal resources. They lobbied for per capita payments from successful land claims, questioned work allocation under federal programs like Civilian Conservation Corps–Indian Division (CCC–ID), and claimed favoritism in the administration of a cattle purchasing program created by the tribal business council. These criticisms echo older complaints and anxieties. The Xo'shga (also described as the Crow Flies High band) were forefathers of the dissident group centered at Shell Creek. The Xo'shga had left the reservation in the 1870s due to a disagreement over the distribution of meat. By the 1930s, the dissidents put considerable effort and time into contestations regarding a $400,000 claim the tribes litigated against the US government. The tribal business council sent delegations to Washington, DC, to attend committee meetings in the Senate and House over the claim as early as 1937, but the slow progress angered the dissident group. They formed a group called Fort Berthold Americans, Inc. in February 1941, and their first announcement proclaimed, "We have waited too long for the pleasure of any office boy or ten shilly shallying Charley McCarthys [sic] to bring the bacon from our $400,000 claim." The Fort Berthold Americans also linked the lack of progress on the $400,000 claims issue to the IRA, stating, "The administration of the so-called Indian Reorganization Act, and legal complications which resulted from the application of the act to the people of Fort Berthold Reservation" had resulted in a lack of general progress and in fact, the group claimed, "conditions are generally worse, and a great unhappiness among our people have resulted."

Despite a tribal council resolution the next month denouncing the "subversive activities of the Chair and Secretary of Fort Berthold Americans, Inc.," a few months later, Oscar Burr and Floyd Montclair traveled to Washington, DC, on behalf of the group—and supposedly the entire reservation—to lobby regarding the Court of Claims bill. When they returned, Superintendent William Beyer reported to Collier, "They are holding meetings in various districts and giving a glowing account of their accomplishments in Washington."[55]

The dissidents aimed to expedite the claims and to distribute the claims money per capita. They industriously circulated petitions for per capita payments, such as in 1939 when they requested that a per capita payment be made from tribal funds. Although their advocated payment would have resulted in a per capita payment of twenty-four dollars per person (according to Superintendent Beyer), the dissidents considered it a possible solution to dire and immediate economic distress. One wrote to North Dakota senator William Langer, "We get stamps for food but a large number of people do not even want food stamps. We want money to buy clothing for our children." The class divisions may seem small to outsiders, but some families struggled to buy food or clothing for children, and among families struggling for meager resources such economic distress created disillusionment with the reservation authority structure.[56]

Some of the dissident rhetoric could be almost comical. By 1940 the council created a cattle purchasing plan to contribute to economic development. It planned to use tribal funds to purchase herds, and youth from the only high school on the reservation (Elbowoods School) who planned to build a ranching career would care for them and receive a portion of the proceeds when the cattle went to market; the tribe would receive the other portion. The dissidents of the Fort Berthold chapter of the American Indian Federation, later of Fort Berthold Americans, Inc., occasionally meeting under the guise of the local American Legion post—and always centered around the Shell Creek community—predicted failure for the plan, wasted tribal funds, and unfair assignments for the opportunity to run the cattle. All these predicted failures, they believed, stemmed from the ills of reorganization at Fort Berthold. The mouthpiece publication of the Indian Agency, the *Fort Berthold Bulletin*, published the following exhortation from Superintendent Beyer regarding the dissident claims:

> We have on this reservation a small number of self-appointed prophets who travel from district to district and attend the meetings that are held to discuss [the cattle purchase plan]. These fellows "prophets" are loud in their clamor, stating that we cannot succeed at any plan—and they use as proof that they, themselves, have not succeeded at any plan. If these "prophets" are your leaders, stick with them, they know the road to the relief department.
>
> Think, and then think again. This is a good reservation, land and water, grass and timber, enough to support all the people here on a much higher standard of living than we have now BUT WHO'S [sic] CATTLE ARE EATING THE GRASS?[57]

The tribal referendum on the cattle purchasing program swung heavily in favor of its implementation. As usual, Shell Creek served as the lone dissident community.

After the electorate approved the cattle purchase program, the dissidents continued to organize, writing again to Senator Langer to request intervention. Floyd Montclair's letter tied the cattle purchase program at Fort Berthold to totalitarianism, dictatorship, and propaganda. His letter ended, "I am ... glad to state that we are not afraid to fight for those things we cherish most. We choose right to live. Not as some foreign ideologists or not the crushing heel of any dictator. . . . We will stand together in this fight for freedom against aggressors." His writing mirrors jingoistic World War II rhetoric. Only, his exposition focused not on German aggression or Soviet activism but rather on a tribal cattle purchase program. The bombast may have emerged from desperation, felt by a minority group on the reservation with a long history of disagreement with tribal leadership structures, fueled by economic inequities and the frustration that accompanies mockery of or silence regarding their critiques. Successful access to cattle as an economic resource underlay a growing class divide at Fort Berthold, and ranchers often worked within the tribal political structure and on the implementation of BIA policy at the local level to protect their land and economic interests.[58]

Contestation of the legitimacy and authority of Fort Berthold's IRA tribal government lasted until the tribes faced something bigger to fight—the

Table 2.4
Cattle-Purchasing Program Referendum Results by District

	No. yes votes	Yeses (%)	No. no votes	Nos (%)	Dist. total	% of total reservation vote
Shell Creek	11	35.5	20	64.5	31	12.4
Elbowoods	54	77.1	16	22.9	70	28.1
Lucky Mound	23	82.1	5	17.9	28	11.2
Nishu	46	100	0	0	46	18.5
Beaver Creek	21	84	4	16	25	10
Independence	16	57.1	12	42.9	28	11.2
Little Missouri/Red Butte	15	71.4	6	28.6	21	8.4
TOTALS	**186**	**75**	**63**	**25**	**249**	

Source: *Fort Berthold Bulletin*, May 1941, Fort Berthold Indian Agency, Record Group 75, National Archives and Records Administration, Kansas City.

Garrison Dam. In the consolidation and exertion of legitimate authority—one of the main components of sovereignty and self-determination practices—these intratribal struggles could only shallowly be classified as "factionalism," or a "structural weakness" that existed as a result of colonialism. These disagreements did arise within the context of colonial dispossession of territory and resources, but such an analysis assumes both an idyllic past and that colonialism holds responsibility for any development, change, or evolution of behavior or thought. The intratribal conflicts at Fort Berthold during the New Deal and early Word War II years show that the development of legitimate authority within a tribal community neither depended on nor had its sole roots in the legislation or bureaucratic practices of the federal government. Communities determined legitimate authority. Tribal members fought, sometimes physically, over being able to define legitimate authority. Their battles over and determinations of the legitimacy of tribal governments opportunistically used or reacted against federal initiatives as they created and set into place the most visceral, concrete components of modern tribal sovereignty.

The New Deal years at Fort Berthold resulted in several changes in practices that comprise modern notions of tribal sovereignty—the exercise and contestation of legitimate authority; the nature of tribal citizenship; the evolution of an indigenous citizenship; and the defense, management, and expansion of territory. Community members—both the acknowledged power structure and dissident groups—shaped these practices, often in battles fought among themselves. The federal government unquestionably modified the physical and political landscape of rural America in the New Deal era, but tribal members seized the legislation's potential to shape and live their own definitions of self-government, membership, and territorial defense.

The IRA did not create authority; it reorganized it, first by staying the heavy hand of federal control in reservation spaces, then by unintentionally creating the discursive space for indigenous communities across the country to organize for or against the legislation. The question of whether the IRA succeeded or failed is simplistic, and we consider a more interesting history when we recognize that Native communities took on an imperfect policy and worked like hell to make it work for them. Whether they accepted or rejected the IRA, indigenous communities across the United States took advantage of the opportunity to define, defend, and regulate tribal territories and memberships.

Land—as a place, space, and territory—embodies a community's past and shapes its future survival. The IRA-organized tribal council saw the delineation, management, defense, and expansion of tribal territories as integral to bolster self-government, prosperity, and security for their community. This exercise of tribal self-definition changed both tribal membership *and* indigenous citizenship. Protection of the tribal land base as a resource for future generations impacted the way the Fort Berthold tribal council defined tribal membership and enacted enrollment decisions. It also resulted in the development of an indigenous citizenship in which neither their US citizenship rights nor their indigenous treaty rights stood as paradoxical to the other.

In contrast to earlier accounts, this history illustrates that federal legislation does not solely drive all this change. What previous analyses termed "factionalism" in fact represents an intratribal contest over the definition of legitimate authority. In the community battles over who deserves to be elected to tribal council, how the tribal council should operate, and what decisions should be legislated and enforced, *all* tribal members, dissident and otherwise, opportunistically used the discursive space created within tribal communities by the IRA to hammer out the extent and boundaries of legitimate authority on the reservation. The Marshall Trilogy, *Ex parte Crow Dog*, Dawes Act, Indian Citizenship Act, and Indian Reorganization Act—the collection of case law and legislation called federal Indian law and policy—may all comprise the timbers and boards of tribal sovereignty. But the lived realities of these policies and laws must be realized on a local level; not even Indian law scholar Felix Cohen could wave a magic wand in Washington, DC, and create tribal sovereignty on every reservation in the United States. Thus, these community-based, family- and clan-fueled tribal political battles are the foundation stones upon which modern concepts of tribal sovereignty rest.

Chapter 3

Indigenous Citizenship, 1940–1945

Like thousands of other little girls across the United States during World War II, Lyda Bearstail spent her wartime childhood sneaking "listens" to the music on the radio supposed to be reserved for the news. She saved to buy war bonds, helped her parents with household chores, and engaged in support activities for the Red Cross. The rhetoric of war—defense, the flag, land, sacrifice, and fighting—permeated her daily life through the radio, the newspapers, and the buzz of conversations among the adults.

But in one respect Lyda stood out from other girls participating in the war effort: her participation in the Fort Berthold "USO." During the war, local chapters of the United Service Organizations (USO) were scattered the country, assembling care packages and welcoming home returning servicemen. But the USO at Fort Berthold, unaffiliated with the larger organization, organized activities that bore the distinct imprint of Fort Berthold's place, territory, and culture. Fort Berthold USO welcome-home activities centered on community dances featuring Native music, dances, feasts, and giveaways for returning servicemen. Lyda remembered how the Fort Berthold group became called the USO:

> I was in [the USO], I was very young. I had to carry a banner that had "USO" on there. They always invited soldiers and here this one, Lawrence Birdsbill, came back, and he said that "your outfit here is like" [the USO he had encountered] when they landed, wherever they landed. Anyway when they came back they gathered—they fed them and they gave them money—and they were called "United Service Organization," so he gave that name to us and they had that on that little banner I

Figure 3.1. Welcome home dance for a returned Marine veteran. North Dakota State Historical Society.

carried when they sang our song when we first came in, and all the committee members would dance."[1]

Dancing in a taffeta elk tooth dress that her *ishawi* (her aunt on her father's side) made her, Bearstail contributed to an event that expressed US patriotism, an affirmation of support and care for soldiers from her tribal community, a celebration of long-standing tribal values that honored men's wartime service to their community, the coalescence of men's and women's work, and a recognition of the importance of both tribal and national place and space. The community dance to honor returned soldiers represents one of many ways people at Fort Berthold developed and maintained a radically indigenous patriotism and indigenous citizenship during World War II—one that connected with and elaborated upon the forms of indigenous citizenship developed during the Indian New Deal. This chapter examines those elaborations of patriotism, citizenship, belonging, and tribal identity to provide insight into Fort Berthold on the eve of the construction of the Garrison Dam.

This chapter first describes the local histories and meanings tied to the land—or place-making—produced by the music, dance, and activities of USO celebrations for returned soldiers. Then, we identify the nexus of human labor within the Fort Berthold landscape that sustained this performance of patriotism and citizenship. Finally, we closely read one element of the event, a flag song, to explore how these enactments of citizenship and patriotism also expressed individual and collective belonging to and possession of the land that constituted "home" for Fort Berthold tribal members. Together, this evidence shows that while larger US narratives of patriotism, work, citizenship, and nation shaped the contours of Fort Berthold community identity, a deeper set of cultural practices relating to history and place-making structured it. These practices and narratives represent the most dynamic elements in the foundations of indigenous citizenship and, thus, tribal sovereignty.

"USO" Dances at Fort Berthold

From the US entry into World War II in December 1941 to the return of servicemen and women in 1945–46, the Fort Berthold community honored soldiers returning after basic training or deployment at a welcome-home dance. The practice drew on longtime community traditions that honored veterans of armed conflict, such as men who protected the villages against Lakota or other tribal incursions. Within the twentieth century, the practice evolved to address new needs and take on new meanings. Clyde Baker (Mandan, Hidatsa) remembered one such dance held for him as a returned soldier:

> There was only one drum in those days, by the way, one drum that handled the dance all night. And from what I hear today—I never did sing Indian—but I was told that there was never one song that was sung twice. There was that many songs that them guys knew by memory. In the wintertime, the nights are long, and that's when they danced all night.... I remember these honor dances because I was home on a furlough and I was given an honor, I remember. At that time there was no government programs around home here, but everyone it seemed like was independent, everybody had a little something—cattle and horses. I remember the people giving me forty dollars, one night, there was three of us home together that one night, and each one of us got forty dollars. This was in 1945, and I suppose today that forty dollars would be like a hundred and fifty dollars. But what I'm getting at here was where did those people get that money, that cash. They didn't have any checks, salary checks coming. But yet they had this value of sharing, I guess. I often thought of that.

Music and dance wove community support, sharing, and economic sacrifice for a returned soldier who had sacrificed for the community. An "economy of meaning that clusters around organized sound," as described by historian John Troutman, the welcome-home dances were rooted in grass dance societies and Omaha dance societies that spread across the northern plains during the nineteenth century—vibrant music and dance traditions that spawned the elaboration of new forms of dance and songs. USO dances also represented a new cultural form, for decades had passed since the last intertribal violence on the plains, and tribal members had lower participation in the First World War than they had in the Second World War.[2]

In the small communities clustered along the Upper Missouri, community members felt the absence of their relatives. During World War II, over 50 percent of the eligible male population served in the armed forces, two and a half times the national proportion of approximately 20 percent. Community newsletters listed the names of the men serving and printed excerpts from their letters, and decades later family members of the servicemen can name the other reservation men who served in their branch, what battles they were in, or when they enlisted. Before soldiers left, relatives prayed for them in English, Hidatsa, Mandan, and Arikara; they prayed for them in church, and over cedar or sweetgrass at home. They prayed for them to return home safely.[3]

When a soldier returned, the reservation at large turned out to celebrate, as relationship and clan ties bound each community to the others. Tribal member Tillie Walker explained, "We're all kind of related you know. We [people from Independence] would go over to Shell Creek if the Missouri River was iced over, and vice versa. It wasn't just the people who lived [in that community], it was broader than that." Each of the small communities along the river bottom had their own dance hall that served as a community meeting space and a place where dances—or "doings"—were held. At Independence, the community dance hall was called "The Soup Hall"; in Lucky Mound it was "Santee Hall." Tribal members trickled, and then flowed, to fill these community spaces. They gathered not only to honor the returned soldier but also to see relatives from another community, eat good food, dance, and enjoy the drum music. Tribal member Rosemarie Mandan, who as a child in Lucky Mound participated in an organization like Lyda Bearstail's "USO," called the "MacArthur Society," described a common scene:

> Especially when someone came home from the service, a soldier, they'd have those big dances for them. . . . I guess the dances back then were

> a little bit different from now. The men would be the ones all dressed, and they danced, and all the women would sit on one side and the men all sat on the other side, and if the women wanted to dance they would dance on the side ... but it was mostly men dancing. But they always had a good time, I remember that.

An older relative brought the returned soldier into the dance hall, and the dances began by welcoming the soldier back to the community. Bearstail noted that her father composed a song for the drum group to sing when they brought the soldier into the dance hall, and the lyrics of the song explicitly referred to welcoming him back.[4]

Northern Plains traditional singing and drumming drives and energizes community gatherings such as powwows, or honor dances like those for soldiers returning from war. Composed of four or five (or more) men who sing in Native languages and English, the drum group creates a powerful sound experience. Some songs have lyrics; others do not. But honor songs, flag songs, and tribally based dance songs usually hold between four and six lines of lyrics, per Plains music conventions. During this period, certain men known for their ability to compose songs made not only songs for social dances but also individual or group honor songs. Only men sang at the drum (and in fact for the Mandans and Hidatsas, only men are allowed to touch the drum), but women who knew the songs sometimes stood behind the drummers, encircling the drum to add a higher-pitched chorus to the words.[5]

Musical practice, as performance and as storytelling, evokes place-making. Music and singing saturated World War II–era Fort Berthold—and not just during community gatherings. Rosemarie Mandan remembered,

> Everybody sang back then, it wasn't just a certain group. *Everybody* sang. I went to sleep many a night listening to my brothers and sons. . . . They would sing. There were all kinds of different songs that you don't even hear anymore, today! There were doorway songs, . . . people had honor songs, . . . what they call *maxewidu*, which is, to me I always say, "That must be the *blues*" [laughs]. Those songs, and of course the dance songs. There was another, a riding song . . . that they sang when they were out riding. People sang *all* the *time*, you know, *everybody* . . . everybody that I knew sang. And there were all kinds of songs, and I remember even personal songs; I still remember Johnny Rabbithead's song, and Finley Blake's and those from Lucky Mound. Because I heard them all the

time, cause they'd always be singing. And when my uncles, like George Youngbird, came to visit, when they'd lay down [to go to bed] they'd just start singing. We grew up with people singing; it's not like that anymore.[6]

Honor songs, doorway songs, maxewidu, dance songs, riding songs—each of these categories evoke tribal members' singing and practice in particular times and particular places. The fact that Mandan remembered so many personal songs from Lucky Mound community members illustrates how songs and music can tie individuals to a specific place within human memory. Tribal member Gail Baker (Mandan, Hidatsa) recalled that the older generation during World War II commonly sang praise songs for other community members. Although most community members during this period spoke Hidatsa, songs began to be composed using English words. One song used popular phrases from the national consciousness regarding the US entry to the war set to traditional musical forms:

> Remember Pearl Harbor
> There's a star spangled banner
> Waving somewhere over there
> My brave soldier boy
> Fighting with the Japs and Germans.

Created by community member Alton Standish (Mandan, Hidatsa), the song must have been popular for people to remember it even sixty-five years later.[7]

The skill and creativity of men who crafted and sang these songs amazed longtime powwow announcer Pete Coffey Sr. "Years ago when I first knew about Indian dancing," he explained, "there used to be only one drum. Only one drum to sing all night long till the wee hours of the morning." He continued, "It's amazing how many powwow songs there is. Like I said years ago there'd be only one group of singers there and they'll sing all night long until the wee hours and never sing the same song twice. And I admire these singing groups."[8]

Dancers also bring emotional heft and excitement to music and create social memory and place. Perhaps for these reasons, traditional Native dance initially evoked anxiety and control issues in non-Natives. In the late nineteenth and early twentieth century, Bureau of Indian Affairs policy had focused on preventing Native traditional dances in all their forms. Bureaucrats and reformers called dances a "moral curse" and "the vicious dance," and they denounced them. According to one critic, the dances featured "acts of self-torture, immoral relations between the sexes, the sacrificial destruction of clothing or other useful articles, the reckless giving away of property, the use of injurious drugs or intoxicants, and frequent or prolonged periods of celebrations which bring the Indians together from remote points to the neglect of their crops, livestock, and home interest." IRA reforms enacted under Collier's direction reversed the ban on dancing and singing, most notoriously expressed in the Office of Indian Affairs' 1921 Circular 1665 under Charles Burke's leadership.[9]

The variety of songs allowed many people, not only the soldier, to participate as dancers. After the welcoming song ended, the organizers seated the soldier in a location visible to the crowd, and the drum group sang individual honor songs. When the drum sang an individual's honor song, the soldier and his relatives danced to the song; when it was over, the gathered crowd put money—whatever they had, or "the best they could do at that time"—into the pot for the serviceman. Community organizations also had honor songs, so when the drum sang Bearstail's USO song, all committee members were expected to get up to dance and put funds into the pot for the soldier.[10]

Although the impetus for this community gathering was serious, the events proceeded with energy, joy, and celebration. Community members were excited over the safe return of a soldier, but they were also probably just happy to gather, visit with relatives from other communities, and eat delicious food. Humor pervades most Native gatherings, and at one dance Tillie Walker (Mandan, Hidatsa) recalled that a middle-aged woman had somehow managed to find a replica of the Japanese flag: "I don't know how she got it, but she took that flag and danced with it. While she was dancing, she placed it like a tail on her *úushi* [Hidatsa word for butt]." At another dance, someone managed to find a cardboard cutout of Hitler, and amid the dancing participants threw it around to each other and stepped on it.[11]

Organizers also fed the returned soldier and the community members who celebrated his return. Bearstail described typical foods, both traditional and some popularized after Euro-American expansion onto the plains: "There was chicken and there was potato salad and there was like Juneberry pudding. And then they used to make these tomatoes—canned tomatoes—they'd put bread in there and they'd put sugar in there, in that. And they'd have rice and raisins. And they had frybread. And coffee. And sometimes pop. And that's what we had." Juneberry pudding was made by boiling locally gathered Juneberries and adding sugar and flour to sweeten and thicken the mixture. For centuries tribal members gathered and dried Juneberries, sweeter than blueberries, during the summer months as the gardens matured—along with large-pitted chokecherries and sour bullberries. Frybread, on the other hand, consisted entirely of the ration staples lard, flour, sugar, and dried milk, and represents the evolution of recipes during the reservation era, when tribal communities received rations as payment for land cessions from the federal government. These foods—along with potato salad, coffee, and canned tomatoes—reference a trajectory of longtime practices around food and feeding the community, reifying community identity and membership through the body. The Fort Berthold community praised women who provided the food "for the quantity and quality of what they supply." Unsurprising in communities whose existence long depended on agriculture, these food practices also remind us that while these gatherings represented US patriotism and citizenship, they built from and upon long-standing cultural and community tradition.[12]

At the gathering's conclusion—after community members danced to their personal songs and gave money to the returned soldier, after the performance of new and old songs, and after laughter and dinner—the drum group sang the returned soldier's individual honor song. Tribal members admired composers for skillfully crafting lyrics and melody for individual honor songs, created for a person after a major accomplishment such as a return from war. Drum groups remembered and sang these songs, which recognized the accomplishments and status of the individual during any subsequent community celebration. The returning soldier's honor song served as the culmination of the event. During this closing song, a soldier's relatives and extended family danced behind him, and the organizing committee members joined them. Before falling into line behind the soldier, his relatives shook his hand, and gave him money or material goods.[13]

The goods given to a soldier could include large-ticket items such as Pendleton blankets or star quilts, and during World War II oftentimes fabric or "yard goods" would be given away. Tillie Walker explained, "The old ladies would have like five yards of goods and it would be trailing behind them. If they had a shawl they would give it to him after dancing. He would then give everything away." The soldier gave away the money and material goods to his father's clan relatives (his clan aunts and uncles), community organizations, military groups, communities, visitors, or someone particularly kind or supportive to him (not a relative). Sometimes families even gave away horses and brought them into the dance hall. Fred Baker remembers those occasions as a young boy of four or five years, because at times a horse got spooked and forced the gathered crowd to scramble to avoid its stamping hooves. Family members and relatives of the returning soldier, however, never received gifts because community members considered it bad form to "give back to themselves." Behind the scenes, women such as the soldier's mother, grandmother, wife, or sisters organized the giveaway, suggesting the clan aunts and uncles who were traditionally given the first and largest gifts, as well as deciding how to divvy up the remaining goods. Walker recalled, "If you have a brother who has gone to war, you make sure you have something."[14]

The community dance strengthened and re-formed community ties as it created a place for community members to gather, socialize, and enjoy themselves. But the dance also honored a young man who had put his life in danger for the protection of the tribal nation and the United States. The songs, dances, food, and giveaways physically and visually represented both to the returned soldier and the broader community the depth of the support and joy that came with his safe return. Finally, these community dances provided the soldier an important tool for asserting community authority in the future—his own honor song.[15]

The gatherings also worked to enfold more people into the community consciousness and life than just the soldier. All participants learned and practiced important skills and community priorities, even if framed by World War II–era patriotism and citizenship. The work necessary to hold such an event contributed to actions and ideas that solidified the individual and community practice of indigenous citizenship—a citizenship just as tied to the history and tradition associated with the tribal land base as to expressions of US patriotism.

The Work of Citizenship: Making the "USO" Dances

When Fort Berthold tribal members enacted their US citizenship *and* their tribal identity through the USO dances, they expressed a novel category and understanding of both identities—national and tribal. In other words, they expressed and practiced an evolving indigenous citizenship. Citizenship is, of course, just as imagined as is the nation. Both are products of the mental work necessary to imagine "community" among a population so large one will never know or encounter each individual. But citizenship—and the nation—also exists outside the mind as a set of practices. Both entail actions that take form in the material world. Indigenous citizenship is revealed via the method and focus of energy and work comprising those "actions of citizenship."[16]

The materialization of indigenous citizenship at the welcome-home dances for Fort Berthold soldiers entangled US citizenship with tribal history, values, and practices. Fort Berthold USO dances were unique, not an imitation of USO events. The dances enacted deeply local practices and ideas with the patina of a nationalist narrative. In fact, the citizenship and patriotism of the USO dances could be expressed only due to interactions with Fort Berthold as a landscape, and as a locally imagined and narrated place. Place-making activities—physical labor that extracted resources from the land, tribal production and consumption, defense and protection of tribal and national territory, and intellectual labor to maintain community knowledge—allowed Fort Berthold tribal members to construct indigenous patriotism and indigenous citizenship. This in turn served as a building block for the expression of tribal sovereignty.

The land sustained indigenous citizenship at Fort Berthold, in the work individuals exerted over the physical space. Gardens, farms, ranches, and natural resources of the land and waterscape supported the USO dances. The delicious foods brought to the community dances needed to be grown, harvested, gathered, herded, slaughtered, and cooked. Bearstail recounts,

> We had to pull weeds, help in the garden. Then we'd have to go pick berries. They had these gallon syrup cans and they had a little handle and they'd tie a string or something on there—we'd have to put it around our necks and they'd send us . . . to pick berries, like chokecherries, Juneberries, or plums. And my aunt used to can, and my mother didn't want to can. She said, I'm always doing something wrong, I might just kill everybody [laughs]. My mother would dry her stuff. We'd have a big cellar right in the house, you know, and my dad would put potatoes in there, and he'd get a great big tub of sand—I don't know where he got the sand but—he'd put all the carrots in there and put it down there.

Before food can feed the body—or serve as one of the pleasurable components of a community gathering—people must gather, process, and store it. The work Bearstail describes is, first and foremost, the work of survival and work for a family. It also signals gendered work, for during this time women grew and processed the food. The work of feeding the body also feeds the family and the community. At a visceral level, this work teaches bodies to use both traditional and introduced methods of food preparation—picking and drying berries that might also be turned into jam or jellies—which sustains the community at gatherings large and small, and thus sustains indigenous citizenship practices.[17]

Men and boys, in contrast, spent much of their lives on horseback. Their work, often ranching, also contributed to the foundation of indigenous citizenship. Gail Baker remembered cattle roundups not only as one of the most exciting times of the summer but as part of his education as a tribal member:

> I had a lot of older brothers and older cousins that'd come there early in the morning; get us up. Our parents never bothered or interfered. When we were sleeping early in the morning our older brothers or cousins would come in and jerk us out of bed or else throw a big dipper of water on us to get us up. That was kinda common. But our parents wouldn't interfere because that was part of our education by our older brothers. The roundup was an ongoing thing with horses or cattle. I can barely remember, back in 1934 or '35, during that drought, there was hardly any grass, so the government bought a hundred-sixty head from the tribe and they butchered them there at the corrals, and everybody made dry meat; they camped there for a whole week. You don't see that kinda stuff anymore, ever. [During] horse roundups in that corral there was over a thousand head of horses in there, cause they came from down south towards Squaw Creek, near what they call String Buttes south of Heart Butte and west and all the way to the mouth of Skunk Creek.

Baker's recollection signals the educational and community importance of the work young men and boys exerted traversing the landscape on horseback, herding cattle and horses—a discipline of the body modeled and enforced by older male relatives. His memories also illustrate how physical markers of the landscape and waterscape—buttes, creeks, the Missouri River itself, and its tributaries—marked the locations of work and community spaces.[18]

The ranching economy and pervasive use of horses created important male social space for families and relatives. Dreke Irwin, fondly remembers the seasonal ebb and flow when he worked with his grandfather as a young boy:

> In summertime, that's when I did most of my help. When I was kinda young there I used to stay out and herd bulls before they put them in with the cattle. Had to keep them separate, you know. Sometimes we took them to the bull pasture.... Everyone in the fall would take their bulls over there and they wintered them. They had guys who probably got paid, would ride out there and feed them, took care of them. Then in springtime, [you would] go back out there, get your bulls back and bring them back but it was too soon to put them among the herd. I used to ride horseback—I was seven, eight years old by then—I would herd them if

they wandered off. I [would] get on my horse and I'd go sit somewhere, you know, and kinda kept them together, let them graze around. When calving time came around, the help I did anyway, at least I kinda had a brand, they'd brand one of those calves for me, that was my pay.

What did Irwin do with the calves he received as pay? "Just stuck them in a herd. A free service, as I was trying to increase my own cattle. I kinda had my own little herd," he laughed, remembering his seven-year-old self.[19]

The Missouri River centered community understandings of place, not least of all because community members followed a *centuries*-old pattern of planting their communities in its river valley. Well into the New Deal and World War II years, people at Fort Berthold used the river and its tributaries to mark place— the location of their birth, where they grew up—and children explored, hauled water from, played in, and swam in the river throughout their childhoods. Tribal members honored this long-standing relationship every fall, when women made cornballs to roll into the river for Grandfather Snake. Edwin Benson's grandfather possessed the right to trap fish, and Benson remembered the detailed process of constructing and using a massive fish trap at the confluence where the Little Missouri met the main-steam Missouri. Late at night his grandfather and friends scooped huge numbers of fish from the trap, stunning them with a hammer and gutting and cleaning them with sharp knives at the river's edge, only to fry them immediately. The delicious taste of fresh fried fish delighted the young boy: "And that's how come I like fish now." These memories—Baker's memory of his grandmother weeping as she rolled cornballs into the Missouri to thank Grandfather Snake, Benson's memory of a late-night feast with his grandfather—are precious. Not only because they denote a location or a time, but because they represent treasured memories of grandparents and relatives.[20] And such memories accrue and accumulate to form an individual's identity and sense of right and wrong—and how humans should live their lives.

Photographs from the BIA's 1942 Report on Extension Work illuminate some of the ideas and practices that contributed to place-making at Fort Berthold and provide insights of how people at Fort Berthold self-identified as indigenous citizens during the war. Tribal members maintained the centuries-old agricultural practices of large-scale gardening and culling the plant and animal resources of the Missouri River valley that sustained their communities through intense demographic and spatial shocks such as Euro-American disease and forced land cessions. Women still used seed varieties of corn, beans, and squash that their mothers, grandmothers, and great-grandmothers developed and refined for the northern plains environment. By World War II, men had assimilated ranching and farming into their lives as community members but maintained the clan and society structures that organized social and ceremonial life in the communities. A BIA survey of the tribe identified that the population had doubled since the turn of the century, from 960 to 1,854, and often families had more economic stability than their white neighbors. And while the reservation hospital knew of one tribal member with cancer, diabetes, kidney disease, and heart disease were largely absent. Community members of all ages still extracted the benefits of the plant and animal species diversity of the river valley environment via hunting, berry picking, gathering coal, and using timber.[21]

Coterminous to these activities, however, the local Indian Affairs bureaucracy worked to redefine the work of gardening, farming, and ranching as part of the patriotic duty of tribal members. The bureaucracy tied work to US citizenship during late reservation era, when the Bureau of Indian Affairs narrated landownership and farming as a route to full citizenship. But during World War II, agriculture and industry became narrated through the lens of wartime patriotism. Under the heading "Food For Victory," the local Indian office exhorted in its reservation-wide newsletter, "We should all take part in producing the needed food products for our family and help our country in the food for victory campaign." Positioned after a detailed listing of tribal members who had invested in cattle or had been particularly successful at planting or "improving" their land, the BIA told tribal members, "Talk will not win this war of all Wars ... nor will guns do it. It is going to take food—lots of it, food that we can raise." The First World War presaged the shift from agricultural work being a route to full citizenship—rooted in the myth of the yeoman farmer's role in supporting democratic ways of life, in the mythology of the Protestant work ethic, and in the fictions surrounding the deserving and undeserving poor—to agricultural work being *patriotic*. But the federal government coalesced and developed this connection during the New Deal and Second World War, when it tied a depleted soil to the depleted economy and human resources in the belief that "human erosion and soil erosion are but twin aspects of a single problem on the land."[22]

Given the larger federal anxieties that tied soil depletion and lack of farm productivity to economic catastrophe, the local BIA's relentless worry over the work of gardening, ranching, and farming and its relationship to "Indian dependency" makes sense. But considering the low "relief," or welfare, rates at Fort Berthold before, during, and immediately after the war, the anxieties expressed in the reservation newsletter were largely unwarranted. As the federal government prepared the national draft, the Fort Berthold office reminded community members, "To those who do not get to go to the front, remember, there are many ways we can serve Uncle Sam. We can work and raise food. We can take proper care of property, and thereby avoid the purchase of repair parts. Yes, an industrious, self-supporting man at home, certainly does his share in helping win his country's war. Let's pitch in and do our part."[23] The Indian Office aimed pleas for self-sufficiency not only to the "man at home." They also directed Native women to "grow a big garden, milk a cow or two, keep some chickens, and then be sure you raise a few pigs for your meat." Homefront rhetoric flourished in directives to grow, harvest, process, and store food for self-sufficiency: "Yes, there are other things to do to help kick the pants off of those - - - - Japs—can and dry all the fruits and vegetables you can this summer. This is also the question of bread—do your own baking at home, it saves money which is hard to get." The end of the passage reads, "We have a real battle to fight right here at home—Let's all fight."[24]

In this context, the images from the 1942 Report on Extension Work illuminate a relationship between continuity and change of practices and ideas around work and identity formulated during this time. In figure 3.2, an older woman in an old-style dress, moccasins, and a sun hat stands with a plow drawn by a horse. A young man or boy is riding the horse, and the stillness of the woman's pose and the smiling discomfort of the young man emphasize the contrived nature of the photograph. A garden serves as the site of the photographs, most likely owned by the woman. Figure 3.3 shows men working with cattle. Their stances read more naturally; their attention is focused on the cattle rather than the photographer.

The work represented in these photographs made place with traditional garden and gathering practices, as well as newer ranching and male farming labor. All, however, deeply modified the land—plowing, fencing, planting, feeding, and weeding. All also required a long-term investment in the health and fruits of the land and the work. Seeds planted in May after the last frost could not be wasted, and calves born in the spring had to be branded, fed, and watched over to provide meat or income later in the year. Once harvested, the food still needed to be processed. Native women like Lyda Bearstail and Rosemarie Mandan experienced that processing every year of their lives and continued a subsistence pattern practiced by generations of community members—canning,

Figure 3.2. Woman plowing, taken for the 1942 Report on Extension Work.
National Archives and Records Administration, Kansas City.

Figure 3.3. Men working cattle at a corral, included in the 1942 Report on Extension Work.
National Archives and Records Administration, Kansas City.

drying, and otherwise carrying food calories from the season of abundance to the season of scarcity.

Fred Baker remembered his work at the Lucky Mound community garden as a young boy: "There was a great big tree that was at the middle of that community garden, and people used come there with their wagons and horses and stuff to hoe their gardens. They would all bring food, and they would share that food with everyone who was there. Kids would be playing; adults would be sitting around visiting and sharing their food. It was a happy time, pretty much an ongoing thing [during the summer]." As Baker relates, the labor itself engendered community. And as he teaches us, the traditional and adopted labor practices happened in gardens, fields, and grasslands, pens, farms, and kitchens—*places*. These places—domestic places, community places, gardens— accrued resonant meaning through the work and practices of past and current tribal members.[25]

Work within and from the lands at Fort Berthold formed a stream of energy, effort, and practice to sustain the USO dances. The labor sustained a pedagogy of community and identity and drew from landscape resources. When Fred Baker found himself awakened early in the morning by a dipperful of water, and then spent his days working cattle in the company of uncles and cousins, he learned through labor the meaning and nature of his identity as a Hidatsa person, and as a Hidatsa man. This dynamic is the essence of place-making. Work on the land—the use and cultivation of its energy—sustains not only individual but community life.

Fort Berthold residents did not directly challenge the paternalistic assertions of the local Indian agency that tied their productivity and labor on the land to their citizenship and patriotism. They received the messages, and the ideologies mattered. But they did not matter nearly as much as the weight of locality and history. Fort Berthold community members performed a culturally specific citizenship and patriotism when they harnessed the resources of the landscape and their labor in it—crystallized at the USO community dances.

The meanings of American citizenship for non-Native communities also changed under the stresses of economic depression and world war. Lizabeth Cohen's works covering the Great Depression, World War II, and Cold War years detail the ways citizenship and patriotism took on new meanings through and were expressed through consumption and production practices. Her focus on urban and suburban life, however, ignores rural America. This is important to note, not least because federal priorities and conceptualizations of rural spaces represent a major variable in the shifting investments in production and consumption. These "hinterland" spaces were—and continue to function as— landscapes that allow urban populations to elaborate their consumption. Fort Berthold, part of this rural landscape like most Indian reservations, benefited from the New Deal's attempt to solve rural poverty. Fort Berthold communities adjusted to national imperatives using preexisting land use and management to weather the change. Such continued reliance on indigenous traditional practices signals that US citizenship and patriotism during these years was contested, modified, and adjusted not solely in urban centers as typically considered. Further, this history complicates the oversimplified political spectrum of conservative-centrist-liberal-radical that assumes as its subject and actor the white middle-class citizen.[26]

Federal entities hammered home those national imperatives relentlessly. Narratives surrounding production and consumption were embedded in the call for Indian "productivity" and "self-sufficiency." The *Fort Berthold Bulletin* reminded tribal members to "stay off relief" via agricultural productivity and thrift:

> It is realized we can not all donate freely to the Red Cross or buy savings stamps and bonds. We can however help our country in another way. Raise a good garden in 1942 for healthful vegetables, milk a cow for the families supply of milk, secure enough hens for our egg supply and raise a pig or two for lard and meat. With this supply of food products you can protect your health and that of your children. Strong healthy people can win a war. Another way just as important is to pay our government debts and stay off relief. This money is badly needed for defense production. Do your country a real service and stay off relief.

The assumption of Indian dependency aligns with the politics of conservation in rural America during the New Deal and World War II years, when agricultural policies began to prioritize large-scale producers and saw small-scale farmers as an economic drag. The early New Deal focused on soil rehabilitation and conservation to strengthen rural economies, but the latter New Deal and World War II years emphasized the expansion of urban consumption to fuel greater demand for rural products. This shift benefited large producers and those who had already begun to invest in corporate or large-scale farming, and federal policy toward rural areas mirrored this trend.[27]

So why the self-sufficiency messages in a community where tribal members had established self-sufficient smallholding farms and ranches due to a centuries-long tradition of subsistence gardening in the Upper Missouri River valley? And when the Native women on the home front had increased reservation agricultural production every year of the war? Perhaps the messages presaged anxiety over the ability of tribal members to adjust to a consumption-based economy. Despite the success in cattle sale income during World War II, resources still pooled around the ranching elite on Fort Berthold. In 1948, a report from the local BIA superintendent noted that in 1946 only 14 percent of Fort Berthold families earned more than $1,250. A next tier (18 percent) of families earned between $750 to $1,250 that year. Far more common, however, were the 35 percent of families who brought in between $250 to $750 a year, or the remaining 35 percent of families who earned less than $250.[28]

Perhaps the anxieties reflected in the BIA messages were, in fact, contradictory. The apparatus of the federal government ballooned in the 1930s and World War II years, and unified imperatives were rare. Further, the transition from the federal system dealing with the economic crisis of the Great Depression to one gearing up for wartime participation created many contradictions in federal policy.[29]

During this time, the Fort Berthold Indian Agency dabbled in this contradictory management of production and consumption. The reservation newsletter conveyed,

> During the First World War, our people, both Indians and whites, responded splendidly in a campaign for the sale of government Bonds. Many thousands of dollars worth of Government Bonds were purchased by Indians, alone, in North and South Dakota. The owners of those bonds did their part in helping win that war.
>
> Now, another call comes from our Government, asking our people to buy Defense bonds and stamps. This is necessary to finance the United States, and to furnish the means to defend our country against those powers opposed to free and democratic government. Let us respond just as cheerfully and liberally as we did in 1914 to 1918.
>
> Defense stamps can be purchased at our local Post Office in Elbowoods.... Employees and others having a regular job, and a regular salary check each month, are urged to buy bonds. Arrangements can be made to buy bonds by paying an installment monthly.

The irony of the encouragement to purchase war bonds—to promote and harness consumption—is that the entire project intended to dampen purchasing power of US citizens to control wartime inflation.[30]

Production and consumption management in the name of patriotism also emerged in the reservation newspaper:

We have heard the saying "Food will win the war." Every day we realize more and more the truth of this saying. This should remind us this spring we should all do our part in producing more food. Improve and enlarge your gardens. Take care of them better than you ever did before. Make this year a record year for the best gardens in the history of the Reservation. Let's help win the war this way.

We should also be saving in our use of the automobile, and use it only when your travel is absolutely necessary. Our Country has a real shortage of rubber and we *must* save on tires and tubes. It is very likely in the near future we will have restrictions placed on gasoline. By doing some careful planning we can all help in saving those materials necessary for our Army and Navy.

The conceptual ties between national defense and agricultural production in rural areas can also be seen in the change in terminology for the programs sponsored by the Agricultural Adjustment Administration (AAA)—the New Deal agency created to manage production and consumption within the agricultural sector of the US economy. The crop acreage allotment program changed from the Agricultural Conservation Program in the 1930s and early 1940s to the Farm Defense Program in 1942.[31]

Rural agriculture policy shifted from the support and maintenance of rural communities to the expectation for rural areas to feed the economies of the industrial sector and urban communities. John Collier—after the start of World War II and amid the BIA's move from Washington, DC, to Chicago as a "non-essential" bureau—subordinated BIA programs emphasizing Indian agricultural training, and instead promoted programs that encouraged Native migration to urban areas with large defense-industry employment opportunities. The BIA as a bureaucratic entity shifted from the maintenance and preservation of tribal cultures to emphasis on Native investment in home front activities such as war bonds purchase and defense-related resources conservation.[32]

This shift in BIA policy occurred in the context of sustained attacks on the Indian Reorganization Act that focused on the "communist" leanings of tribal reorganization governments and the termination of policies that discouraged of Native cultural and social traditions. One such congressional attack from a North Dakota congressman stated, "The so-called Wheeler-Howard Act attempts to set up states or nations within a nation which is contrary to the intents and purposes of the American republic." Such rhetoric—especially from North Dakota representation—inspired the Fort Berthold Tribal Council to draft and submit resolutions in support of the IRA to Congress.[33]

More interesting than the attacks themselves—or Collier's and the BIA's responses—is that perhaps the attacks were correct. On the surface, Figure 3.4—one of a series taken from the BIA's 1942 Report on Extension Work that document the 4-H displays in Fort Berthold communities—conveys compliance with national messages on Indian self-sufficiency, or even the importance of rural production to feed urban consumption as an expression of citizen patriotism. Devoid of people, such photographs detail the fruits of agricultural labor from the reservation communities of Elbowoods, Shell Creek, and Nishu—all under the visual auspices of the local 4-H club and the American flag. Neat shelves of the "best" produce grown by children in the community—onions, potatoes, pumpkins, and huge squash—as well as canning jars shine. Such images, in the

Figure 3.4. Shell Creek community 4-H produce display in the 1942 Report on Extension Work. National Archives and Records Administration, Kansas City.

context of calls for war bond sales and Red Cross victory drives, could showcase a community that merged a long-standing agricultural tradition with the imperatives to perform Indian and rural self-sufficiency and production for a wartime economy.

But the USO dances complicate these images. With those dances as context, these bureaucratic images show us how community members sewed the mantle of patriotism and US citizenship to fit over *preexisting* tribal practices of production and consumption. The production and consumption work practiced for the USO dances represents a distinctly nonstate organization of both. Giveaways, the provision of food produced and collected from the community at large to attendees, community-pooled money for soldiers, and the culturally specific engine of the gatherings (namely, traditional music and dance) illustrate a community that *ignored* the model of production and consumption recognized and valued by the state. It also draws upon earlier, deeper understandings of survival, community, and membership founded upon the resources of a local subsistence-oriented community economy organized and structured by a tribal web of kinship and responsibility. This culturally specific consumption and production did not necessarily reject the wartime consumer economy. It did, however, provide a counternarrative within the boundaries of Fort Berthold with considerable cultural weight. It also implies that indigenous citizenship—rooted in the soil, in the work to harness the resources of the landscape, and in alternate organizations of production and consumption—transformed national rhetorics and symbols of US citizenship and patriotism into an intensely local practice and ideation.[34]

Indigenous citizenship also framed defense and protection work. Tribal members invested in the defense and protection of the tribal and national community—and the lands held by both. High enlistment numbers in the general population were mirrored within Native America, and approximately twenty-five thousand Native Americans served in World War II. The armed forces did not segregate Native Americans as it did African Americans, so our casualty rate mirrored the national average, but due to a much higher service rate—50 percent of eligible Fort Berthold men—the reservation also stood to lose a much higher proportion of its servicemen.[35]

Collier proudly promoted Native participation within the theaters of World War II and emphasized reconciliation between Native and white soldiers. The symbolism and iconography of Natives and whites fighting for the same nation during confirmed not only Indian-white rapprochement, but the triumph of US democracy. Wartime propagandists used this symbolism to contrast the supposed freedom and democracy in the United States with Axis fascism and dictatorships.³⁶

Armed forces news services enjoyed highlighting Native soldiers within the ranks of American forces. The Fort Berthold community newsletter copied an article from the *Army News Bulletin* about tribal member Nathan Little Soldier that read in part, "'Chief Wahoo' Soldier, our North Dakota Indian boy, is really whooping it up as he puts the boys of the Fourth Platoon through their paces. Soldier, as one of the batteries non-coms, is proving to be just what his name calls for." US popular culture celebrated Native soldiers for their participation, and simultaneously stereotyped them as savage warriors. The patronizing text quoted by the Fort Berthold newsletter reflects a comic rendition of militarized stereotypes of Native American men to portray a unified war effort within the United States—and the incorporation of characteristics previously feared in service of the US wartime cause. Another army publication mused, "A red man will risk his life for a white as dauntlessly as his ancestor lifted a paleface's scalp." Non-Natives highlighted these qualities to reinforce mythologies of the righteousness of the United States, the successful assimilation of Native soldiers, and the supposedly innate wartime skills that perpetuated tropes of the savage Indian warrior.³⁷

It pleased white society to narrate Native men's participation in the war effort as a triumph of incorporation. But the work of the soldier—defense, protection, sacrifice of safety and comfort, and the monotonous work to assist a large army to function—meant deeper things to Fort Berthold soldiers and their relatives. The same newsletter that published the story about Nathan Little Soldier also listed all the Fort Berthold men in service:

> Army: Roy Atkins, John Baker, Louis Baker, Jr., Theodore Baker, Paul Bateman, James Conkling, Donald Goodbird, Archie Hopkins, Lloyd Howard, Fred Huber, Nathan Little Soldier, Victor Mandan, Daniel Many Ribs, Wilfred Medicine Stone, Fred Morsette, Lawrence Sears, Roger Shell, Frank Sherwood, Lee P. Smith, Mason Two Crow
> Navy: Louis Felix, Jr., Carl Sterud, Peter Sterud, Jr.
> Marine Corps: Claude Huber, Perry Ross
> Air Corps: Guy Bateman, Albert Charging, George Howard, Jr., Percy Rush, Quentin Simpson, McRoy Star

Other boys, who are contributing their services during the present war, as follows:

Army: David Grinnell, Lawrence Birds Bill
Navy: Joseph Bell, Kenneth Deane, Lawrence Good Bear
We are all proud of this long list of our boys who have entered the service of our country.

Fort Berthold, as a community, valued each name, remembered each person. This excerpt evokes more than pride in their service, or an echo of national narratives. It asserts, like African American and Japanese American soldiers and communities, a claim to the nation. Male bodies as defenders and protectors formed the foundation of this claim, but it also grew from community participation in the most important political processes of the time.[38]

But before these young men ever left the reservation, for their names to be listed in a community newsletter, community elders protected their bodies and their military labor. Parents of soldiers paid tribal elders, who held medicine to pray for the safety of their sons. The prayers said over them, at times accompanied by the transfer of an eagle plume or the right to paint one's face, held a distinctly Hidatsa or Mandan or Arikara meaning rooted in a long history of defending tribal communities and territories. Relatives particularly took pride in Native soldiers' service—one family photograph from the war era shows an elderly grandfather, Joseph Youngbird, and four of his grandsons. The young men pose in their uniforms, and their grandfather poses in his full traditional regalia, including a warbonnet.[39]

Male wartime service meant hardship at home. When Rosemarie's brothers went to fight in the war, she found herself saddled not only with her usual duties but also with theirs. "We had to do men's work, and help my mother get horses, put harnesses on the horses, cause everything back then was with teams. And then we even helped cut hay. I remember that one summer my mother and I cut hay, stack it and all of that; oh yeah, it was hard. And we still had to have gardens," she recalled. And the possibility of death continually loomed over servicemen and their families. Dreke Irwin's uncle, Clarence Spotted Wolf, served in the army, and his uncle processed his worries over breakfast made by Dreke's grandmother, "'I'll be going into the service,' he'd say, 'I got the feeling I'll get bumped off over there,' he'd kinda say. Then his parents would say, 'Don't say that!' you know. 'I don't know, I'll go over there, I'll make it out of there' [talking

Figure 3.5. Joseph Youngbird (Hidatsa) poses with his grandsons in their military uniforms.
Courtesy of Reid Walker.

like his uncle], it's like he had that premonition. Sure enough, killed in Luxembourg, Germany. He was in a tank war. I think about that every now and then." Dreke prefaced the statement, "I was about eight or nine—when I was eleven, I think he got killed, and six months after that my grandma passed away, she had cancer."

Edwin Benson's older brother served in the army in Germany for over three years. Benson recalled, "I was lonesome for my brother, he was the only kind of mate I had at home, you know." When he heard his brother was wounded, Benson related, "That was the first time in my life I ever prayed. . . . I told the Lord to bring my brother home. 'I want him here with me,' I said, 'so he can help me haul hay,' I said. [laughs] That was the first time I'd ever prayed." The armed forces sent young men who had never even been outside of North Dakota across oceans to fight—and some of them, like Clarence Spotted Wolf, died in those foreign places. Every family member faced this terrible possibility, so it makes sense they worked so hard to celebrate and honor them when their sons, brothers, and uncles were lucky enough to return home.[40]

When soldiers returned, USO community dances held in their honor expressed the community appreciation of their World War II service. In preparation for the dance, someone made each returned soldier his honor song—a slower-beat, solemn song that referenced his name and accomplishments, and perhaps his branch of the armed forces. Men wrote the songs for other men who defended and protected their community with their lives. They made the song expressly for the returned soldier; but his family members and descendants could potentially use it as their own honor song for generations to come. The honor song commemorated the individual but also served as a form of community memory and history. Each honor song linked the individual soldier to tribal history, values, and defense. Further, community members held the songs in their memories years afterward, indicating that the honor songs are history—history sung, practiced, and honed by a community.

Most people grew up hearing and singing a wide variety of songs, and community members considered the men who made unique and beautiful honor songs as highly talented—not only for their ability to create lovely and moving music and lyrics but for their ability to memorize and faithfully reproduce a long history of tribal and intertribal songs. Longtime powwow announcer Pete Coffey Sr. described honor songs:

> Some of them have words in them, what we call honor songs. Some individual would like to have an honor song and they select some man, designate some man, say "I would like to have an honor song, can you make me an honor song." "Sure." That's where I say I admire these people; they'll never refuse you. And they'll make one for you. It might be an ordinary powwow song, but they'll find some lyrics to fit it. We had a lot of those honor songs during the war years, when everybody went, the young men went to services.

Long after they passed away, community members remember men like Thad Mason—"He was kind of the Rogers and Hammerstein of Independence"—and Billy Baker as master songwriters.[41]

The intellectual and cultural labor of honor songs placed the individual—and their descendants—within the tribal landscape; they made individuals part of the "place" even as they allowed their bodies to perform and constitute part of the communal meanings of that place via participation in the honor song. The honor song contains a statelier beat. The form of the music ensures that the person narrated by the song dances in a formal way around the common dance arena, and social conventions require that spectators rise to their feet as the honor song is sung and danced. But the work of honor songs does far more than simply ensure solemnity and respect. The process of crafting honor songs transforms individual experience (military service) into symbol (defense, protection, service to community), which is then remade into an object (the lyrics and music of the song). This object is then used to evoke experience through its performance, through the complex physical embodiment that contributes to "molding experience into symbols and then melding symbols back into experience." Honor songs create place by answering the question of "what did this body do?" as they are performed. The songs remind community members of the physical sacrifice performed via male bodies, so that the individuals become reminders of the importance of service to the community. Further, each time the song is sung, it indexes the place where it was originally given, the communal recognition the soldier receives, and a specific history. Pete Coffey Sr. described the historical role music serves when he explained, "I always tell the people that people will die, or leaves will wither, or something's going to give, but powwow songs never die; as long as you can remember them, they go on and on and on."

Place is not merely a container through which we move. The movement of our bodies *creates* place as we speak, walk, ride horses, ride in cars, dance, or sing honor songs. This is how the meanings ascribed to the physical environment—a physical environment that *includes* our bodies—become communal.[42] The work of "defense" and "protection"—as formulated during and after World War II—became another important type of work, or community practice, which solidified both community identity and ideations of patriotism to the larger United States. This work illustrates the distinctive characteristics of indigenous citizenship at Fort Berthold.

The creation of honor songs for returned veterans—the assignment of stories and place to their bodies and the incorporation of their actions and physical bodies into the Fort Berthold as a *place*—represents intellectual labor and energy by the men who made them. The songs were neither easy to make nor to remember. Song makers held within them—during a time when few could access audio recorders—the memory of both the song created and how it differed from other honor songs, as well as the physical memory of how to sing it. The honor songs taught children community values and marked individuals as part of a shared community history. The artistic skill of the songs and their makers' labor to create and maintain community structures of memory and recognition lives on entirely due to the efforts of tribal members. This expression of tribal patriotism could happen, in part, because after the IRA Native groups across the country no longer faced a stark choice between their claims of rights as citizens and their cultural heritage.[43]

Finally, USO community dances taught children about the importance and practice of kinship networks at Fort Berthold. Lyda Bearstail participated by carrying the USO banner in the Shell Creek community dances, but the family and clan relationships structured her participation. The USO chose Bearstail based on her family relationship with adult organizers; and her ishawi made her moccasins and taffeta elk tooth dress for the dance. Bearstail remembered, "That's what aunts did a long time ago. Your father's sister or your father's cousin would dress you. They'd bring you, like my aunt brought me that dress and moccasins and belt. She dressed me so I could dance. And that's the way they did it a long time ago." Older community members expert in family and clan relations orchestrated the entire community gathering. Elders knew who should get the first donation during a giveaway: a clan aunt or clan father—meaning one's father's clan brother or sister—and importantly *not* a family relative. Singers knew who possessed the right to sing certain songs, when songs should be sung, or the appropriate way to pay a group of singers for rendering a personal honor song. Through performance, practice, missteps, and observation, events like the welcome-home dances for returning soldiers taught the praxis of Fort Berthold community life to young men serving in the armed forces, and to children like Lyda Bearstail. And because Fort Berthold community members practiced this intellectual labor within the context of citizenship and patriotism, this knowledge and its use became enfolded into not only tribal membership but also US citizenship.[44]

The local foundations and interpretations of indigenous citizenship at Fort Berthold—the physical labor that extracted resources from the land base, the unique tribal expression of the ideal management of production and consumption, the meanings attached to the defense and protection of tribal and national territory, and the production and maintenance of community knowledge—also hinges on ideas of land and territory, or what lay outside community and tribal boundaries. The following section uses a uniquely tribal expression of patriotism and citizenship—a flag song—to explore how Fort Berthold community members understood their territories and what lay beyond their boundaries.[45]

Imagining Territory: A Fort Berthold Flag Song
The enactments of citizenship and patriotism at welcome-home dances also expressed individual and collective belonging to and possession of territory, or

the land that constituted "home." But what is not "home" always helps to define "home." The following flag song, widely used at Fort Berthold gatherings, indicates the importance of land and territory in the creation of citizenship. Flag songs are used to begin large public gatherings like powwows—an example of an organic fusion of US citizenship and patriotism and community or tribal identity. The melody for this particular song is considered beautiful and elegant and has traveled far and wide across Indian Country. Drum groups from many other reservations reproduce the melody, often without knowledge of the original words or concepts.

> Awa hiróo mada maaragabixe
> *[From] this land, our flag*
> Ihcagita icíiawa
> *Only it alone is very strong*
> Maihá ida awagoa nagabiha-waguc
> *In the middle of the enemy's land it's waving high in the air.*

Community members originally translated the song's lyrics from Arikara to Hidatsa, and translate the Hidatsa to English as, "Our flag is the strongest, it's waving in enemy land," or "Our flag is the only strong one; that's why it's waving in enemy territory."[46]

The iconography of the flag saturates flag songs, which are used to invoke respect and solemnity, and to reference the bravery, courage, and sacrifice implied in military service at the beginning of a social gathering. Long before the modern era of the state, territorial claims—and the violence used to achieve territory—structured the use of flags. The physical characteristics of the US flag documents the claims, annexations, and incorporations that succeeded due to violence, often toward indigenous groups—whether represented in the thirteen red and white stripes representing the thirteen colonies, or in the fiftieth star that marked the incorporation of an illegally annexed country far outside the territorial logic of the US mainland.[47]

Native use of the US flag—via artistic or craft representation, flag songs, and as a physical presence at social and community gatherings—*seems* to ignore those dynamics of violence and wrongful claims. But its pervasive use within Indian Country lies not in community dismissal of past wrongs, but in positive, concrete claims on ancestral lands within US territorial bounds. These land and territory claims gain currency via Native service during wartime, but are rooted in the memory of Native dispossession. The appropriation of the US flag as metaphor, icon, and banner, is a place-making strategy in the face of state assertions of space.[48]

But before we venture far afield, let us return to the text of the Fort Berthold flag song.

> Awa hiróo mada maaragabixe
> Ihcagita icíiawa
> Maihá ida awagoa nagabiha-waguc.

Community members used the song for cultural purposes unique to the reservation, yet it expresses patriotism and an investment in American citizenship. The fusion of these can happen due to the imagination of a place outside of "us"—which in this case means outside the United States—explicitly drawing on older understandings of the enemy territory of another tribe. The words evoke both loneliness and pride, via the dual invocation of a US flag flying by itself in enemy territory, as well as the idea that people are talking about how the flag still flies in an unfriendly space.

The icon of the flag within the song also symbolizes the bravery and strength of those who serve in the armed forces—the flag flying alone in enemy territory implies the determination and power of those who fight under its auspices. The conduit of this fusion of icon, metaphor, legend, and national place-making—perhaps the only reason it can happen despite the history of colonialism—is the land. "*[From] this land, our flag / Only it alone is very strong / In the middle of the enemy's land it's waving high in the air.*" The presentation of a shared home territory *and* an imagined enemy territory allows community members to express citizenship to claim the rights that status confers; to claim patriotism and love for a nation that also represents territorial dispossession; and to give deep and meaningful recognition to the sacrifices of community members who endangered their lives in the name of national priorities.[49]

Land as a metaphor to express tribal citizenship, patriotism, territory, and sovereignty evolved over many years. World War I, the Great Depression, and new possibilities realized after the Indian Reorganization Act created fertile ground for this conceptual cross-fertilization. The physical and intellectual labor of both local and national place-making allowed tribal members to imagine and express a more unified and cohesive ideation of US citizenship. Fort Berthold tribal members remade national narratives of rural economies and tribal communities to frame the practice of indigenous citizenship. This work, this strategic appropriation and the persistence of culturally specific practices, refashioned local expressions of national citizenship and patriotism. In doing so, it also remade one of the key components of modern tribal sovereignty.[50]

The "USO" dance for returned soldiers represents a nexus of community and cultural labor. Food preparation, songs, giveaways, and the dance itself created place for Three Affiliated tribal members to solidify and reenact indigenous citizenship. Indigenous citizenship literally grew from the landscape—itself a nexus between human labor and the physical environment—expressed through bodily labor associated with farming, ranching, preparing food, dancing, or creating and performing song. As tribal members practiced these things, family and community ties grew stronger—as did the citizenship and patriotism during a time of war. This rich social context, thick with meaning and a shared history, allowed people at Fort Berthold to co-opt the anxieties and directives of the federal government to fit community needs and goals.

These practices and ascription of meaning to the landscape, to the body, or to community actions lie at the heart of indigenous citizenship. For citizenship was never a category imposed upon a blank, faceless indigenous population; Native communities appropriated symbols and meanings of citizenship and patriotism to serve their needs. In this labor, Native communities shaped and asserted their own identities and structures of authority and power. The community places created by dances, honor songs, and giveaways render the priorities of the federal government irrelevant—if only for the brief time in which a community gathers to celebrate the bravery of its members—and the places detailed in this chapter allowed community members to sow and nurture the seeds of self-determination and modern notions of tribal sovereignty.

This indigenous citizenship, coalesced during the Indian Reorganization Act era and elaborated upon and performed during World War II, would be tested. At the center of the coming conflict was the loss of thousands of acres of prime agricultural land—the Missouri River bottom that sustained Fort Berthold community members for generations beyond counting. This loss of land and resources would alter the trajectory of community understandings of place, space, territory, and citizenship.

At this juncture, the Three Affiliated Tribes had rebounded from a population low of only 960 tribal members at the turn of the century to reach 1,854 members. They had weathered the invasive Indian Affairs bureaucracy of the reservation era, major land takings by the executive branch of the federal government, and the Great Depression and huge drought of the 1930s, and they had sent high numbers of tribal members to fight in World War II. Dr. Herbert Wilson, who worked on the Fort Berthold Reservation for decades, characterized members of the Three Tribes as "remarkably healthy, robust people, and of course, they were still self-sufficient for the most part. They grew their own food, gathered wild fruits and berries, and ate wild game. Diabetes was unknown, kidney problems were unknown, and heart disease was very rare, as was cancer."[51]

As early as 1943, it was clear that immense change approached—not only to the broader United States, but to the land and communities at Fort Berthold. Fragmented rumors of possible plans by the Bureau of Reclamation and the Army Corps of Engineers to dam Awáati circulated and accrued on Fort Berthold shores. On November 14, 1943, the tribal council passed a resolution to oppose a "Lower Dam":

> WHEREAS: the Three Affiliated Tribes of the Fort Berthold Reservation depend very largely on their bottom lands along the Missouri River for their welfare, and there appears no other region obtainable as satisfactory substitute for agricultural and timber industry; and
>
> WHEREAS: a dam below the Fort Berthold Reservation is being contemplated for future action by the Congress of the United States in cooperation with the State of North Dakota, which action, if realized, will destroy by permanent flood all the bottom land of said Reservation, causing untold material and economic damage to the Three Affiliated Tribes; and
>
> NOW, THEREFORE, BE IT HEREBY RESOLVED: by the Tribal Business Council, in a meeting assembled, duly and regularly called, a quorum being present, and voicing the adverse opinion of its constituents, that it opposes the present plan of constructing a dam below the Fort Berthold Reservation or any other plan which will destroy the flood areas of the Missouri Valley.

Roosevelt did not sign the federal legislation authorizing the Pick-Sloan Plan until December 1944, but Fort Berthold leadership had heard of the bill.[52]

Tribal members also felt the foreboding. Rosemarie Mandan remembered, "When we were still walking to school . . . they already had sticks, sticks with those ribbons, all over. . . . They were already surveying." She continued, "I was too young at the time, but I remember my mother coming home one day, and she said, 'I just heard the most *terrible* thing,' she said. 'I heard they're going to build a dam and that water is going to cover that hill.' I remember that, you know."

Chapter 4

The Deluge, 1945–1952

An Associated Press photographer captured the moment Secretary of the Interior Julius Krug signed an agreement between the Three Affiliated Tribes and the Department of Interior, selling one-third of the Fort Berthold Indian Reservation for thirty-three dollars per acre (fig. 4.1). The accompanying caption in the May 21, 1948, *Washington Post* read,

> Lo, the Poor Indian . . .
> TRIBES GIVE UP LAND—George Gillette of the Fort Berthold Indians, covers his face and weeps as Interior Secretary Krug signs a contract by which three tribes sell the best part of their North Dakota reservation to the Government for $5,105,625. The land will be flooded by a dam and reservoir project. Secretary Krug said that while the contract was fair, it gave him no happiness to take part in a reduction of Indian land reserves. Said Gillette, chairman of the tribes' business council, "Right now the future does not look good to us."[1]

In the photograph a group of besuited men stand gathered around a desk at which another man in a suit signs a paper. The men peer at the desk, at the piece of paper, and their sight lines intersect where pen and paper meet. Only two men look elsewhere, and one of them—then tribal chairman George Gillette—covers his eyes with one hand, the bottom half of his face visibly contorted, while his other hand holds his glasses. Published in the *Post* on May 21, 1948, the photo was reprinted in newspapers across the country.

The *Minot Daily News* quoted Gillette at greater length,

> You will excuse me if I say that members of the tribal council will sign this contract with heavy hearts. With a few scratches of the pen, we will sell the best part of our reservation. Right now the future does not look

Figure 4.1. Tribal chairman George Gillette (Arikara) covers his face in anguish while others look on as Interior Secretary Krug signs a contract by which the Three Tribes sell one-third of the Fort Berthold Indian Reservation for $5,105,625. *Left to right:* Ben Reifel (Lakota), Bureau of Indian Affairs superintendent at Fort Berthold; Gillette; Joseph Packineau (Arikara, Hidatsa), Elbowoods district; James Hall (Hidatsa), vice chairman; Levi Waters (Arikara), Nishu district; Mark Mahto (Mandan), Red Butte and Charging Eagle districts; (partly hidden) George Charging (Mandan), Lucky Mound district and tribal council treasurer; Earl Bateman (Arikara), Nishu district; and Ralph Hoyt Case, tribal attorney. Associated Press.

too good for us.... We have faith that Congress will recognize that this contract gives the Fort Berthold Indians only part of what is due to them. The truth is, as everyone knows, our Treaty of Fort Laramie, made in 1851, and our tribal constitution are being torn into shreds by this contract.[2]

Gillette described the forced sale of Fort Berthold tribal lands taken via eminent domain—a legal privilege of the United States as a sovereign power. The reservoir created by the Garrison Dam, the second main-stem dam constructed under the Pick-Sloan Plan, would submerge the taken lands. Built at the edge of the Fort Berthold Indian Reservation and completed in 1954, the Garrison

Dam cost $300 million and remains the fifth-largest dam in the United States. Garrison flooded over 150,000 acres of prime grazing and agricultural land, and every community on the reservation. The reservoir's rising waters forced more than 80 percent of Fort Berthold residents to relocate, and destroyed infrastructure such as school buildings, a hospital, and community centers.

To create the Garrison Dam, the US government used eminent domain to take treaty-guaranteed land. Because treaties are mutual recognitions of sovereignty, the eminent domain taking of Fort Berthold lands indicates the willful disregard of sovereign power. Novelist, Indian activist, and scholar D'Arcy McNickle—also a former commissioner of Indian affairs—elaborated, "The Indian tribe was put in the category of private landowner, against whom the state could proceed; compensation in money was made the equivalent of ethnic and cultural identity. The process, in time, can only lead to the extinction of the Indian people as a separate and identifiable thread in American Life."[3]

Perhaps appropriately, then, most of the men in the photograph gaze both at the man signing the document, Secretary Krug, and the pen frozen in its journey across the page. The composition of the image confirms the source of power, the centrality of state authority, and the exercise of federal sovereignty at the expense of tribal sovereignty. The photo circulates in academic works and textbooks, usually deployed as an illustration of the human costs of hydropower projects, federal development projects in the mid-twentieth-century western United States, or midcentury federal Indian policy.[4] The photograph's historic and contemporary function, however, centers on it as an exhibit of the Garrison Dam and the communities it flooded.

Photographs are often used as unsophisticated illustrations (especially by historians), but every photograph also signifies a hidden history, one that complicates the image, makes it richer, and imbues it with meaning. These histories cannot be read in the assortment of individuals, objects, or landscapes displayed in an image, for the potential and scope of its mass production often flattens the photograph and ensures its misreading and mischaracterization. In some ways, then, a photograph mimics the functions of a place as a physical marker of history and culture that requires expertise to narrate and interpret it and needs time and careful consideration. Under the caption "Lo the Poor Indian," for example, the photograph elides the real-life qualities of George Gillette. His childhood on Fort Berthold attending both the Congregational church and Arikara ceremonies, at which his elders smudged him and prayed over him to cleanse and protect him, disappears; his journey through off-reservation boarding schools, from Bismarck Indian School to Flandreau Indian School to the Haskell Institute vanishes; his twenty-two years in public service as an unpaid tribal council member, even as he ranched to support his family, evaporates; his work as a lay minister at the Snowbird Chapel, his hymns sung in Arikara and English, fades into the background, remembered only by those closest to him.[5]

This chapter attempts to create dimension and texture for this photograph—so that we can imagine the sound of the camera's flash bulb, the scrape of a ballpoint pen across thick paper, the smell of wool suits and Brylcreem, and the physical pain that accompanies the attempt and failure to hold back tears. This photograph becomes more legible when we take time to understand how Fort Berthold people grappled with and relentlessly refused to relinquish elements of their sovereignty in opposition to the Garrison Dam. This history of community protest against the Garrison Dam further developed the practice and ideation of indigenous citizenship at Fort Berthold—a product of long tribal histories, and in response to the threat posed by the dam.

Torrent: The Pick-Sloan Plan

Too much water is a problem, especially when it gathers from many different directions. At the end of winter, for example, the combination of melting snow and one intense rainstorm can create a flood. At first, the river rushes just a bit faster or slightly higher. But as the miles of river upstream gathers runoff from acres of surrounding lands, what seemed like a slight rise in the river quickly becomes alarming. In these moments, rivers become scary, swollen with violent rushing water that rises and rises and rises. In the 1940s, the Pick-Sloan Plan was like a flood—not only because many rains and streams fed into a rising, inevitable rush of water that was the Pick-Sloan Plan, or Missouri Basin Program, but also, because while a flood is a systemic event, it is experienced locally and only those who suffer under its impact truly understand its power. The political process that created Pick-Sloan started innocently with a few drops of rain, but by 1943 it became a torrent—much like those that flooded Lower Missouri states and were used to justify the creation of a Missouri River valley hydrological project known as the Pick-Sloan Plan.

Some say a flood inspired Colonel (later General) Lewis A. Pick of the Army Corps of Engineers. The wet 1943 springtime produced three weeks of flooding within the space of a month and a half. The flood hit in the middle of US involvement in World War II, and Lower Missouri states sustained $6,500,000 in direct damages and $1,300,000 in indirect damages. Supposedly, Pick jumped up on his desk as the floodwaters immersed the streets outside corps offices and yelled, "I want to control the Missouri!" at his subordinates. The flooded Omaha airport runways upset the army supply chain, and the House Flood Control Committee called a special meeting to question Pick. They quickly passed a resolution directing Pick to prepare a report on flood control, which he completed three months later in August 1943 and rushed to the House Committee on Rivers and Harbors.[6]

Long before the '43 floods or the advent of the Pick Plan, W. G. Sloan from the Bureau of Reclamation had researched and prepared a comprehensive plan of his own for the Missouri River basin. The Flood Control Act of 1936 and the Reclamation Project Act of 1939 had authorized the bureau to complete a comprehensive study of Missouri River multiple-use developments, and when news of Pick's pet project reached the bureau, Sloan hurried to finalize his plan, begun at least five years prior. Each agency issued its plan in August 1943. The Army Corps of Engineers' plan focused on Lower Missouri levees and massive main-stem dams on the Upper Missouri; the Bureau of Reclamation's Sloan Plan would have built reservoirs on Awáati's tributaries to make collection basins for irrigation, land reclamation, power production, and increased navigability. The Pick Plan largely benefited farmers and urban areas in the Lower Missouri basin states, and his plan located the five main-stem dams in Upper Missouri states, each at the edge of an Indian reservation. Pick's plan ensured that Native communities would bear the greatest loss of land.[7]

Pick began visiting Lower Missouri River states to sell his plan in fall 1943, and in the summer of 1944 both agencies pushed their own proposals in Congress. President Franklin Roosevelt and the Missouri basin farmers unions both preferred a unified, comprehensive effort for basin planning, ideally under a single agency—a kind of "Missouri Valley Authority" (MVA) to mirror the New Deal's Tennessee Valley Authority (TVA). But critics of an MVA were loud and persistent. During wartime, some feared the creation of another New Deal–oriented "superagency," and, as usual, western interests feared federal power almost as much as they sought federal relief and subsidies. Critics argued that an MVA threatened private enterprise, and that an aggressive executive endangered state sovereignty and congressional control.[8]

A month after Roosevelt's administration came down in favor of an MVA, the corps and the bureau combined their plans, retaining 110 of the 113 projects from both plans. Secretary of the Interior Harold Ickes panned the inflexibility displayed by the corps's refusal to reconsider the scope of their projects, noting,

"The Corps' reputation for arrogance . . . is legendary, and every effort that has been made to induce the Corps to listen to recommendations made by the ablest civil engineers in the country has been resisted with an obduracy that is beyond belief." The National Farmers Union president, James Patton, described the newly formed Pick-Sloan Plan as a "shameless, loveless shotgun wedding." Congress, now unfriendly to Roosevelt directives, also contained western congressmen who worked hard to ensure the Pick-Sloan merger devastated the MVA option. It worked. Roosevelt signed the Flood Control Act of 1944 (P.L. 78-534) on December 22, 1944—a scant four months before he died.[9]

The deeper currents of Pick-Sloan, however, emanate from a new apogee of bureaucratic consolidation and centralized power in the federal government that emerged in the late nineteenth and early twentieth centuries. The federal government's ability to imagine "space" put broad social visions of the West into practice through aggressive exercise of federal sovereign power over its territorial base. Beginning with the Land Ordinance of 1785, federal policies long aimed to map, understand, rationalize, and administer western lands as territory. During the nineteenth-century expansion into the territorial interior, these spatial strategies centered around the question of arid lands and irrigation. This spatial work included federal land policies such as the 1862 Homestead Act—which encouraged agricultural settlement on arid western lands unsuited to eastern farming techniques—and the 1877 Desert Land Act—which subsidized irrigation of arid western lands to spur settlement and demand for railway service across the continent. These acts—among many others—disposed the government to subsidize western irrigation and land use. At the turn of the century, conservation advocates influenced Theodore Roosevelt's presidential policy, leading to the creation of the Bureau of Reclamation in 1902 under ideas that emphasized "the fullest necessary use of resources by the present generation, their development, prevention of their waste, and their utilization for the benefit of the many and not merely for the profit of a few."[10]

By the New Deal years, Progressive Era conservation evolved into the bleaker question of soil rehabilitation. During the economic and ecological breakdown of the Depression and the Dust Bowl, New Dealers began to equate the ecological health of rural lands and the economic health of US agricultural areas with the ability of the country at large to emerge from the Great Depression. The ecological and economic crises of the period created fertile ground for Roosevelt to reinterpret and further expand the power of the executive and federal sovereign power. The 1936 creation of the Great Plains Drought Area Committee typified this interventionism. A direct response to the intense drought years of '34 and '36, the Great Plains Committee surveyed agricultural and economic conditions in the Great Plains states and produced a unified set of recommendations on policies to rehabilitate both the soil and economy of those areas.[11]

US engagement and victory in World War II also shifted federal policy priorities. When the United States began to mobilize its war machine before its official entry into the war, an earlier focus on rural soil conservation evolved into an emphasis on production—supposedly to help rural areas produce raw agricultural products efficiently, agricultural policies needed to shift away from small farmers to favor large agricultural producers. These policies prodded the rural poor toward factory work in major wartime industry cities and ensured that only large producers would realize agricultural profitability. Thus, World War II and late New Deal policymakers no longer considered the subsistence agriculture practiced by Three Affiliated tribal members—praised and encouraged in federal Indian policy for the previous fifty years since the Dawes Allotment Act—a viable rural economic system.[12]

The postwar United States also flexed its colonial and imperial powers. The federal government of the 1890s—which worked to claim territory in a newly quelled northern plains via the Missouri River survey—held more centralized power and become cockier. US imperialist success before the Second World War and the country's shared victory in the conflict further decreased federal interest in substantive engagement with indigenous land rights. Instead, most divisions of the federal government pushed for incorporation of indigenous lands such as those in Alaska and Hawaii, the appropriation of Native lands for wartime projects, and the development of all possible natural resources within the economic territory of the United States. All these efforts represent aggressive assertions of federal sovereign power.

US waterways and energy development policy mirrored this trajectory. But whereas the federal government saw soil conservation, reclamation, and rehabilitation as necessary to *maintain* the nation's economic health, federal waterway control symbolized economic modernity and progress. During the early decades of the twentieth century, hydroelectric projects linked waterway development to relatively cheap, clean, and low-impact power production. Exploration and survey blossomed once hydro projects became not just economically viable but profitable. The 1918 development of the Wilson Dam over the Tennessee River at Muscle Shoals, Alabama—later elaborated upon via the Tennessee Valley Authority—led to the 1920 Federal Water Power Act, which created the Federal Power Commission and coordinated hydroelectric power projects in the United States. New Dealers promoted federal investment in hydropower to boost job creation and to provide rural electricity. Federal planners sold the Hoover Dam and the TVA as projects with both the short-term potential to combat the immediate economic disaster and long-term potential to build a healthier economy.[13]

The Tennessee Valley Authority allowed the federal government to practice the politics and mobilization of hydroelectric development during the New Deal; afterward, the federal government aggressively created massive hydroelectric dams throughout rural America, especially in arid and semiarid zones. And while state and federal governments rationalized these hydro projects with assertions that the dammed waterways represented a common resource to be developed for the "common good" or public interest, the implementation typically benefited the career trajectories of politicians as frequently as they considered the impact on the communities to be flooded. The hydro projects also conformed to the longer history of nation-state–driven challenges aimed at indigenous land rights extending from territorial wars to reservation confinement, to allotment, to railroad cessions. US development policies idealized and transported many TVA strategies to nations in Africa, Latin America, and Asia, and promoted hydroelectric projects as symbolic of modernity and progress—even as the projects guaranteed that periphery economies remained in debt to the economically powerful in ways that decreased the actual benefits of cheaper electricity to the affected communities.[14]

The Missouri River floods of 1943 and the administrative jockeying between the Army Corps of Engineers and the Bureau of Reclamation amplified these deep currents of federal policy. A veritable flood of dam-building policy resulted, against which the Three Affiliated Tribes struggled for nearly a decade. The Bureau of Indian Affairs, fighting its own administrative battle for survival after the disintegration of the New Deal bureaucracy, failed to inform the Fort Berthold tribes of their potential land losses until 1947, by which time the Fort Berthold Tribal Council was already knee-deep in negotiations. The first reservation to deal with an aggressive Corps of Engineers—the administrative unit driving the main-stem dam portion of the Pick-Sloan Plan—Fort Berthold became a test case not only for the corps in dealing with recalcitrant Indians but for other tribes affected by the legislation. By 1951–52 when the waters of the Garrison Reservoir submerged the foundations of houses that had been laboriously and at times chaotically moved to the top lands in the two preceding years,

Congress had legislated the communities of Fort Berthold out of one-quarter of their total land base and 94 percent of their agricultural lands. It did not happen, however, without a fight.[15]

Levees: The Fight against the Garrison Dam

For tribal chairman George Gillette, the meeting of pen and paper in the "Lo, the Poor Indian" photograph did not come as a shock. Rather, a decade of struggle culminated in that moment. It must have felt unbearable to Gillette as the authority of federal sovereign power quenched tribal rights when the pen began its journey across the paper. Perhaps he remembered the lushly timbered bottomlands, the beauty of the graceful S curves created by the Missouri River as it cut into the earth of the Great Plains. Gillette and the other tribal leaders present had ridden horseback through those bottomlands, to herd cattle or visit relatives or ride to community dances and council meetings. During those rides, whether in the harsh, below-zero windchill of winter, among the soft fuzzy crocuses and blooming tiger lilies and echinacea of spring, or in the heavy sun and sweat-drying winds of summer, they had eaten cornballs and cracked jokes or sung Hidatsa, Arikara, or Mandan riding songs with other men as they traveled or herded cattle. The same hands that held Gillette's glasses and covered his eyes had branded cattle, built fence, and steered his horse through the Fort Berthold landscape. As a carpenter trained at the off-reservation Haskell Institute (now Haskell Indian Nations University) in Kansas, he knew the satisfaction of using his hands to smooth rough wood and build useful things, like his family's house in the Beaver Creek community in the Missouri River valley. As a pastor, he used his hands to write sermons and hold hymnals written in both English and his first language, Arikara. The simple beauty of these things must have wrenched a fissure in his chest as he faced the prospect of their inundation.

As the ink dried on the page, Gillette removed his glasses and shielded his eyes with his hand. A camera flashed and froze a moment of pain and grief. Gillette—and all the men with him that day—had battled the Garrison Dam for years. They represented only a small portion of those who would grapple with its implementation.

> Rosemarie: I graduated high school, 16, went to Haskell, 18, I had my first job at Belcourt for two years. . . . At 21 I decided to go to college, so I was going to the University of New Mexico. So that's how long it took. All the fighting, the struggling, the trying to save the land, negotiations

and the meetings.... My Uncle Ben [on the tribal council] used to be going to DC and [my parents were always] trying to give [my uncle] some money—they never had money. So I went to college, I was 21 when they had the big powwow at the powwow grounds in Elbowoods, because that was the last time the people were going to gather [pauses]. [Voice shakes] And I had my friend, I brought her with me, she was one of my non-Indian friends from university, and she was there for that powwow I remember. Anyhow that was the last thing, that big gathering, I remember. From then things started to dismantle.

The fight against the dam and its construction was a grueling, decade-long marathon of activism, fundraisers, local political organization, conflict, and navigation of the national political scene. In its midst, tribal members grappled emotionally with how their lives might change. Edwin Benson remembered his elder clan brother:

In our way, Crows Heart he was my older brother, he said, "My little brother, come here."... I went and sat beside him. "Now," he said, "I want to tell you something. They tell me they're going to flood this all out. No such a thing," he said. He named different creeks, "They're really deep; they'd have to fill all those up before the water would come up here."... And after he died a little while later, it was no problem to fill that river valley up, that bottom land.[16]

The fight against the Garrison Dam was like fighting a flooding river: at first it seems unreal that the rains or snowmelt upstream will produce any change, but as the current gets higher and faster it soon becomes clear that to have anything left, you need to start throwing up levees. Tribal leadership changed four times during this period; every two-year election cycle installed a new tribal chair; the tribal council found legal representation, then fired them and brought in new counsel; eight official and four unauthorized tribal delegations visited and sought time with Senate and House subcommittees; the council held hundreds of community meetings to seek feedback and hear complaints. The federal government's compensation package shifted from lieu land offers to cash settlements, and by the end of the decade the tribal council found itself in hearings defending timber and mineral rights it had never ceded or relinquished. Tribal member Robert Lincoln described the process as being "much like the hen and her young fighting off the hawk that is sweeping down to attack."[17]

Soon after the 1943 floods and the inception of Pick's aggressive promotion efforts for the Army Corps of Engineers plan, the tribal council passed a resolution against any dam that would flood Fort Berthold lands. Signed by then tribal chairman Carl Sylvester, it read in part,

> WHEREAS: a dam below the Fort Berthold reservation is being contemplated for future action by the Congress of the United States in cooperation with the State of North Dakota, which action, if realized, will destroy by permanent flood all the bottom land of the said Reservation, causing untold material and economic damage to the Three Affiliated Tribes; ...
>
> NOW, THEREFORE, BE IT HEREBY RESOLVED: by the Tribal Business Council ... that it oppose the present plan of constructing a dam below the Fort Berthold Reservation or any other plan which will destroy the flood areas of the Missouri Valley.[18]

The concerned tribal council telegraphed Commissioner of Indian Affairs William Brophy in early 1944 to request a meeting over the proposed dam site. If he responded, his response is not preserved within the federal archives.

Community organizations, including the long-adversarial group organized by a dissident core of tribal members from Shell Creek, shared the tribal council's concerns. Fort Berthold Americans, Inc. presented a written document that opposed construction of the dam in June of that year. Regardless, Roosevelt signed the Flood Control Act of 1944, which authorized the creation of the five main-stem dams along the Upper Missouri including the Garrison Dam, in late December 1944.[19]

Only a month before Roosevelt authorized Pick-Sloan, Fort Berthold elected a new tribal chair: thirty-eight-year-old Martin Cross, a dogged politician who descended from important tribal leaders. Under his leadership, the tribal council passed a Resolution Further Opposing Garrison Dam, which mustered several arguments:

> WHEREAS; [construction would] force approximately 200 families to move from their permanent homes ...
>
> WHEREAS; the cemeteries of our forefathers will be destroyed with it all our memories and kind remembrances of the burial places that have been held sacred for all; ...

Figure 4.2. Four-time tribal chairman and leader of the "No" faction, Martin Cross (Mandan, Hidatsa). North Dakota State Historical Society.

WHEREAS; and deprive approximately 250 boys from our reservation who are now serving in the armed forces of land rightfully theirs; . . .

WHEREAS; we have permanently located on these lands, and our forefathers also have lived on these grounds and it is the hopes and plans of our children and their children to occupy this land continuously forever; and money or exchange for other land will not compensate us for the land, land marks, and sentimental attachments.[20]

The arguments, posed in the form and language of a sovereign authority, mobilize tribal notions of place and sovereign territoriality—the mention of homes and burial places and "land rightfully theirs"—as well as an evolving indigenous citizenship, as seen in references to military service and aboriginal land title. The components used to argue against the implementation of the Garrison Dam come from, and perhaps comprise, the arsenal of tribal sovereignty. After the passage of this second resolution in June 1945, Cross and tribal council secretary Floyd Montclair met with the local BIA official C. H. Beitzel and Colonel Pick to discuss the effects of the project on Fort Berthold. After their meeting, the trickle of activity became a deluge.[21]

The tribal council sent a delegation to Washington, DC, to testify before the Senate Committee on Indian Affairs and protest the construction of the Garrison Dam. Council members Martin Cross, Jefferson Smith, Martin Fox, and Earl Bateman took a train to Washington and arrived October 4 on a shoestring budget. Clothed in suits gathered from charity missionary barrels and partially funded by their neighbors going door-to-door collecting quarters and dimes, they were met at Union Station by Felix Cohen, the foremost federal Indian law scholar of the twentieth century. Cohen coalesced the modern field of federal Indian law via his 1941 *Handbook of Federal Indian Law*, in which he brought coherence to a diverse range of treaties, statutes, and decisions that spanned hundreds of years. Cohen found the delegates' lodging and accompanied them to their October 9 hearings before the Indian Affairs Committee (he also submitted a memorandum a week later to the committee confirming that the Three Affiliated Tribes possessed the legal ability to request an injunction to prevent unlawful interference with their property). A few days after their return from the capital, the tribal council authorized Cross and council member Jefferson Smith to engage an attorney to "prosecute the Tribal opposition to the construction of the Garrison Dam, and other details that may be involved."[22]

After their hire of attorney Ralph Hoyt Case, the Three Affiliated Tribes achieved a small victory late in December 1945, when a rider to an expenditures bill halted spending on Garrison Dam construction until a settlement with the tribe was reached. The rider put greater pressure on the tribes to negotiate and presumably agree to a settlement. The tribe also hired an engineer to analyze and submit a report on an alternate dam site; he submitted his report in March 1946. The first set of compensation negotiations focused on lieu lands—lands offered by the War Department to the Three Tribes in lieu of those flooded by the Garrison Dam. (The proposal would be akin to Canada offering the United States lieu lands above Idaho and Montana for the annexation of Washington State.)[23]

The offer enraged the community. In the only meeting Pick held with community members at large on Fort Berthold—fairly characterized as a disaster—tribal member James Driver, the last tribal member born at Like-a-Fishhook, rejected the idea:

There are some things that are dear to me, above all others. For instance, the land I am standing on is dear to me. From time immemorial, we have resided on this land. The land beneath our feet is the dearest thing in the world to us, and I am here to tell you that we are going to stay here. We refuse to be flooded. As members of the white race, you have come from across the pond as newcomers to this land. In the years that have come and gone, the time when our chief Four Bears was alive, he made treaties with your government that promised this land would be ours forever. Forever! What confuses the Indian is how he and the white man can have such a different interpretation of that word. We are here today to remind you that we were on this land long before the first white man came, and we are going to remain here forever.[24]

Other community leaders echoed Driver's sentiments. Respected tribal member and longtime community judge Daniel Wolf, a man once described as having "long years of living among Indians as a member thereof, [that] instilled into his mind an experience of thoughtfulness, and all due consideration of angles that eventually reach a common point," asserted, "There is no land that compares to what we have here."

The tribal members' statements so angered Pick that he stormed out of the meeting and thereafter displayed what amounted to a personal grudge against the Fort Berthold communities—he advocated, for example, to prevent tribal members from liquidating their timber and oil resources in the taken area. Simultaneously, local white communities of Killdeer and Stanton protested the taking of their lands for the lieu lands offer. This route seemed a dead end—especially as the corps' Pick-Sloan eminent domain land takings aimed to take reservation lands, not those of white communities.[25]

The Army Corps of Engineers arrived at Fort Berthold to begin work on the Garrison Dam in April 1946. And although Martin Cross protested and petitioned Congress to halt construction, community demands effected no relief. Community anger also shifted to tribal leadership. Tribal members voted out Martin Cross in the November 1946 election and voted in George Gillette as tribal chair. Community members may have believed Cross cooperated too fully with an arrogant Corps of Engineers and War Department. Soon after the election, the council-at-large rescinded tribal cooperation with the War and Interior Departments to conduct land survey and appraisal work, a move Cross bemoaned in a letter to the chief engineer in the Office of Indian Affairs. "I do hope I was doing the right thing. Some of my political friends have called me weak-kneed in this move to lend cooperation," he wrote.[26]

Less than a month after George Gillette became tribal chairman, the secretary of war made a formal lieu land offer to the Three Tribes. The secretary of the interior—supposedly an advocate for tribal communities within the federal government—wrote a paternalistic note to accompany the lieu lands offer that stated, "I feel that it is necessary for me to call your attention to the fact that the Garrison Project, as one element of the Missouri River Basin Plan for flood control, irrigation, navigation, and power development, has been approved by the Congress, and that an appropriation for construction work has already been made. In the circumstances, the lieu land offer of the War Department should engage the serious consideration of the Fort Berthold Indians."[27] The lieu lands offer led to a spate of meetings on Fort Berthold over the course of one week in December—one in each of the seven major reservation communities. Despite snow and a bitingly cold winter—which in North Dakota in 1947 could mean blizzard snowfalls of nearly four feet and temperatures as low as minus-twenty-eight degrees Fahrenheit—community members determinedly traveled to each meeting to oppose the lieu lands offer. Six days after the last and largest community meeting at the Elbowoods Agency Council Hall on December 10, exhausted tribal delegates traveled to Washington, DC, to meet with top Interior and War Department administrators. They reported the community rejection of the lieu lands offer and the tribal business council resolution to reflect community opposition.[28]

After the secretary of the interior also formally rejected the War Department's lieu lands offer in January 1947, Congress moved to another compensation strategy: cash. On July 31, 1947, Congress passed P.L. 80-296, based on consultations with War Department representatives, that offered a $5,105,265 lump-sum payment to the Three Tribes. Congress passed P.L. 80-296 only a few weeks after the visit of a *fourth* tribal delegation that specifically testified against a cash settlement. Mark Mahto, a sixty-year-old Mandan tribal council member from Shell Creek, gave fiery testimony:

> The quickest and most merciful way to exterminate the three tribes is by mass execution, like they did to the Jews in Germany. We find it strange that the treaty made between you and the aggressor nations of Japan and Germany are more sacred than the treaty you made with the three tribes. Everything will be lost if Garrison is built. We will lose our homes, our

communities, our economy, our resources.... If you are determined to remove us from our land, you might as well take a gun and put a bullet through us. The principles that we fought for in this last war, right beside you, was for the very homes, lands, and resources that you are trying to take from us today.

Mahto's commentary remains incisive. It also reflects a defense of tribal sovereignty, one in which the treaties signed with tribes should be held to the same standard as treaties signed with Japan and Germany. By the time Mahto reached home, news of the passage of P.L. 80-296 already arrived at Elbowoods, and he sat through an emergency council meeting on the legislation, according to one chronicler, "in stunned silence." Congress not only disregarded his testimony but also presented a deeply inadequate compensation offer. Congress expected the five million dollars to cover not only compensation for lands taken but relocation costs of individual families and the entire tribal infrastructure—a hospital, cemeteries, roads, schools, and Bureau of Indian Affairs agency buildings. If the cash payment intended *only* to compensate for lands taken, it would have amounted to $1 to $2.50 per acre at a time when even mediocre grazing land in North Dakota was valued at five to seven times that amount. Congress gave the tribes five months to consider this cash offer for their bottomlands, and if they rejected the offer, they would be forced to seek compensation via federal courts. It was a major blow.[29]

Resolve frayed, and preexisting community fractures widened. The first rift, however, came not within the tribe, but with its attorney, Ralph Case. In a September 25 meeting, several community delegates and council members expressed strong displeasure with Case's effectiveness. Ben Spotted Wolf, from Lucky Mound, doubted Case's abilities: "When this question [of cash settlement] came up some time ago we knew we would have a fight. Our Tribal Council was asked to seek help to fight and the Council selected a lawyer, Mr. Case, but for some reason we heard on the 31st of July that he lost and had his back broken. We and he have lost in disgrace." George Parshall of Shell Creek was even more withering not only toward Case but also toward the federal government:

We know we hired a man to oppose the Garrison Dam and during all this time Mr. Case has spoken to us in favor of the Dam. He should not do that. Instead, he should be finding out how to oppose the Dam. He has pointed out the advantages of the Dam. This afternoon he has taken up three hours of our time speaking of the Garrison Dam. He has told us nothing about how to oppose it. Offers made by the Government in the past have not been fulfilled, it would be the same in this case. We cannot break the laws of our forefathers. We will hold onto them until we drown and go out of sight.

Although some present at the meeting supported Case's efforts, the overall atmosphere teemed with anger and betrayal. Martin Fox of Charging Eagle added, "If our attorney Case can't oppose the Garrison Dam he should resign."[30]

The delegates adjourned the meeting without resolution and resumed two days later. They continued to pointedly question Case, and even asked where he had been when Congress passed P.L. 80-296. In the middle of this council meeting—unannounced, unwanted, and uninvited—entered General Pick and North Dakota congressman William Lemke. After Case's introduction, Pick told the assembled leaders he and Lemke happened to be "making a trip through the Reservation" and stopped to see the tribal chair and superintendent. He "hoped the people would reach a satisfactory settlement."

Pick and Lemke may or may not have been on a rescue mission on Case's behalf. Clearly, however, they sensed the fraying tribal cohesion and sought to exacerbate matters. Lemke spoke paternalistically about "his good Indian friends" and emphasized the need for a settlement "fair to everybody." Pick, already no friend to the people of Fort Berthold, reads as patronizing and arrogant.

Immediately after Pick and Lemke left, the slow erosion of a cohesive tribal politics intensified. Martin Cross, who attended the meeting as a tribal member as he no longer held office, offered a challenge. He rose from his seat and stated, "I want admission of defeat from Attorney Case, from [council member] Jeff Smith and the Tribal Council. Would you, Mr. Case, publicly admit defeat?" The tribal council meeting minutes then note, "At this point, the Chairman [George Gillette] told Martin Cross he was out of order and requested him to take his seat. Mr. Cross wanted to offer a resolution which was refused by the Chairman." As the federal government increasingly disregarded tribal sovereign power, tribal politics became chaotic.[31]

In October 1947, before the Three Affiliated Tribes accepted or rejected a settlement, the Army Corps of Engineers began construction of the Garrison Dam.

The Garrison Dam began to seem inevitable. The cash settlement offer necessitated the survey and assessment of tribal lands. In the remainder of 1947,

Bureau of Indian Affairs staff from the newly created Missouri River Basin Investigations (MRBI) unit visited homesteads, surveyed land, and interviewed tribal members about their lands, assets, and future plans. The MRBI completed its Social and Economic Report on the Future of the Fort Berthold Reservation, North Dakota, on January 15, 1948. As the assessors and surveyors worked, the personal disputes of tribal politics intensified. Martin Cross and Floyd Montclair, who served on tribal council together from 1944 through 1946, unified with several supporters and agitated for tribal members to vote no on the clearly inadequate cash settlement compensation package legislated in P.L. 80-296. At the September 1947 meeting that Pick and Lemke crashed, conflict between Martin Cross and the tribal council surfaced. Now, it mounted.[32]

The "No group" spearheaded by Cross and Montclair concentrated in the Charging Eagle and Shell Creek districts—districts long suspicious of the Bureau of Indian Affairs and (as seen in chapter 2) dissidents of the Indian Reorganization Act in the mid-1930s. Outsiders considered Shell Creek a fractious, rebellious community, divided among itself. The Xo'shga, or Crow Flies High band of Hidatsas, who revolted against reservation era confinement to live in Montana (the army later rounded them up and brought them back to Fort Berthold), settled in Shell Creek and maintained a unique community attitude. Cross's faction aimed to prevent a clear majority, as a majority of eligible Three Affiliated tribal members had to vote to approve the compensation package. The alternative, however, was dangerous: no compensation at all for the lands taken. In May 1948, the tribal referendum on the P.L. 80-296 compensation package passed with 65 percent of eligible voters voting "yes." In truth, in practice, the vote did not represent a choice; it represented the decay of the last possible barrier against the Pick-Sloan flood.[33]

This chaos and heartbreak is the context necessary to understand the photograph of tribal chairman George Gillette with his face buried in his hand, next to Secretary of the Interior Julius Krug as he signed the contract that authorized the sale of the Fort Berthold Missouri Valley lands. The federal government had steadily forced the people of Fort Berthold to sell the heart of their reservation.

Those voting "no" continued to agitate in meetings held far from the eyes of the elected tribal council. In November 1948, tribal members voted George Gillette out of office, after he had been forced to oversee the sale of lands he and everyone he knew held dear. Carl Whitman Jr., a man a decade younger than either Gillette or Cross, replaced him. Only thirty-five years old when elected chairman, Whitman was described a few years later by a visiting anthropologist as a "swarthy Clark Gable" with a "moustache" and "faint, knowing smile." During his tenure as tribal chair, Whitman built strong relationships with other council members as well with the Fort Berthold superintendent, Ben Reifel, a Lakota tribal member from the Standing Rock Reservation. He and other council members balanced political advocacy in Washington, DC, with the earthy, hands-on engagement necessary in tribal politics—perhaps because the "No" faction posed a persistent challenge to their political authority.[34]

Soon after Whitman's election and the sale of the Fort Berthold bottomlands via P.L. 80-296, Cross began to hold unofficial meetings in districts to advocate for a per capita payment of the cash settlement payment. By late August of 1949, Cross organized an unauthorized delegation to Washington regarding the distribution of settlement monies that competed with the tribal council delegation in the capital at the same time. Cross characterized the tribal council as "unwilling to permit settlement of differences at home" and asserted

Figure 4.3. Three-time tribal chairman Carl Whitman (Mandan, Hidatsa).
Courtesy of Kathy Whitman.

that "the Indian Office personnel has been around making appraisals of lands, homes and improvements, but they have never told us or anyone how much we will receive." Cross justified his unauthorized advocacy on behalf of two hundred tribal members who signed a petition asking for per capita disbursement of the taken lands settlement. His testimony—wandering and at times self-aggrandizing (he claimed in defense of Case that the current tribal council had proved "yellow," and noted, "I often wonder if I and Mr. Case had worked together on this we probably would have had a better showing")—purported to represent the disenfranchised and the poor of Fort Berthold. As he translated for tribal member Martin Fox from Arikara to English during the testimony, the statements he cultivated also made racial accusations. Fox's testimony—orchestrated by Cross—asserted, "They got this group of men and members of the tribal council that are mostly comprised of half-breeds and they took some other half-breeds along [to give testimony in DC] and they are using that money while they are denying the original, the genuine Indian."[35]

As Cross and his "No" crew organized rump delegations, Whitman and the rest of the tribal council struggled to maintain political legitimacy in Washington as they disseminated information and reached out to community members at home. The erasure of mineral, timber, shoreline, and hunting rights in the proposed P.L. 81-437—the official act that legislated the taking of the Fort Berthold bottomlands—particularly concerned the standing tribal council. This attempted erasure of Fort Berthold treaty rights over natural resources illustrates the growing conservatism of Indian affairs in the Cold War era, and a serious erosion of tribal sovereign power. Congress refused, even as it attempted to remove tribal resource rights, to accept the independent valuation of the taking area. P.L. 80-296 appropriated a little over five million dollars, though tribal council testimonies and supporting memoranda to Congress valued the land at over twenty million dollars. P.L. 81-437 eventually tacked on an additional $7,500,000 for compensation for the bottomlands taking, bringing the total compensation to $12,605,625. But in late October 1949, Congress passed P.L. 81-437 with no explicit acknowledgment of tribal rights to natural resources.[36]

As this transpired, the no-vote faction fixated on a per capita payment of the cash settlement, regardless of the final amount or natural resource rights included. These members asserted that the current tribal council's plan for compensation ignored landless tribal members, or those not directly losing land within the taking area. Because the tribal council prioritized loans and relocation assistance for tribal members who held lands within the taking area, tribal members already economically disenfranchised through the loss or sale of their allotted lands worried whether they would see compensation for the loss of communal tribal lands. Cross and Montclair continued to organize rump delegations to demand that any cash settlements for the taking area be disbursed per capita. One such rump delegation early in 1950 led to fears from the elected tribal government that Congress could use any per capita disbursement of the cash settlement as a rationalization for tribal termination or the transfer of service provisions—welfare, health care, and other programs—to the state of North Dakota.[37]

Congress passed H.C.R. 108—also known as the termination policy, enabling the termination of the federal-tribal relationship for certain tribes and the tribal status of thousands of their tribal members—over three years later in 1953, but its response to the rump delegation demands for per capita disbursement presaged the legislation. Whitman's reports from Washington to the tribal council and the tribal community after this latest rump delegation became frantic, as congressional responses to Montclair's testimony emphasized Congress's "pre-termination" version of the implications of a per capita payment. Whitman described congressmen asking Montclair "if he meant dividing the tribal assets—he said yes. Mean[ing you] want to get $3000 apiece. He said yes. Indians are competent? Yes. If that's the case, no need for the Indian Service. Let's turn them loose—no need to reestablish the agency." Whitman explained that as the bulk of federal monies came from eastern taxpayers, eastern congressmen could be resentful of large blocks of money going west.[38]

The rise of conservatism in Washington, DC, and the political missteps of the rump delegates forced the elected tribal council to work fast and hard to achieve tribal ratification of P.L. 81-437, the official act to take the tribes' Missouri valley lands—despite the council's misgivings regarding its terms on rights to natural resources. After a tribal vote ratified P.L. 81-437 in early March 1950—525 tribal members voting yes, or 55 percent of eligible voters in favor of ratification—the tribal council passed a reluctant ratification resolution that asserted its rights to natural resources even after P.L. 81-437 was signed.[39]

The tribal communities remained doubtful and confused over the course of events. The "No" faction continued to circulate a petition that demanded per capita distribution of compensation monies, and in response Whitman and the tribal council conducted lengthy community meetings in each district to explain their resolutions and their long-term strategy to seek tribal rights over natural resources lost in P.L. 81-437. The elected tribal council conducted over fifty-five district meetings by June 18, 1950, and field notes from the meetings illustrate the intense commitment necessary to explain the tribal council's stance, the political process, and the possible pitfalls of per capita distribution. The meetings lasted for hours, and community members who attended expressed a wide range of grievances, fears, and anxieties regarding their relocation due to the Garrison Dam. Council members explained not only their own political decisions but their engagement with federal and state politics—all while they empathized and gave advice regarding personal concerns. A broad cross-section of the tribal community attended—women, men, elders, young adults, English-speakers, and those who needed translations of anything in English—and the proceedings illuminate tribal communities desperately following a complicated and disempowering political process, while simultaneously caring for their families and preparing to relocate. Complex negotiations with government representatives had to be translated into Mandan, Hidatsa, or Arikara for elders unable to follow the discussions in English. Community members and their tribal council representatives spent long hours in discussion and dialogue. Field notes for one meeting observed, a "kerosene lamp is brought in and lighted."[40]

The political wrangle over the per capita disbursement became explicitly framed via blood quantum. Dissidents claimed that the elected tribal council was filled with "half-breeds" who only promoted the interests of other "half-breeds" while disempowering the "full-bloods" in the tribal political system. Per capita disbursement proponents argued that poorer tribal members would not survive without per capita monies: "The people who signed the petition had no flour, no nothing—so these are the ones that signed—the very poor." The tribal council and their supporters variously portrayed per capita proponents as thoughtless, irrational, or selfishly focused on payment for themselves in the "here and now" rather than on consideration of what was best for the tribe as a whole and into the future. Many fought the per capita issue by suggesting that the disbursement should happen only if those who received it terminated their tribal membership. Cross maintained his per capita stance, continued to promote it in Washington, and justified it with the rhetoric of race, blood quantum, and political disempowerment—ironic given that his own mother was non-Native. His rhetoric proved persuasive to a majority of tribal voters; in November 1950 they reelected him as tribal chairman, replacing Whitman.[41]

As the per capita debate continued, tribal leadership pursued aid outside of the lackluster BIA and Department of Interior. Carl Whitman sought help from the University of North Dakota during his first term as chairman from 1948 to 1950. Decades later, he remembered,

> I became chairman at the time the Garrison Dam was under construction and the water was backing up. As I've said before, I had two mandates. One was to bring about a better settlement than the one the Engineers were offering, and the other mandate was to bring about a mass relocation of 95% of our people in the most orderly fashion and the shortest time possible. [For] the latter I futilely went to UND for, brain, backup support; and nobody showed up there, none of the department heads showed up for a meeting, except for Dr. James Howard, an archaeologist.

One of the local Congregationalist ministers, Harold Case, sought the assistance of Rev. Galen Weaver, a national activist in the Congregational Church. Through Weaver, noted anthropologist Sol Tax and several of his graduate students initiated his Fort Berthold Action Anthropology Project, a group that produced much of the writing about the difficulties associated with the relocation due to the Garrison Dam. Tax would later collaborate with D'Arcy McNickle and establish, not only a series of summer Workshops on American Indian Affairs that would help ignite a generation of Red Power activists, but also the 1961 American Indian Chicago Conference, a huge gathering of tribal leaders and community members from across Native America that also played a part in convincing Native youth that they needed to establish their own activist path. But at this juncture, Tax sent his students to observe in several venues, not necessarily to act. Robert Reitz embedded in the local Bureau of Indian Affairs to assist with planning the move from the river valley to the prairie, Robert Merrill engaged more at the community level, but Edward Bruner essentially moved into the community of Independence with his wife. Their field notes reflect their relative distance from day-to-day community life, with Bruner and Merrill displaying much more empathy toward community members amid the unfolding tragedy.[42]

The National Congress of American Indians (NCAI) also wrote guarded letters to senators in support of the Fort Berthold communities, to advocate for the adoption of amendments that would "lessen the impact of this catastrophe upon the Indians." The NCAI has never, perhaps, been an organization of firebrands (in the 1960s they sloganeered, "Indians don't demonstrate"); their language in these letters confirms this reputation. "The defects [in P.L. 81-437, which appropriated $12.5 million for the taking of the bottomlands] are of three kinds," NCAI acting secretary Ruth Bronson (Cherokee) wrote, after opening the letter assuring Senator Joseph O'Mahoney that they did "*not* ask for any increase in this amount." She continued,

> The first [defects] are those which injure the Indians or deprive them of something valuable without corresponding benefit to the Government. I am certain the Committee did not want to injure the Indians gratuitously. The second kind are technical defects that might permit some individual landowners to enjoin the flooding of the reservoir. For the government's own protection these constitutional loophole should be plugged up before the Act is accepted. The third group of defects are mere logical inconsistencies, some of which may interfere seriously with efficient administration.

The remainder of the letter addressed some of the most hateful provisions of P.L. 81-437, such as the transfer of mineral rights in the taken areas to the government and the prohibition of the use the compensation money to hire attorneys to represent the tribe. The letter reflects the careful lobby of an organization that sought to create and preserve positive relationships with elected officials in an increasingly conservative era. Regardless, even this overly respectful letter produced few results.[43]

When the Army Corps of Engineers completed the dam and the waters began to rise, October 1, 1951, was set as the final date to move from the Missouri River valley. A huge farewell celebration was held in Elbowoods to say "Goodbye to the Valley." Rosemarie Mandan recalled that big powwow, the last time the people gathered in the river valley—during the interview, her shaking voice forced her to pause. "That was the last thing, that big gathering," she recalled. "From then things started to dismantle." The deep loss in Rosemary Mandan's voice and George Gillette's tears came from the same emotional root: an irrevocable attachment to land, formed over countless generations, fused to individual and collective identities, with a power that could cause a heart to rend.[44]

Deluge

> You white people have been here three-hundred years and yet have no sentimental attachment to any section of our country. . . . With the Indian, it is different. He is protected by a treaty more sacred than any

law congress can promulgate. I love to visit the graves of my departed relatives and friends at least once a year. I love to visit the spot where my father fasted to obtain the favor of the Great Spirit. This I can't do when all the sacred spots are flooded. If there be any people in these United States who are entitled to sing, "My country 'tis of thee, sweet land of liberty," it is the American Indian people. Yet, when I sing "America," I feel like crying, because I don't see any liberty or justice. (Mark Mahto, 1946)[45]

The vicious scramble to throw up political levees against the Garrison Dam attempted to stem what seemed like an inevitable flood. Fort Berthold community members experienced it as a deluge, a cascade of water that covered their lands. A deluge cannot happen without water, but it also cannot happen without something flooded—*land*, covered like a biblical flood, landmarks disappearing above a dammed watershed. A deluge also evokes changes in the meanings of sovereignty, and what constitutes "public good." For example, Marx and historians of the end of the French monarchy use the quotation from Louis XV, "Après moi, le déluge" to evoke a revolutionary change in sovereign legitimacy and authority.

As Mark Mahto's analysis at the beginning of this section illustrates, community members often touched on all these ideas evoked by "deluge"—flood, the interplay between water and land, emotional attachments to the land taken by the Garrison Dam, their status as citizens, and the federal recognition of not only their citizenship rights but their treaty rights. Assertions concerning treaties between the federal government and the communities of Fort Berthold align with tribal assertions of American citizenship, clothed in the rhetoric of patriotism and nationalism but formed by cultural norms and community history. This citizenship, founded on indigenous subjectivity *and* identity, was also embedded in the landscape the Army Corps of Engineers planned to flood. This indigenous citizenship demanded that the US government recognize Native citizens' equal standing with other US citizens, and to honor treaty agreements with the Three Tribes.

Testimonies about the importance of land as place, history, and tribal resource center every protest against the Garrison Dam. The testimonies convey deep emotion, as in the testimony from Mandan/Hidatsa tribal elder James Driver that began the first (and only) at-large meeting General Pick held with indigenous community members from the reservations his dams would flood:

> I hear that you have come here to ask us to give up our lands. I am an old-time Indian. I have little knowledge of the English language. You will understand me when I tell you that there are some things that are dear to me, above all others. For instance, the land I am standing on is dear to me. From time immemorial, we have resided on this land. The land beneath our feet is the dearest thing in the world to us, and I am here to tell you that we are going to stay here. We refuse to be flooded.[46]

Pick did not even look at the community members who spoke to him. His frustration likely rose when community testimony asserted the impossibility of providing alternate lands or monetary compensation for those to be taken by the Garrison Dam. Daniel Wolf, the former tribal judge, told him, "I doubt his word because they have fooled us. They have never lived up to their promises. There will be no land in comparison in what we got here. Now if we are located by force somewhere else, this land to be inundated, the Indian people will pass away with loneliness and sadness. I am opposed to flooding this reservation. You will have to kill me to take me from my land."[47] Pick responded after a few more equally defiant speakers by storming from the meeting. Months later, a local newspaper recounted Wolf's testimony, with a sad coda:

> At the May meeting many Indian leaders voiced their opposition to the dam. Among them was Indian Judge Daniel Wolf, chief of the Water Buster Clan. Aged, wrinkled, and crippled, Judge Wolf waved the Fort Laramie Peace Pipe under Pick's nose and shouted, 'You'll have to kill me to take me from this land.' Pick and his men were unmoved by the Indian's words. Judge Wolf is now dead. He died in his home last July and is buried in the Catholic cemetery at Elbowoods.[48]

As the fight against the Garrison Dam intensified, community testimony also flagged the timber, coal, and grazing resources to be inundated by the Garrison Reservoir. At a Nishu community meeting, an objector to the lieu lands offer stated, "Reservation has been developed through the past CCC program to where it is an ideal livestock set-up with its timber for shelter, lignite beds and timber for fuel, reservoirs, rivers, streams and developed streams for stock water, etc., all of which are not duplicated in the lieu land offer."[49] At a meeting in Charging Eagle, Mandan tribal member Edna Atkins reflected on the importance of soil and land to communities that farmed in the Missouri River valley for hundreds of years: "The soil cannot be compared with any other area. We raise practically every known variety of corn, beans and other produce that can be raised in any garden. The lieu land cannot be compared to Reservation when it comes to producing gardens. For this reason I don't want our lands flooded by the Dam."[50] Atkins's statement also references the agricultural achievements of the Three Tribes in their development of many varieties of corn and beans, and shows how the literal soil linked to tribal identity and pride.

Tribal members' narratives connected their tribal history to agricultural practice to specific *places*—imbued with history and culture, sites that served as an index for the shared history of the Three Tribes. Anthropology graduate student Robert Merrill interviewed tribal judge Peter Beauchamp (Arikara) in 1950, and Beauchamp made a point of taking him to the Old Scout Cemetery— the burial place of Arikara scouts who served under Custer. As Beauchamp showed Merrill the cemetery, he not only told stories about tribal history and culture but also wondered aloud what it would be like when a place so rich with both was covered by water. "[Beauchamp] asks where'll there be a place where we can come all together and see these things [graves and monuments]. We don't know." After Beauchamp described a sundance site to be inundated, Merrill's field notes describe the conversation:

> He describes and points out Fishhook Village: they lived all together— close—along the bluff (very low bluff)—and there was a trading place and a slaughter place for beefs and warehouses at the edge where boats came. And down where those trees are (down on flats below the bottom land now farmed) is where they had their gardens. And in that little place they grew so much corns, beans, and squash that it would tide them over the winter; they did it right—they worshipped when breaking the ground, and at seeding, and for rain and to all the things of nature. And they had crops enough on that little land to feed all the people.[51]

More would be covered by the lake than what could be counted, measured, and replaced. Tribal testimonies described how the rising waters of the Garrison Reservoir would immerse places, old battle sites, garden boundaries, cemeteries both marked and unmarked. James Driver of Shell Creek asserted in one community meeting, "The Army's job is to fight wars, not build dams to flood out people like us. This land is our home, our people are buried in the hills of our lands. We are opposed to leaving our homes."[52] Graves of ancestors recurred as a trope in protest testimonies, the human lifecycle of old age and death tied to the experience of raising children and the need to plan for future generations.

At a Nishu community meeting to debate the War Department's lieu lands offer, one tribal member asserted, "I object to leaving my land and home where my children have walked and played. I can almost see their cute footprints as they left them in the growing into adulthood. Where can the Army find a place as good as our lands. If there are such lands, the whites would not give them up. Our cemeteries will be molested—here where we have placed flowers on the graves of those who have gone on ahead of us."[53] Community members associated the land as a resource and home with raising children, family life, and the human lifecycle—and thus also linked land to ancestors, family members, and their gravesites. What are graves and cemeteries other than places human communities set aside to remember—to remember who used to live, but also their actions? The human body interred in the earth transforms that site, that land, and that soil into a powerful *place*—a place through which personal, familial, and community histories can be remembered and retold.

Tribal members found unfathomable not only the loss of the physical soil but also the loss of landmarks and places that indexed crucial cultural and community histories. This shared history—and, in the case of cemeteries, literally interred in the landscape—structured their tribal and community identities, and how they defined themselves as human beings.

Such identities—like all identities—evolved. During the New Deal and World War II years, tribal members tailored US rhetorics of nationalism and citizenship over their tribal and community identities as Mandans, Hidatsas, and Arikaras. The result was a particular brand of indigenous citizenship that recognized their standing as American citizens and as tribal members whose collectivity held a unique relationship with the federal government. Tribal members used this indigenous citizenship to claim rights, and though it had many and enduring roots, the prospect of inundation by the Garrison Dam also began to shape this citizenship and community identity. Protest narratives used indigenous patriotism, developed during World War II around male service in the armed forces, to highlight the injustice of the Garrison Dam. One of the first arguments against accepting the War Department's lieu land offer at a Nishu community meeting explained, "The War department is the very agency that took our boys in the war to help others fight for their homes and the boys now return to Fort Berthold Agency to see 350 of their homes to be taken by the Army Engineers for the Garrison Dam."[54] As with other racial and ethnic groups such as African Americans and Asian Americans, the community deployed male military service during wartime to demand full citizenship rights, and as a rationale to combat the Garrison Dam it pervaded community meetings, negotiations with federal officials, editorials, and congressional testimonies. One tribal member commented at a Lucky Mound meeting, "It will be taking away from our young men the very thing that they fought for in the war just ended." Mandan tribal member Edna Atkins asserted, "It seems that Army Engineers have not upheld the things our boys in the war fought for and we felt our boys would come home to something that was theirs but it looks like their services to our country were useless. I object to anyone coming and appraising our land we are the ones to do this. We are not naturalized Americans, we are real Americans. The man pushing this should go to another country where force is recognized." These citizenship claims via military service were not an assimilated American patriotism. For example, Atkins's statement also asserted, "[If the government] were planning to take our lands they should have come to us first. We were the first owners of the land." Her reference to "first owners of the land" specifically recognizes indigenous status—which she does not see as contradictory to her rights as a US citizen.[55]

Further, no community members advocated for an erasure of their tribally specific relationship with the federal government, if only because they feared the loss of the economic rights due tribal status. At a Nishu community meeting, a woman identified only as Mrs. Jackson Ripley humorously stated, "I was so mad when I heard I'd become a citizen. It was up to the Agency—they gave me a purse—I was a white lady—but its [the purse] been empty ever since. Do you want to be like me? It attacks everything: pigs, chicken, clothes, furniture.... Per capita payment invites becoming a taxpayer." Mrs. Jackson Ripley referred to an actual, physical purse, a remnant of the bureaucracy of Indian affairs of another era. The use of the term "citizen Indian" in the late reservation era referred to tribal members deemed "competent" to manage their own affairs—resulting in fee-simple ownership of their allotment, control over their own finances, and US citizenship. The status, as well as the fee-simple title to their land allotment, often led to land dispossession, as tribal members typically could not access the loans necessary to buy farming or ranching equipment; without that option to build income, property tax payments became untenable. When the Office of Indian Affairs conducted so-called last arrow pageants of assimilation on reservations throughout the 1910s and 1920s, Indian men who had received fee-simple titles to their land through allotment would shoot their "last arrow" before crowds of fellow tribal members who did not yet hold fee-simple title to their lands. Tribal members receiving their fee simple dressed in traditional regalia, shot their "last arrow," then entered a tipi and changed into "civilized"—Euro-American—clothing. The local Indian agent would then place the person before a plow and tell him to take the handle, stating, "This act means that you have chosen to live the life of the white man—and the white man lives by work." Women, however, neither shot an arrow nor stood before a plow; the Indian agent gave them a purse. To the BIA, Mrs. Jackson Ripley's purse signified US citizenship, assimilation, and landownership. To her, however, it signified an empty status as a taxpaying US citizen, stripped of indigenous treaty rights—a poor imitation of the indigenous citizenship evolving within tribal communities.[56]

Later in the same meeting, Mrs. Byron Wilde commented, "Now Senator Malone—he agitates to set the Indians free. But we are free. He means to make us taxpayers. A letter came the other day saying that. What are they after? They're counting our lands. They aren't satisfied with what they've cut off. They still want to get what little we've got. That land is more of an asset for you or me than anything you possess."[57] The testimonies asserted indigenous patriotism and US citizenship claims while also recognizing and asserting the value of their *different* relationship and status in the eyes of the federal government. The value of this tribal-federal relationship lay in its recognition of their aboriginal land rights—the freedom from state and federal property tax on tribal land serves, of course, as a legal recognition of the fundamental territorial difference between fee-simple landownership and "Indian land" held in trust by the federal government.

The assertion of uniqueness and specificity went beyond tribal land status. An unattributed statement from a Lucky Mound community meeting reads, "The Mandans of the Three Affiliated Tribes have as part of their heritage an obligation since time immemorial that pledges them to migrate upstream as a manifestation of progress. This obligation is seriously respected by the Mandans in their present day ceremonial life. A shrine in its commemoration is located on the reservation. To 'move back' to the lieu area is a violation of this sacred trust."[58] Those perceived to abandon this cultural specificity could face subtle criticism, as when Merrill's field notes at a Congregationalist Church committee meeting recorded community members' gentle teasing directed to those who changed their last names from those that sounded indigenous—such as Little Owl and Sitting Crow—to "white" last names.[59]

Discrimination, and in particular a long history of white-on-Indian racism, also produced a boundary line between white and Indian, American citizen and

Native American citizen. Structurally reinforced when the War Department took Fort Berthold lands via eminent domain—a privilege of a sovereign power in the name of the supposed "public good"—tribal members narrated these boundaries as they made sense of the changes that rolled over them. Joe Packineau Jr., the vice chairman of the tribal council in 1950, encountered graduate student Robert Merrill and his advisor Sol Tax at a baseball game in the Elbowoods community in early June 1950. After waving his hand to indicate the valley, Packineau commented, "Isn't it lovely." Merrill and Tax agreed. Merrill's field notes record,

> He says what a shame it is to flood it—we agree—then describes how Indians are a settled people while Whites if they can get more money, will move like that—snaps fingers. What a tragedy to force Indians out when they're settled in such a nice place. Then says Indians are discriminated against—Sol demures—then Joe describes how he's been in Wash. many times and how "you feel it inside that you're not given a good deal"—look at all the dams on the Missouri flooding Indian land—and all the things cut out of the bill—and not enough to compensate for the moving.

The snap of Packineau's fingers creates its own conversational boundary, an indication of the difference between Euro-American ties to land and Native ties. Packineau explains this boundary between white and Native not only due to a different relationship with the physical landscape—he bears witness to its structural reenactment, as he experienced it as a tribal leader in Washington, DC, forced to plead the case of his community and his lands before white senators, congressmen, and federal administrators.[60]

Later, Merrill wrote a letter to his wife in which he described his afternoon with tribal judge Peter Beauchamp that relayed his shock over encountering the long history of white racism toward Fort Berthold tribal members, for in their conversation Beauchamp recounted treaty violations, children being sent away to boarding schools, racial violence, and other acts of racism. Merrill wrote, "And I got such a tremendous outpouring of the most intense distrust, suspicion, and complete lack of understanding of Whites in his recital of everything that has happened to the Arikara (that's his tribe) from the time of Custer on—and the incidents—they practically break my heart—the things that were done were incredible enough—but the Indians had not the slightest understanding of what was happening to them or why—it was a series of incomprehensible injustices." However, Fort Berthold tribal members understood much more than

Merrill gave them credit for—and likely much more than Merrill understood—he was grappling with the racism of white society from the opposite position for the first time.[61]

White society treated Fort Berthold tribal members and their claims differently; that difference contributed to their identity formation. But community identity *and* subjectivity—the internally driven process through which tribal members expressed the intersection of myriad external forces that tried to shape and label them—created a unique assertion of US citizenship. Their protest of the Garrison Dam mobilized all possible identities to save their land: their identity as US citizens, as members of a tribe with a specific relationship with the federal government, and as Mandans, Hidatsas, and Arikaras whose lands continually re-narrated to them a unique cultural and community history. Tribal members used all these valences to prevent their inundation and used them as an organic but cohesive set of rights claims as indigenous citizens.

The persistent demand that the US government respect past treaty agreements comprises a final, integral ingredient to this formulation of indigenous citizenship. "Sovereignty" was not a term much used during this period in discussions of Native communities in the United States. But the tribal sovereignty discourse harvested to fuel gaming initiatives and the self-determination of extractive industries in the 1970s and 1980s evolved from seeds planted earlier, and not only by the Marshall Trilogy of the 1820s and 1830s or Felix Cohen's *Handbook of Federal Indian Law*. Marshall and Cohen translated the insistence on self-determination into language that the US legal system could understand, but tribal communities such as Fort Berthold *crafted* it when they fought for treaty rights, land, and resources—the components of tribal territories. In the 1950s, tribes and tribal members may not have framed rights claims in terms of sovereignty per se, but they *did* demand that the United States fulfill its treaty rights. The two rhetorics and two arguments are interwoven.

Former tribal council member Carl Sylvester wrote an essay titled "The Voice of Flood-Threatened Indians," in which all these concepts circulated—the importance of and emotive ties to the landscape at Fort Berthold; the richness of tribal subjectivity and the way in which the landscape and its landmarks continually reinforced it; and a set of claims of rights as citizens that did not erase indigenous identity, but used indigenous land title to bolster those claims and assert a moral (rather than purely legal) imperative to recognizing them. "We base our objection [to the Garrison Dam] mainly," he wrote, "on several fundamental reasons."

One is that the threatened portion is our best part in the reservation, comprising the bottom and bench lands in the proposed flood area. . . . The landscape will be radically changed.

Another reason is that many spots are cemeteries for our dead, beside those that are marked off in recent years. It is impossible to dig all these up for replacement elsewhere. Then again, our soil is sacred to us, in that our ancestors fought tooth and nail for it, in order that we, their progenitors, might dwell therein, and in turn protect and perpetuate same for our future offspring.

. . . More than a hundred years ago, the Supreme Court of the United States rendered an opinion that the Indian was not here by the grace and permission of the white man and his Constitution, but the Indian was here first, and that fact precluded making laws pursuant to the Constitution, without the Indians' consent.

. . . We, as aborigines and autochthons, hold that the soil in our possession is our to have and to hold, and that any power to take it away without our consent is immoral and a gross injustice.[62]

The demand for recognition of treaty rights could be belligerent. Such as the scathing analysis James Driver provided quoted earlier in this chapter. Perhaps Pick stormed out of that community meeting because Driver had concluded his statement, "I have seen a good many white people with bald heads, and when a person is in that shape, he is usually the most gifted liar in the country. His promises are taken with a smile, but they are not worth the paper they are written on."[63] Tribal testimony before Congress invariably recounted the treaty history of the Three Affiliated Tribes with the federal government that began with the 1851 Fort Laramie Treaty and catalogued all subsequent land cessions. Testimonies from tribal members in community meetings, though less meticulous, also asserted tribal treaty rights and indigenous land title to combat the Garrison Dam. Some, like Martin Fox of Charging Eagle, asked, "What manner of Govern't is this that we live under that our treaty rights are not respected? . . . I want the government to pay the Three Affiliated Tribes all the debts it owes through [treaty] obligations before we are drowned out." Edna Atkins of Nishu went further and questioned, "Why doesn't the government keep a record of what it took from us [as the original owners of the land] as well as keeping a record of all the cost of things it has done for us. The government had not kept its obligation but the Indians have kept theirs even when verbal. The government keeps telling us that it does things right, why didn't it come to us before the Garrison Project was half completed."[64]

Tribal members mobilized treaties and a newly defined government-to-government relationship in their protest testimonies. This framing undermined the paternalistic guardian-ward rhetoric often employed in contemporary interpretations of the treaty relationship and built the foundations of modern notions of tribal sovereignty. Former tribal politicians used the Indian Reorganization Act, barely over a decade old, as a conceptual device to claim tribal land rights. Former tribal chair Carl Sylvester explained in one meeting, "The Indian Reorganization Act came along and gave us some freedoms. We thought we had some rights and before someone wanted to come in they should ask the Council but without such consent engineers came in and made surveys. . . . I felt the Indian Reorganization Act guaranteed us possessory rights but this appears to be violated by the Congress. Tranquility and justice supposedly guaranteed us by the Constitution of the United States is being violated."[65] Tribal delegate J. B. Smith strategically invoked the IRA to Democratic congressmen when he testified, "When this Democratic Party assumed domination of the country they offered us that new bill [IRA]. Shall we embrace the Government[?] We did. I worked hard for it. We took it on. They said expand, expand, and that there were wonderful opportunities. For those reasons we accepted the New Deal. And now what is going to happen to us. We are going to be ruined."[66]

Treaty rights. Aboriginal land title. The sacredness of soil that grew gardens and held the bones of ancestors and even the memories of the footprints of children. Mandan religious imperatives. Citizenship claims. "Real" Americans. The Indian-white racial divide. Military service. These tribal ideas circulated and gained currency because they analyzed the practices and experiences of Fort Berthold tribal members. The mobilization of this constellation of ideas, claims, and arguments birthed an indigenous citizenship founded upon tribal subjectivity *and* identity. The interior and exterior discourses that constituted identity had their genesis in a landscape that narrated Mandan, Hidatsa, and Arikara culture, deep and recent histories, and familial ties. During a crisis to protect the tribal land base, community members asserted individual and community rights based on a history of treaties and a new government-to-government relationship institutionalized by the Indian Reorganization Act. This dynamic is the basis of indigenous citizenship.

The eminent domain taking of Fort Berthold tribal lands in the name of the public good represents a clash between tribal and federal sovereignties. Federal policies focused on the development of territorial resources in the name of modernity, progress, and the continued elaboration of federal power within its territories. But these policies did not necessarily need to diminish tribal self-rule, or sovereignty, at Fort Berthold. The federal government made choices and enacted decisions that valued Native lands and lives less than those of their non-Native neighbors.

When the hope for an equitable or just compensation evaporated, the endless rounds of lobbying and negotiation devolved into infighting narrated by race and class. Community members rejected the lieu lands offer, possibly because they could not fathom that an even more injurious solution would be legislated: financial compensation. The people of Fort Berthold employed every weapon in their arsenal to fight the Garrison Dam, including the mobilization of the rhetoric of indigenous citizenship in combination with the space for "self-rule" carved by the IRA, and treaty rights that emphasized a government-to-government relationship. These remain some of the key elements in the theoretical and practical constitution of modern tribal sovereignty.

This context preceded the "Lo the Poor Indian" photo caption that began this chapter, but it is not all we need to know. George Gillette, the man crying due to the sale of his community's beloved bottomlands, served his community as a tribal councilman at Fort Berthold for twenty-two years, then in the Bureau of Indian Affairs for the next sixteen years. A Congregationalist minister, his favorite hymn was "Higher Ground," and he gave sermons and sang in both English and Arikara. He possessed a playful sense of humor and made his young daughters laugh by wiggling his ears at the dinner table or "walking like George Jefferson before there was a George Jefferson." Decades later, his daughter Florence Gillette Brady, characterized her father's iconic photograph: "He was hurting. Hurting, hurting. It hurts me to look at it, I guess, because it was all decided even before he became chairman. And he got the blame." Gillette's eldest daughter, Barbara Roy, responded, "He always had the best interests of the people. He was caring. To the whole community, that's why they show him crying. He was thinking about everybody."[67]

This photo, its context, and associated histories are not regretfully nostalgic exhibits in the "larger" story of US history; they are its living flesh.

Chapter 5

Relocations, 1952–1960

By 1952, federal contractors began to remove frame houses from their foundations, load them on flatbeds, and pull them up roads to new homesteads; behind, they left the gaping holes of foundations, which filled with water as the reservoir continued to rise. Other houses could not be moved, and the water inundated them. As tribal members packed their houses, confusion and the lack of a clear destination exacerbated the intense political turmoil. Class divisions also narrated as racial divisions contributed to political and social chaos and intensified tribal members' dissatisfaction with the distribution of tribal resources. Most tribal members experienced narrowed financial choices, and lack of capital complicated relocation logistics. Relocation and reestablishment on the prairie entailed more than individuals or houses—cattle and other livestock needed to survive on the top lands, families needed to drill or develop wells or springs, and communities had to rebuild the infrastructure of homesteads and towns. Simultaneously, tribal members struggled to say goodbye to the beloved places of their everyday lives, and to adjust to life outside the river valley. The requirements of this emotional, social, and physical labor guaranteed that identity and tribal self-determination at Fort Berthold would change. Maintenance of community life took a back seat to family survival, and individual struggles intensified the disagreements over how to ensure community survival. The loss of the river valley meant not only the loss of some of the most valuable agricultural land in the state, but the loss of a home, the places where children or grandparents had walked, where loved ones were buried, and where tribal members had built their lives.

Yeses and Nos

By 1950, the dissident group on Fort Berthold coalesced into a camp called the "Nos"—so called because they voted no on nearly every major tribal initiative

Figure 5.1. Houses pictured in the flooding of the Fort Berthold Reservation, ca. 1950. Rev. Harold W. Case Photograph Collection. Courtesy of the North Dakota State Historical Society.

since reorganization. They voted no on the IRA, and as we saw in previous chapters agitated against the makeup of the first IRA tribal council. They also voted no on a tribal cattle purchase program, and no on accepting the cash settlement for the bottomlands after legal opposition to the taking had failed and the lieu lands offer fell through.[1]

One tribal member described the tribal factionalism:

> It started with the Wheeler-Howard bill—the Yeses wanted self-government and government help and the Indians to be cattlemen and farmers, while the Nos didn't want self-government, didn't seem to want to be farmers or cattlemen and didn't like the Indian Service—think that all the doors ought to be locked and the whole thing burned up. And they would sign the contract (meaning PL 437 I think, not the Army contract but maybe that also) because they said you didn't know what you would get for your land or your houses and might not get money in the end. The no's wanted fee patents and per capitas. But now there aren't so many no's—they didn't like the cattle program either—the 2% tax and all—but now they're joining about ½ are in now, so there aren't so many. At Independence there are 53 families and only about 8 are No's. The No's are at Elbowoods, and Nishu, and Beaver Creek (and Red Butte?). There is a lot of quarreling and fighting and jealousy—it's not

good—they don't like the cattle getting on land not leased, nor cattle anyhow.²

Led by Martin Cross, the Nos blamed the tribal council for selling the bottomlands and accused the council of taking tribal funds to fight in Washington against the Garrison Dam with nothing to show for it. Frustrated over a tribal business council resolution opposing H.R. 81-8411, a bill to distribute the cash settlement for the bottomlands to tribal members per capita, the Nos felt that use of the cash settlement for anything but per capita payments would only benefit the "haves" and ensure that the poorer people on the reservation would not "get their fair share" of the woefully inadequate compensation monies. Perhaps a symptom of the reservation class structure, the No group saw the Yes group as the only beneficiaries of tribal economic development initiatives, a "favored few" who "got all the money at the expense of the whole tribe," with nothing left for "small-time operators." One community member noted to an anthropologist,

> That council, all they think of is cattle, not people. There are cattle people who have been getting loans for twenty years and still get them—they shouldn't do that—once or twice ought to be enough—and then let other people get a chance. . . . But they only help those who have cattle. It's all politics—only white ones—ones with blue eyes like the Fredricks and the Halls. . . . They discriminate against the full bloods like us.³

The No group narrated the class divisions as racial divisions and claimed that only the "half breeds" or those with "blue eyes" benefited from tribal loan programs. Meanwhile, some in the Yes group expressed impatience "with those less highly motivated"—"with the indigent, the 'reliefers,' the 'lazy' and 'unambitious.'" Edward Bruner's field notes characterized one tribal member as "in the No group and his reasons are obvious. He feels that the money in the tribal funds go to a favored few, and he is not the type that would benefit from any tribal program."⁴

In an analysis that the new Fort Berthold superintendent never submitted to his superiors, R. W. Quinn wrote:

> With the use of these funds in a great tribal development program, they see themselves subjected from now on to the domination and control of those who have called them lazy, shiftless, ignorant and lacking in ambition, and who have told them that their present poverty is due to their own lack of effort and ability. They see all the resources of the tribes

going into an organization of effort according to principles that their denouncers have accepted and they have not.... It is to be expected, given the situation, that this group would prefer, and would support a man who proposed, a per capita payment of the $7,500,000.

Such a man arose during the turbulent period of negotiations over compensation for the losses which were to be suffered due to impoundment.[5]

The Yes group held political and economic power since IRA reorganization. Anthropologists and Bureau of Indian Affairs employees debatably identified them as the more "acculturated" tribal members, but by and large they *had* in fact benefited from the economic and political system more than others. These members, however, attributed their economic stability not to nepotism or unfair lending practices, but characterized persistent hard work as the reason for their success. One tribal leader from Independence told anthropologist Robert Merrill,

> You know, Bob, the only people that are suffering on account of this long delay when nothing is happening and nothing is getting done, are the more aggressive people. The people that just don't want to be bothered to take care of themselves, and want other people to take care of them—they are the ones that are going to benefit, and there is just an awful lot of people who are beginning to say, well, if that's the way it's going to be, this program's going to drag out and out, long and long, and we're not going to get anything out of it, well, to hell with it, let's take what we've got coming, and they're crossing over to the other side.[6]

The inundation loomed. The Army Corps of Engineers told the communities that in the fall of 1953 the water would swell and cover key roads by the spring of 1954. Worse, the land assessment data illustrated that far fewer people and livestock could be sustainably maintained on the remaining reservation lands than originally estimated. BIA employees hammered this point home in community meetings to plan for the relocation.[7]

Martin Cross and Carl Whitman became lightning rods for public opinion during their time on the tribal council. In 1950, Whitman was tribal chair and Cross was not on the council; but the past success of rump delegations orchestrated by the nucleus of the No group encouraged Cross to organize a trip to Washington to testify in support of a bill authored by North Dakota senator

Quentin Burdick. Burdick's bill legislated the per capita payment of the cash settlement to Three Affiliated Tribes members. Cross lobbied Burdick for the legislation in response to the planning process organized by the Yes group. In the Yes plans, of the total $12.5 million compensation for lands taken, the tribe would earmark $7.5 million for a revolving loan program to reestablish agricultural families, a land consolidation fund, a long-term loan program to finance housing for nonagricultural families, and well development. The No group capitalized on long-standing distrust of the Bureau of Indian Affairs and class and race tensions to oppose council plans to maintain a portion of the tribal compensation money as a communal resource. It also fed community fears that a group of powerful leaders capitalized on previous economic opportunities at the expense of the needy. After the tribal council passed a resolution *against* the Burdick per capita bill, Cross organized a rump delegation to testify in support of the per capita bill. This controversy over the allocation of compensation for the bottomlands illustrates a community-wide shift from understanding the taken area as a *place*—as a living marker of history, culture, and identity—to a space. The relentlessly rising waters turned the taken lands into space quantifiable, bounded, interchangeable with other parcels, and worth a finite amount of money.

The per capita movement advocated by Cross and the Nos solidified the commodification of what had once been a place of unquantifiable value and atomized its worth. The per capita proposal, in an echo of the logic of the Dawes Act and presaging termination legislation, forced individuals to make a choice based on their fears of the worst-case scenario—do you want minimal individual compensation for a beloved homeland, or do you want no compensation at all? The Cross faction circulated a petition demanding a per capita distribution of the tribal compensation monies, which collected signatures from one-third of the eligible voters and was then used to encourage Burdick to sponsor the aforementioned per capita legislation, H.R. 81-8411. The faction also used the introduction of said legislation to spur their presence in Washington as the "true voice" of the Three Affiliated Tribes. Cross testified,

> I will concede that if the funds were made available in cash payments, one or two of the Indians might not get much good out of their respective shares of the money, but this should not be an excuse or hindrance to place the funds in trust status. I do not believe in penalizing all the Indians on account of one or two.

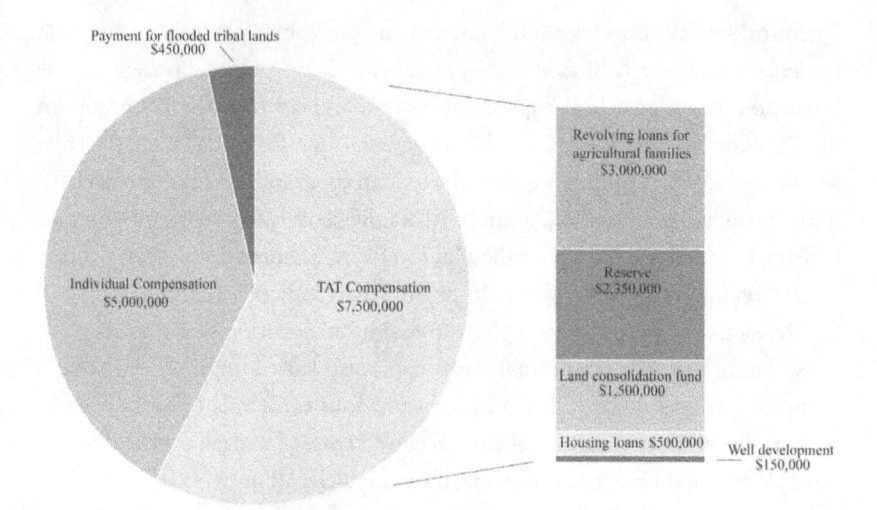

Figure 5.2 Overall allocation of compensation for lands taken by the Garrison Reservoir, and proposed Tribal Business Council plan for $7.5 million of the compensation monies not earmarked for individuals.

I protest any efforts by certain parties who laid careful plans to prevail upon the U.S. Congress to turn over to them these said funds, which are legally and rightfully belonging to the Indians. Undoubtedly, these parties planned for themselves well-paying jobs in handling of the funds for us.[8]

The dissident group had honed its tactics in the fifteen years since the IRA. The deluge of their homes intensified community emotions. The petition, as it encouraged distrust between tribal members based on class divisions narrated as racial divisions, appealed to local congressmen after the BIA made it clear it gave little credence to the No complaints. Off the reservation, a conservative turn in Indian affairs and in national politics ensured that politicians and administration eagerly heard criticism of the BIA and an IRA-organized tribal government. In fact, Commissioner of Indian Affairs Dillon Myer welcomed the prospect of relocation of the people of Fort Berthold and its potential to end their relationship with the federal government.[9]

Cross and his supporters organized a 1950 rump delegation that typifies their opposition to the tribal council's plan for the compensation monies. Cross brought with him several elderly tribal members who identified as "full-blood"—a claim to authenticity, such as when one rump delegate asserted in the introduction to his testimony, "I, Chester Smith full-blood Mandan...

oppose placing Tribal funds in control of the Tribal Business Council because any funds administrated by them never reaches below their class.... It means goodbye to the fund as far as we are concerned." The rump delegation testimony asserted the squander and mismanagement of tribal funds—specifically mentioning the cattle-purchasing program and trips to Washington that they claimed amounted to "pleasure trips for the members of the Council since they do not accomplish anything to justify the costs to the Tribes." Smith also asserted, "In regard to Garrison Dam controversy and the settlement in connection with this problem, we the bona-fide Indians did not have much say in the matter, the so-called patent in fees Indians took leading roles in the negotiations. We did not want to sell our land or properties, but it was these people who sold us down the river on pretext of representing the Indians." He suggested that the members of the tribal council even be barred from holding any office in the BIA and that they "be denied any share of the proceeds from Tribal benefits." His was an intensely personal criticism of tribal leadership.[10]

Another witness, Philip Atkins (Hidatsa) asserted that nepotism structured tribal loan program decisions:

> The Tribal Loan Committee is composed of five members. It happens in this case that four members of the Committee are closely related by blood and through marriage, the fifth member has sold out to them by going along with them. They have connived the functions of the committee by making and giving out loans and repayment cattle to themselves and their relations first, of course we protests [sic] such actions in vain. It is my understanding that some of these exceed $10,000 each. This fact does not leave much money left for others to use.... Those of us not related to them have been ignored. Our requests for loans are rejected time after time. They are very much prejudiced against those that are not in with them on their actions.[11]

Beyond the personal, tribal member William Dean (Arikara) compared the current tribal authority structure to dictators and linked it to communism, saying, "We Indians detest and fear Communism and dictators, but the Communists may well have established a beachhead in our midst. We have had a taste of dictatorship under the present Council."[12]

The tribal council justified its work against the per capita bill based on the impact of a per capita distribution on the rights of minors and future generations of tribal members. In a June 1950 tribal council meeting, tribal chair

Carl Whitman spoke about how a per capita distribution would mean, "900 children's money will be dissipated." Council member Ben Heart agreed, saying that it would squander the money that should be kept "for the children and those who will be born." The rush to act included passing a resolution that said that anyone who wanted a per capita payment of the settlement money could receive a per capita but would be disenrolled from the tribe. Only two representatives voted against the resolution, Ben Heart and Hans Walker Sr. This move further inflamed the No leadership and tribal members susceptible to such rhetoric. And although Whitman said at the end of the meeting, "It's good to have opposition—that's democracy, and if you didn't have [it] we'd get lax," the actions of the tribal council that day provoked resentment.[13]

The rump delegation of the per capita bill amplified tribal fears. In notes taken by a Bureau of Indian Affairs employee after the Senate hearings on Burdick's per capita bill, Cross told the employee that "he wanted to get his statement and that of the others into the record because 'election is coming soon.'" The $7.5 million in tribal compensation money had not yet been appropriated, and it was unlikely the secretary of interior would approve any per capita disbursement; neither Cross nor Burdick expected passage of Burdick's per capita bill. Cross's rump delegation to Washington solely intended to undermine the sitting tribal council.[14]

It worked. A month after Cross's testimony, the tribe held elections. Voters reelected three councilmen, including Carl Whitman, and voted in three new council members, including Martin Cross. The tribal council election for chairman resulted in a split vote: five for Whitman, five for Cross. Unable to break the deadlock, the tribal council decided a tribal referendum should elect the chair, and in late September tribal members voted for Cross by a margin of 323 to 225. The people had spoken in favor of Martin Cross, and also in favor of a per capita distribution of tribal compensation money.[15]

Tribal politics got uglier. Direct personal attacks on Martin Cross and Carl Whitman saturated public meetings, dependent on the venue and audience. At one gathering a Whitman supporter stated,

> Someone patted our leader (Martin Cross) on the back, and he doesn't need it (deserve it). This man (referring to C. Whitman) worked for that program and we got our program. And then they say that *this* man (M. Cross) did everything.... If I have to get per capita at the price of being cut loose—No! I don't want a guy in Stanley to grab my land when it's

taxable. These people (those for per capita) aren't ready to say, "Mr. Spalding, give me my share and I'll get out." But they drag the rest of us with 'em.... Let's have a man who'll stick with us (meaning C. Whitman). He's not Gros Ventre [Hidatsa]! He's part Ree [Arikara]! I know!

The daily shrinking land base and per capita compensation distribution debate intensified tribal politics, particularly fears about the impact of a per capita distribution on members' tribal status and thus the status of their allotted lands. The same speaker later said, "This per capita business has ruined most of our people. Some years back a few people became citizens, and my dad was one of them.... We had to struggle to keep our own homes. I don't think a one of those guys is living on his allotted lands now." Such statements suggested somber gatherings. Sol Tax's graduate student Edward Bruner noted that after a meeting at Nishu,

> After the meeting sandwiches and pastries were passed out to all present along with juneberries (canned) and sugared black coffee (weak). The pastries were bought sweet rolls, doughnuts, and fried bread (deep fat fried).... Men passed these things out around the circle in the galvanized metal tubs. No one thanked anyone for anything, and about the only thing I heard was when Franklin Howard came to me with the Juneberries he remarked that this was a real Indian dish.[16]

Little genuine communication existed between adherents of the two factions. Personal accusations spread beyond council members and colored interactions between tribal members at the meetings. At one open forum, a tribal member named Walter rose and spoke in favor of a per capita payment. Anthropologist Robert Reitz's field notes read:

> He went through a long harange [sic] about how the old council had given loans to friends and relatives and no one else, and that he had applied several times for a loan and had been turned down, and that there was no chance for most of the people to get any good out of this money, money which was really theirs and belonged to them, and was quite bitter about his accusations, most of which were directed against Carl Whitman and Fredericks, Hans Walker and Jim Hall.

In response, council member Ben Youngbird got up to answer him, "and told him that while he never should have brought up the subject in public, as long as Walter had made those accusations, he was going to answer them." He told the assembled group that while the tribe approved the tribal member's loan application for cattle, Walter had not put away enough feed for the cattle, so when it came time to issue them the tribe refused his request because "he wasn't prepared to take care of them." In response, the tribal member again rose and accused Youngbird of not having enough to feed his own cattle—an accusation Youngbird provided further information to refute. More community members began to participate, such as when a Mrs. Frank Chase said, "Walter should be the last one to stand up and make these kind of accusations." She reminded him of an incident after he had become a US citizen, in which he had invested all his money in milk cows, and "immediately after, during the winter, these milk cows, make good land marks . . . laying there dead." She sarcastically concluded, "and that that's the kind of judgment he was able to exercise, although he insisted on getting a per capita saying he was capable of handling his own money."

It got worse. She then remarked, "Walter was no good, had never worked, never would work, and never would be any good, and that all he was good for was to beat up and make false accusations against people." In response to this painful dressing-down, "Walter got up, and with an injured air, said that he had thought this was going to be a friendly meeting, but that if this was the way it was going to be he was going to go home, and he left."[17] This type of reciprocal shaming illustrates the erosion of community cohesion; it was a slow, painful, heartbreaking process.

Nerves frayed. Even the local non-Native Catholic priest felt the stress. When one of the anthropologists embedded in the BIA asked him about the relocation of the Nishu Catholic church to the residual lands,

> he became very excited and said there was no reason why that shouldn't have been accomplished long ago—that he wasn't trying to take the water hole from the Indians, that he would see to it that they had access to it, and he gave me all sorts of reasons to the point that his purchase wouldn't affect them adversely in any way, and ended with the accusation that Franklin Howard and Ben Young Bird and those people down at that end are just trying to get a hold of everything for themselves and corner everything and set up a little empire down there—that's all they're trying to do, they've been trying to do that all the time.[18]

The community experienced myriad stresses as members moved their homes, health care facilities, roads, and graves. At the same time, tribal leadership also dealt with further bureaucratic violence from the Army Corps of Engineers, which during relocation argued that *non-Native* landholders within the taking area should be paid out of the monies appropriated by Congress for the taking of Fort Berthold tribal lands. In response, the tribal council passed a resolution stating, "(1) that no part of the $12,605,625 . . . may be used to pay for any lands, interests in lands or improvement owned by nonmembers of the Tribes in the Taking Area of the Reservation, but said lands should be paid for out of Army appropriations; (2) that in the payment for inherited interests in lands, the Council will recognize as 'heirs' . . . only bona fide enrolled members of the Three Affiliated Tribes."[19]

The tribal political attacks, national political maneuvers, and defense of the already-insufficient compensation monies against the machinations of the Army Corps of Engineers took a toll on Martin Cross. His alcohol use began to interfere with tribal business. One tribal council member recalled a meeting the council attended at the Aberdeen, South Dakota, BIA office when only three councilmen appeared for a ten o'clock meeting because, "only three of them were sober enough to show up." Robert Reitz's field notes related,

> Martin Cross had called up about ten o'clock and asked Mr. Spaulding to postpone the meeting until two o'clock in the afternoon. Mr. Spaulding announced this to the three saying that all the men gathered there to meet there were specialists in their field and this was costing the taxpayers of the United States an awful lot of money to bring them together, and that here were only three gentlemen present, and from what he could detect from over the phone, the chairman was pretty drunk.[20]

Gossip about Cross's struggle with alcoholism circulated within the Fort Berthold community, and for some it overwhelmed his achievements as tribal chairman. As his disease intensified, tribal police arrested him several times on drunk and disorderly charges—which fueled criticism and forced tribal law enforcement to justify the incarceration of the highest tribal leader. Unfortunately, the nascent state of treatment for alcoholism in this era rendered his illness a tool used by his political opposition to discredit his leadership.[21]

The rise of waters behind the Garrison Dam, petty machinations of the Army Corps of Engineers, stress of relocation of 95 percent of the population, intensified factionalism, personal attacks, and a leadership vacuum created a crisis in tribal authority. Nearly forty years later, a seventy-nine-year-old Carl Whitman reflected in an oral history interview on how change in the nature of tribal leadership partly fueled the political turmoil. He pondered the weaknesses of a majority-rule system. "You can't convince the guys that lost, the voters whose candidates lost, you can't convince them that they did wrong. So it's split the tribe in many ways. Not just politically, but religiously, educationally, biologically, and also the full bloods and the mixed bloods, and the rich and the poor, all kinds of ways, economically." During the upheaval of relocation, tribal politics grew fraught with reciprocal shaming and blaming for community woes. One satiric editorial from 1952 titled "Observations of a Hillbilly" quipped,

> The present Tribal Business Council is nothing less than a blight on the face of progress. . . . Former leaders who have passed on who could neither read nor write were more effective, forthright, and capable than most of this crew. . . . Certainly they do not set an example for anyone by sitting around and bragging.
> . . . I hereby announce my candidacy and solicit your vote and support. If elected, I will make every effort to erase any prestige built up in the past in representing the people. Immediately after being sworn in, I shall contact all my influential friends in Washington DC for a per capita (payment) of cheap whiskey, wine and beer. . . . I will completely ignore any person or organization that is interested in the welfare and destiny of the present, younger and unyet [sic] unborn generations. . . . And finally, I shall express the desires of my constituents from as many jails as I can enter. My only shortcoming is that I cannot brag well. This, to my regret, seems to be the major qualification for this position of trust. Sincerely yours, Paige Baker Sr.[22]

The federal government's forceful taking of the tribes' most precious resource—the Missouri River valley—shattered political authority. Communication within communities and between leadership deteriorated, and the political infighting aimed not to control the reallocation of land, but to control the allocation of tribal compensation money. As the federal government threatened and eventually gutted the tribal land base, authority came to be expressed through the control of tribal monies.

Moving

For her summer job as a teenager, Rosemarie Mandan helped administer the relocation of her relatives' graves from the bottomlands. She remembered, "You had to get in touch with family, 'Where do you want it to go,' because we were being *dispersed* to these places where nobody *lived*. These places, where we are, like Mandaree, there was nobody there [at that time]. . . . So, nobody! And that's where they were coming to from the bottomlands, which were so fertile, and all the trees; it [the river valley] was just the most beautiful place."[23] The Three Tribes had clustered their communities in or near the river valley for their entire known history and knew the prairie lands that comprised the residual lands of the reservation far less. People at Fort Berthold remained "unfamiliar with the nature of their holdings" in the residual lands of the reservation—and in some cases had "in fact, never seen them" or even regarded them as "foreign." This familiarity with the river valley mirrors Sitting Rabbit's visual representation of the Missouri River, in which the Missouri River centered the landscape and settlements; the farther away you look from Awáati on Sitting Rabbit's map, the less detail exists to guide you through the landscape.[24]

The move to the prairie lands practically represented a move to the unknown. The federal government forced over 90 percent of the 420 families living on the reservation to move from the taken lands, inundating one-third of the arable land on the reservation. When tribal members moved to the top lands, they lost natural resources that supported a subsistence lifestyle—wild game, berries, lignite coal for fuel, and wood for timber and fuel. The move constituted less than fifty miles for all involved, but it required a transition from the shelter of the bottomlands to the harsher, unprotected climate of the prairie. A description of the relocation by then Fort Berthold superintendent R. W. Quinn reflected, "In some instances, community organization and associations will be completely shattered by this type of movement." Quinn never submitted the memorandum, but its contents indicated at least some bureaucratic understanding of the changes to come. "The population of Shell Creek, perhaps the least acculturated of all the groups, will probably be the most dispersed. Extended family groups which have lived close together for generations, and family groups which built up close associations and emotional ties, will be separated to scattered holdings in the residual segments. Membership of the various Societies—the Antelope Society, the Water Busters, will no longer be members of one community."[25]

Non-Natives refused to understand the true scope of this change. Superintendent of Indian Affairs Dillon Myer saw the forced relocation, "however unfortunate it is for the Indians," as an "opportunity to make a new start and not repeat the past mistakes." Both local and national white populations hoped for the end of the Bureau of Indian Affairs and the end of federal treaty responsibilities as a side benefit to the relocation. Local white populations opined on the relocation and showed their deep ignorance regarding the present and past of their Native neighbors. The *Killdeer Herald* editorial staff—a newspaper from the town of Killdeer, North Dakota, approximately twenty miles from the reservation border—characterized the relocation resulting from the Garrison Dam as an "opportunity" to make tribal members "full citizens." The paper remarked,

> Let them own land. Let them have their homes and farms and cattle. Let them raise their families as they wish subject to the conventions of modern living. Let them vote. Let them drink. Let them pay taxes. Not half citizens enjoying only the fruits of democracy, but the responsibilities as well. Nothing makes good citizens as fast as responsibility.... 1952 is a good time to start modernizing our Indian Bureau and its methods, ultimately, and none too soon, resulting in its demise.[26]

Non-Native definitions of citizenship held no room for the indigenous citizenship developed and practiced at Fort Berthold; white North Dakotans felt no responsibility for the treaties signed by the US government, even though they owed their livelihood and very presence on the plains to those treaties. Today, many non-Natives still possess no conception of treaty rights and how the land and resource rights of indigenous communities might entail a historical trajectory different from their own.

The local Bureau of Indian Affairs remained sometimes willfully clueless in its understandings of what the river valley meant to members of the Three Tribes, and some of its reports to superiors evince scant empathy for tribal members. In one such report, Fort Berthold superintendent R. W. Quinn wrote,

> One of the most serious problems we face in implementing the relocation of the people of the reservation is their negative attitude towards moving out of the valley.... They know they must go, but you often hear such phrases as "displaced people," being "flooded out," "When that water comes we got to go" and "I sure hate to leave this place." They seem to regard the $7,500,000 settlement as payment for their tears and not a means of expediting their movement.

Quinn's obliviousness continued, "They are prone to start meetings off with statements of numerous citations of violations of government pledges of the past and completely disregard the problems of the future until they are brought out and laid on the line."[27]

Tribal members found it difficult to imagine a viable future for their communities. Tribal judge Peter Beauchamp, speaking with anthropologist Robert Reitz, mentioned prophecies shared with him by an elder tribal member:

> Old George [Grinnell] had said that in the Gros Ventre [Hidatsa] beliefs, when the Missouri River began to flow westward, and when the large game animals began to go away, and the native birds desert this land, and when the small animals in the brush began to grow horns—at this point the judge laughed and said, "Silly things like that[." W]hen these things happen they signify the end of the three tribes—that it would show, or rather tell, that the time had come when the would begin to dissolve and they would come to an end as a people—it would be the end of them.[28]

Beauchamp also described his foreboding associated with environmental changes. He noted the presence of new plants, the disappearance of birds such as the plover and the curlew, and even the disappearance of coyotes, which, in his youth "used to run in packs from fourteen, fifteen, sixteen of them together. At night they would seek out the top of a hill, and sit in a circle, then one would get in the center of the circle and lift up his throat and nose and bark at the moon, then the others would join in the chorus, but that now if you see a coyote he is usually alone—they are very few and scattered."[29] Beauchamp worried that such changes presaged the end of his communities. This feared dissolution of the tribes directly connected to the loss of land. But the tribes had already lost nearly 95 percent of their land base by 1910. So perhaps the change in the landscape—the land, water, and human presence that had sustained the Three Tribes for thousands of years—represented another aspect of what tribal members most feared and felt with such foreboding.

The people of Fort Berthold could not see their forced relocation and the loss of their lands as an "opportunity." The loss of tribal lands, of every settled community on the reservation, did not represent the loss of a generic parcel of land measured, marked, appraised, and bought. It represented the loss of a past—a past archeologically traced for a millennium, and in oral tradition traced to the beginning of time. It also meant the drastic contraction of a viable future. Reitz recorded an exchange with tribal member Charlie Parshall in his field notes: "Charlie figured the old Indian ways are about to go and that the relocation will be the end of them. After the people relocated there will be a new set of people living closest to one another and even these will not be very close. They will have a difficult time visiting one another in the way they are now accustomed to.... He says when they relocate the land will be scarce." The conversation ended with Parshall telling Reitz, "Really, the land is pretty poor. With the taking of the river bottom the best of the lands went."[30]

Such conversations allude to the *fears* of the community, not their practical reaction to the reality of deluge. Tribal members sorted through unending personal relocation logistics during a time of deep uncertainty. One elderly tribal member, Mrs. Duckett, worried she did not yet know how she would support herself. She spoke of three possibilities: "1. She would like to settle [in] the new Elbowoods and start a hotel or tourist court.... 2. She would like to start a village store in the hamlets like Beaver Creek where extended periods of isolation often leave them without sufficient supplies. 3. She would like to get some cows and chickens like they had before her husband died."[31] In the face of the unknown, tribal members persevered and tried to plan for a radically changed future.

The convoluted relocation logistics required appraisal of tribal members' lands and acceptance of that appraisal before the formal sale of their lands. Simultaneously, individuals and the BIA had to identify lands in the residual reservation for exchange or purchase—a situation complicated by a half century of allotment. Already, the fractionation of some inherited lands split between so many descendants of the original allotted tribal member left parcels as small as thirty-six feet by thirty-six feet. Field notes from one community meeting illustrate the complexity of fractionated holdings:

> There are over 240,000 acres in the western segment and according to a survey made, there are 64 economic units within this segment which would indicate that the segment will be able to support 64 families. Under the various allotment acts during the period beginning 1900 until 1929, there was 3401 allotments made. Under the various allotment acts, some of you received 320-, 160-, 80-, and 40-acre allotments. Some of you received three allotments, some two, and some on, and others received none. Immediately after the allotments were made, the heirship problem present itself until today there are some allotments that have over 100 heirs; there are some persons interested in over 100 allotments.[32]

Only after the completion of such intricate land dealings could tribal members begin the physical move. The move often included the transportation of a house and everything in it and the establishment of infrastructure to support a household in the new homestead. Tribal members had to drill wells or develop springs; fence pasture or field boundaries; create roads to their new house sites; dig outhouses and establish plumbing; build corrals, sheds, and barns; and move livestock.

The initial per capita payments did not cover relocation costs. Most of the initial per capita met immediate rather than long-term needs. One tribal member spent his entire per capita by August 1951 and, according to Bruner's field notes, had "nothing left. He spent 1200 for pick up which neither he nor Edna can drive. Then a wagon, farm equipment, pony for his son Richard's boy Fred, 200 went for a cook stove, 225 for a washing machine, 100 for groceries, 25 for a horse, 100 or so for a water barrel." He could not remember how he spent the rest. An elderly tribal member bought a treat for his grandchildren with the initial per capita payment. "They gave us a thousand dollars apiece," Clyde Baker (Mandan, Hidatsa) remembered,

> a lot of us, well, I guess all of us, never saw that kind of money. And I remember hearing about one of the old guys that used to have braids, he came from old Fishhook Village, he wanted to buy, well he bought a nickelodeon for his grandchildren. And when it was delivered they found out that he didn't have electricity [chuckles]. But that's what we were doing with our money, you see, we didn't know how to handle big money, you know.[33]

Not everyone nickeled-and-dimed away their initial per capita. One tribal member invested in a small community store in Shell Creek. Bruner's field notes documented,

> [The owner's] sister was there and they had a loud speaker on a car and were playing Indian records, some Sioux songs, some Hidatsa, and a few Western records thrown in. There were also some Sioux from another reservation. I noticed that when William Bell's song was played, his son started to dance along. Lee is really going to town with this store, he wants to get a cooler, juke box, and hamburger stand. It certainly seems to be a focal point.[34]

He hoped to set up a community store on the top lands after the river valley fully flooded.

Before the relocation, the BIA classified families as "agriculturalists," "potential agriculturalists," "off reservation," "placement," "government employees," "welfare," and "estates not probated." BIA administrators then matched families to the amount of land they possessed within the taking area and classified them based on Missouri River Basin Investigations (MRBI) land appraisals. Table 5.1 roughly outlines the land-based class system that functioned on Fort Berthold and shows that most tribal members held lands that would be compensated within the $1,000 to $7,000 range. The class system also skews toward the lower end of the landholders, and only a few tribal members held land in enough quantities and quality that they appraised at more than $15,000. The bottom-heavy class structure meant that most tribal members felt heavy economic costs of relocation, for the lack of high-value land likely mirrored a lack of capital that could insulate individuals from relocation costs.[35]

Inefficient and paternalistic Bureau of Indian Affairs staff exacerbated the financial stress of relocation. Reitz noted in his field notes in mid-1951, "The Aberdeen office has returned all pending land transactions for a statement by the buyer and seller as to the status of oil rights. This brings the land acquisition program and the consolidation of economic units to a halt, of course." The local BIA staff could be autocratic and opaque in their dealings with tribal members. The BIA land agent, identified only as MacSpadden, was a "very bull-headed and an opinionated person, who decided how things should be done and then had people do it that way," and unnecessarily complicated matters for tribal

Table 5.1
Compensation by Status

	$1–$500	$500–$1,000	$1,000–$2,000	$2,000–$4,000	$4,000–$7,000	$7,000–$10,000	$10,000–$15,000	$15,000–$20,000	Over $20,000	Total
Agriculturalists	7	13	25	27	32	31	21	11	7	174
Potential agriculturalists	3	4	8	15	13	3	9	1	4	60
Off reservation	50	27	43	43	35	5	4	1	2	210
Placement	11	14	20	25	17	5	6	2	2	102
Gov't employees	1	8	7	4	5	1	0	0	1	27
Welfare	5	8	7	19	17	16	10	4	3	89
Estates not probated	3	0	3	6	3	5	1	0	0	21
Totals	80	74	113	139	122	66	51	19	19	683

members when he forced land appraisal and sale decisions upon them. According to Reitz's field notes,

> Old George Howard, who was getting a divorce from his wife, had promised her some land. MacSpadden decided that George Howard should give her some land that was in the Taking Area so she would get cash money, and merely informed George that this was what he was going to have to do, in no uncertain terms. George felt that he had to comply, and he did. Mac did the same thing with Walter Stink Face, and in Walter's case he didn't even give Walter the appraisal of his property to approve along with the vast number of appraisals that have gone through and been approved and served as a basis upon which people have been paid for their land in the Taking Area. Walter's case of appraisal was still sitting in his folder, and [the BIA agency staff] had come across it merely by accident, and it had never even been forwarded. This is because Mac wouldn't deal with them, and so Walter complied which was to give his wife some land without knowing the appraisal value of any of it.

MacSpadden even told the local Catholic priest, Father Reinhardt, to "go ahead and move his church and not to worry and that all would be taken care of.... He instructed Father Reinhardt to do it though the usual sale hadn't been consummated, and the deed approved, and in the face of a tribal council resolution which had tabled the original sale of the land to the person from whom Father Reinhardt had bought it by the tribes." Whether MacSpadden made the process more difficult for tribal members, or illegally easy for the local priest, his behavior added to the confusion and stress of relocating from the bottomlands.[36]

Of course, not all BIA employees showed such disregard for tribal and individual rights. Many staff members labored to reduce the confusion of the relocation process. They collaborated on community meetings with tribal council members in each segment, to disseminate information about the land appraisal process, the assessment of residual reservation lands, and community needs such as road construction, well development, and assessment of the carrying capacity of each new segment of the reservation. The reservation would be divided into four segments once the waters rose, each isolated from the other. The physical separation of each segment created logistical problems for health care, law enforcement, and other essential services. The Missouri River ran between communities before, but the Garrison Reservoir created a far larger separation. Today the reservoir completely isolates the Twin Buttes segment from the rest of the reservation, and tribal members must travel off the reservation to reach that segment, as illustrated by map 5.2.[37]

BIA employees disseminated complicated and at times overwhelming information, meant to inform decision making by community members as they planned their relocations. The BIA told tribal members to keep in mind the physical features of the terrain and the "potential cost of maintaining such a road" when requesting road locations. The bureau also gave disappointing news about the carrying capacity of each segment. Its 1947 assessment told the community at Independence that the western segment would support over one hundred families—a figure later revised to sixty-four families, and only if the land was developed past the current carrying capacity for thirty families.

Government planners assessed the soil of the residual reservation lands into seven possible classes based on texture, depth, and the slope of the land: "A 9 foot fall in 100 feet was not desirable and automatically would place the land in the grazing class." The reservoir would cover most of the most fertile soil class. BIA administrators told community members at Independence,

> The class I-II and III soils were arable soils. Class I is the soil which is found on the bottom lands and which will eventually be lost in the Taking Area[.] Class II land would also be inundated except for about 40 acres in the entire western segment. Class III land was the only type available in the western segment and was at its best not very good farm land. If farmed this type of soil required extensive soil conservation practices.... Class IV land is good grazing land but can be used for forage production. Class V land is the marshy land which is absent in the Western Segment. Class VI land is good grazing land. Class VII not as good as your Class VI. And VIII is the badlands and is absolutely worthless.

Tribal members struggled to stay afloat in the flood of complicated and disconcerting new information.[38]

The much lower carrying capacity of the residual lands forced dispersed settlement on the reservation. The low quality of residual lands made the combination of an agricultural or ranching lifestyle and the continuation of pre-Garrison community life diametrically opposed to one another. BIA relocation policy assured a scattered settlement pattern, with families separated from each other on self-contained homesteads. The BIA developed water resources on the residual lands "in locations that would invite the uniform utilization of the land"—ensuring that family homesteads remained physically distant from each other as never before experienced in the history of the Three Affiliated Tribes.[39]

Moving was messy. Choosing land, moving a house, and establishing a household in what amounted to a foreign landscape took years, and tribal members lived in constant uncertainty. Rosemarie Mandan remembered the chaos:

> Oh there was a turmoil! Because you had to decide where you wanted your house. I remember my sister, Antelope Woman, she had her house, was in Red Butte, so they were going to move to Mandaree. . . . that's where she moved do. So in order for that house to come there, they had to move it across the ice (cause it was rugged over here on the west side) and bring it all the way over here to Lucky Mound, and it stood there by the store until the ice froze again, and then they brought it across. And then of course there's no water [at the new homesteads], so they had to dig wells for wherever they were going to put their house, and they [the company being paid to drill wells] got paid according to the feet. And of course they would go down as far as they could, to make money, the ones that did the digging. And I remember all these people complaining about the water because they had to pump pump [for water] and their feet would go up in the air. I remember that, it was really rugged. It was a time of turmoil.[40]

One tribal member, Louise Holding Eagle, returned to her home after a birthday celebration to find that in her absence the Army Corps of Engineers had moved her house, barn, and chicken coop—she had driven down her driveway to find an empty field where her house used to be. She remembered, "I know one lady who had to chase her house on horseback." Houses sometimes sat on the prairie for days or weeks on end and became easy targets for thieves who ransacked them for belongings that looked antique to sell to dealers. In this way, some families lost all their family photographs, beadwork, quillwork, or other items treasured for generations.[41]

The houses sat on prairie roads between their old homesteads in the river valley communities and new homesites on a prairie; between a community life that accrued meaning and form with the development of a vibrant indigenous citizenship practice, and an unknown future. The vulnerability of those homes, unmoored from their foundations—to wind, snow, rain, or thieves—mirrors the vulnerability felt by community members as they anticipated a greatly changed future. Tribal members struggled through the turmoil of moving—making land deals under duress, relocating everything from graves to houses to people, and administering a sudden influx of cash—and faced a future as unknown as the prairie lands to which they moved. They worked to make sense of the enmeshed sweeping environmental, community, and family changes.

Saying Goodbye

Lyda Bearstail—then called Lyda Black Bear—still served as the banner carrier for the Shell Creek "USO." From June 15 through 17, 1953, she carried the USO banner for a celebration in the Shell Creek community for the last time. Shell Creek set aside these dates for a celebration to bid "farewell to the valley" in anticipation of the rising waters of the Garrison Reservoir. The community printed programs that detailed the history of Shell Creek and the Xo'shga band specifically, then listed key members of local organizations and described the packed schedule. Community contests like sack races, tug of war, "saddle horses neck reining," a "3-year-old youngsters candy race," a "pop drinking contest for women of 55 and older," and a "women's tent-pitching contest" filled the mornings during all three days of the celebration. In the afternoons, the reservation superintendent or the local schoolteacher gave speeches before the powwow started in midafternoon. Community members butchered beef and served meals for a free event open to the public. Amid political infighting, chaos, and the anticipation of sweeping change, some aspects of community life remained vibrant.[42]

The historical narrative presented in the program centered Shell Creek in the history of the Three Affiliated Tribes, from the time when the Crow Flies High band refused to stay on the reservation up through the passage of the IRA and Drags Wolf's support of the Wheeler-Howard Act. The historical narrative closed with the words, "Today we are saying Farewell to Shell Village; Our Grandfathers, Where They Walked. But the work and the spirit of those who have gone on before are with us, as we face the future to build the new and better life for those who are to follow." The farewell celebration evoked as much sadness as it did enjoyment. The reflection "Today we say farewell to the village of our fathers, as the waters of the reservoir rise to flood our ranch and crop lands, our homes and firesides" reflects the loss of homes and community places associated with the unique history of the Crow Flies High band, a band that held onto its singular character and outlook from the mid-nineteenth century

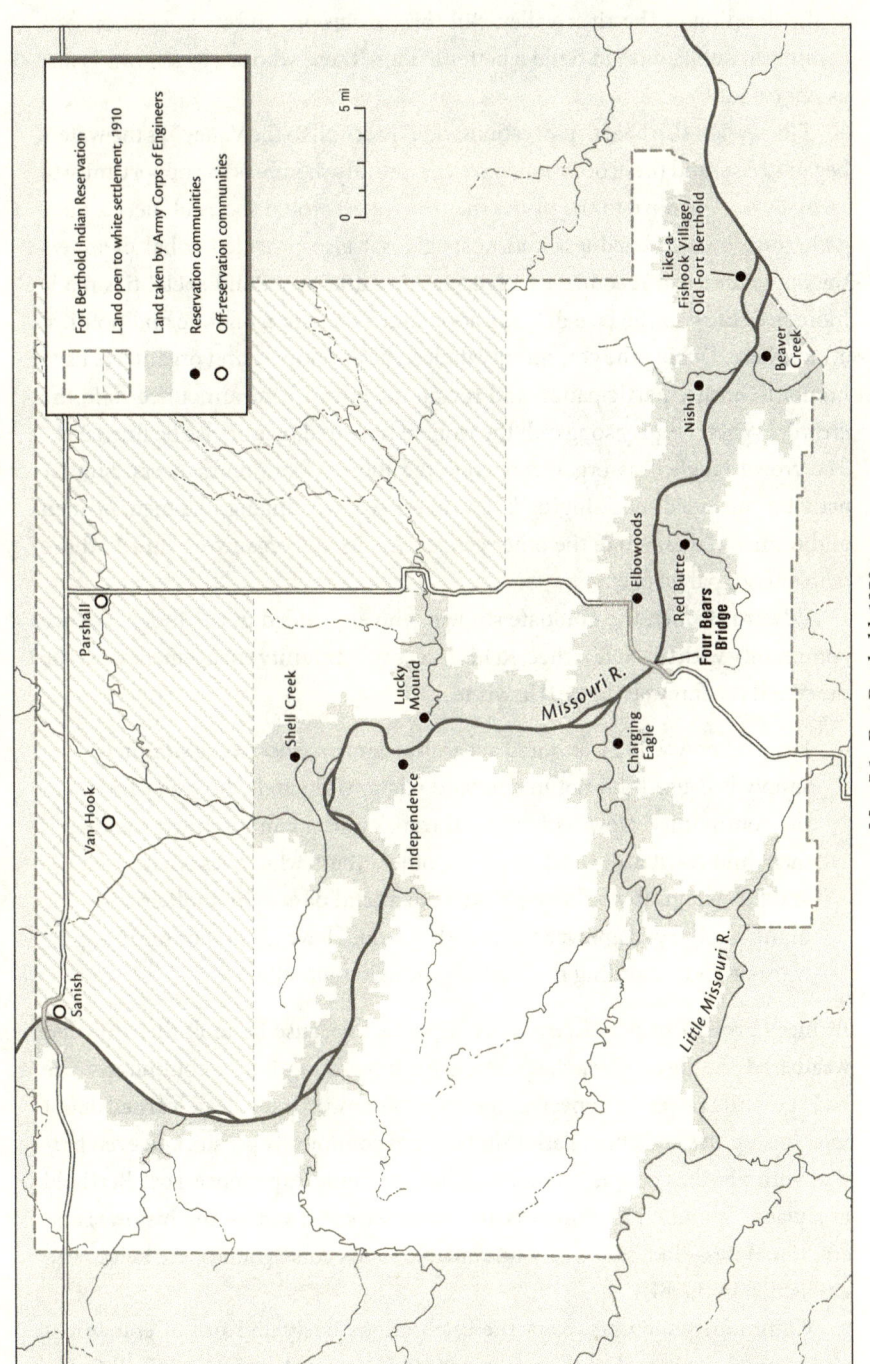

Map 5.1. Fort Berthold, 1950.

to the flooding of the river valley. But the conclusion, and its invocation of a community obligation to build a better life for "those who are to follow," is just as important.[43]

Elbowoods also held a reservation-wide "Farewell to the Valley" as the waters began to rise, and these occasions gave community members the opportunity to formally say goodbye to the places that the waters would soon submerge. Such gatherings included sadness and nostalgia but also provided tribal members the opportunity to reconnect with each other and to solidify social ties made more necessary in the face of dislocation and a chaotic economic and political atmosphere. During the community dance, the announcer and organizers used humor to ensure participation and rev up the crowd. One announcer told the crowd, "When we play songs, all the women have to dance or else be fined 25¢." The crowd laughed as organizers collected money from nondancers. Similar activities included men singing like women, women singing like men, or men and women dancing like the other gender. Again, the organizers "fined" those who did not participate.

Edward Bruner, the graduate student who embedded in the Independence community with his wife, reflected his level of community engagement when he described the farewell dance. He wrote,

> I can see now why I was bored at the first dance earlier in the summer—simply because I did not understand relationship and who was who in the community. Now with a literal translation, I can catch the excitement and spirit and watch with the others there who gives what when and for whom. It would be pointless to attend dances in another community and try to analyze them as they would have no soul or meaning without understanding the vital ties intracommunally.[44]

Bruner's growth in perspective only happened because he took the time and weathered the discomfort that came with integrating into a community. He had spent time deep in conversation with community members, learned about relationship ties and clan relationships, heard community gossip, and even partied with another couple one night. Thus, he could experience Fort Berthold as a place—a union of landmarks and waterways and stories and histories and emotional ties—in a way likely unavailable to his colleague Robert Reitz, who embedded in the BIA.

Community members kept the celebrations lively and full of enjoyment and worked the crowd of their own accord. At one celebration in Shell Creek (not the final celebration, but in the last few years before the communities were flooded),

> Rosie Crow Flies High seemed to be the most active gal at the dance. She came around with a pole and made all the women get up and dance. This was always done in a jovial spirit with a lot of laughs and joking. Often the women would refuse the first time only to get up and dance after one or two proddings. No woman refused to dance after being prodded.... When Rosie came around with the pole she joked with Pearl Edna and Cookie who were sitting together about how Louis Brown acted as announcer. Louis had to name all the school kids who were being honored, and about half of the 14 kids were named Crow Flies High. Louis couldn't get the name straight, he changed between Crow Flies High, Crows Flies High, Crow Fly High, etc. The women thought this was a good joke.[45]

Rosie Crow Flies High would, in the 1970s, serve as the chairwoman of the Three Affiliated Tribes tribal council. Her social acumen and lively participation in the community of her birth probably helped her establish a solid base of political support after the relocation; surely, her experiences during the relocation also shaped her priorities and experiences as she worked on the council.

Individuals also said goodbye to the river valley privately. Rosemarie Mandan's father (Hidatsa, Mandan) visited the old Like-a-Fishhook Village site as they readied to move. He went to the site of his mother's earth lodge, where he was born. Before the land flooded, tribal member Mary Elk (Hidatsa) took photographs of different places in Shell Creek, the community where she grew up. Unfortunately, her house burned with the pictures in it, so she lost all the photographs of her childhood home. "That's what hurts me," she said. "You never can replace any pictures. You lose them once you lose it all." Saying goodbye to the taken lands lasted for years afterward. Decades after the flooding completed, my grandmother, Myra Snow (Mandan, Hidatsa), stopped at the shore of the reservoir nearest to the community in which she grew up. As she looked out over the water, she began to cry, sobbing. Throughout most of the oral history interviews accessed for this research, community members refer to things left behind and covered by the water, from houses to tractors to gardens.[46]

Loss defined the move to the prairie. Land and water center tribal narratives of our loss. Dreke Irwin (Mandan, Hidatsa), a well-known powwow announcer, served in the armed forces when the dam flooded the river valley; he returned to a drastically changed landscape. "What I always missed was that timber and that river," he remembered, "and all that rich ground; fertile." He noted that prairie soil is full of clay, "gumbo," and more fit for pastures than for fields. Tribal member Mary Elk—respected for the knowledge and dedication to the position she held in the Antelope Society—agreed. "All those things we lost," she said, "they can never replace, no matter how much money they give us. They can never replace the good water and land we lost."[47]

Phyllis Cross, the oldest daughter of Martin Cross, who after the relocation earned her nursing degree, offered journalist Paul VanDevelder her analysis:

> Our thinking failed us because suddenly our landmarks, our social and physical landmarks, the framework for everything we were, was gone. Our identity derived from our villages. Those were destroyed. We were born into very dynamic and complex social networks that connected those identities across forty generations. Those went when the villages went. When everything was gone, there was no one waiting to help us put the world back in order. No jobs, no communities, no gardens, no homes. Gone.[48]

Community life changed irrevocably. Clyde Baker (Mandan, Hidatsa) believed that "all that kind of life was left down there, in that valley, because we were all mixed up here, some of the White Shield people came over and lived with us in Mandaree." The change in communities, the sudden discontinuity ensured that "our way of life just changed, like daylight to dark, the change." Intimate family ties weakened, particularly the time spent "visiting" relatives, which Baker blamed for how "today our kids don't hardly know their relatives today, nothing like they used to." Rosemarie Mandan agreed and described how a whole generation of children attended boarding schools due to the closure of the reservation schools. Sending so many children away to boarding school, "just broke up the whole family system, it sure broke it up. Since everyone was going away, they didn't learn their language, so the language is not spoken anymore.... It's really a shame, because that culture, it's tied in with the language. There's no getting around it."

Mandan's memories of her father or her grandmother telling tribal oral tradition or family stories during winter evenings to a log house full of neighborhood children filled Mandan's childhood; her father read books like *Silas Marner* or *The Christmas Story* and retold the books in Hidatsa. In her perspective, loss of culture represented the biggest change since the Garrison Dam flooded the river valley. Mandan reflected, "And we were all separated. I was no longer close to my cousins, I wasn't close to where my grandparents lived.... Broken up, just broken up." She continued,

> We know all those things [tribal stories and family histories] because we were still at home. And just think if we had left, we wouldn't have all that family history, and all those other things my dad used to tell us. He used to take us outside and tell us legends... see, those are things we don't have anymore. See in our little log house, the neighborhood kids would all come in and sit down and he would tell these stories, legends; or those coyote tales.[49]

As the tribes relocated from the river valley to the prairie, the federal government implemented the twin policies of termination and relocation. Both policies—along with the concurrent P.L. 83-280—eroded tribal community life and landholdings across the country. Termination policy anticipated the end of the trust relationship between the federal government and tribes. The loss of tribal trust status sought by the legislation would effectively eliminate tribal sovereign powers. The termination shortlist included the Three Affiliated Tribes alongside the Menominees and the Klamaths, and the threat of termination hung over the heads of every tribal group in the nation. At the same time, Dillon Myer—the soulless bureaucrat who oversaw the implementation of the Japanese American internment camps—asserted that if the tribal government thought itself able to manage the compensation monies from the federal government, then the Three Affiliated Tribes no longer required a treaty relationship or the "supervision" of the BIA. Myer also mobilized the Bureau of Indian Affairs to encourage tribal members to relocate from reservations to major urban areas, such as Denver, Chicago, Los Angeles, Minneapolis, and Seattle.[50]

In the context of the economic and social turmoil of the move from the river valley, relocation to a major urban area became, if not attractive, perhaps necessary to survive. Few jobs and the end of a functional subsistence agricultural economy pushed tribal members to leave the reservation for their economic survival. Half of the tribal population participated in the relocation program by the early 1960s. Even on relocation, however, times were tough. Gail Baker remembered about life after the Garrison Dam: "One of the biggest changes was that it really split us up. They sent a lot of them on relocation, too, for jobs. But it's pretty hard when you don't have education to go on relocation and try to get a job, you're going to get the bottom job."[51]

Bureau of Indian Affairs bureaucrats exacerbated the chaos and used it to advocate for immediate termination of the Three Tribes. In a 1955 report, the agency asserted, "The tribes are now enjoying the highest level of resources in their history," before concluding, "We can see no particular gain for the Indian people by delaying the institution of a planned withdrawal of all special government services. The shock of such a program will have immediate repercussions, but the negative effect of such reaction can be considerably reduced if the problem is properly presented in positive terms."[52]

Political life on the reservation remained troubled. In addition to unending conflict between the Cross and Whitman supporters, the physical relocation of tribal members to new communities threw the voting process into disarray. Because by the 1954 election most people lived at their new homesites, the relocation nullified the previous districts. Meanwhile, voters had not yet approved the plan for new segments. Its approval required a successful tribal referendum with participation of at least 30 percent of the eligible voters. Thus, the entire 1952 tribal council stayed in power until voters approved the new segment voting amendment in September 1956, so Cross and his faction "remained in office for more than two years after the expiration of his second term." Whitman regained the chairmanship, but Cross's control of the council ensured that it remained dominated by the Nos—and stayed in power during the most important years in deciding how to administer and distribute the compensation money for the tribes' beloved river valley.

Broken. Mixed up. Split up. A change from daylight to dark. The Three Affiliated Tribes experienced a radical shift in our territorial base, and Fort Berthold life changed with it. The reservation divided into five segments, with five towns serving as the central locations for schools, clinics, and community centers: Parshall (Northeast Segment), White Shield (East Segment), New Town (North Segment), Mandaree (West Segment), and Twin Buttes (South Segment). Awáati, the Missouri River, which once served as a connection between communities, swelled and bloated after the Garrison Dam to separate each segment from the next, to create a reservoir today named Lake Sakakawea. A 1953 cover of the *Fort Berthold Agency News Bulletin* depicted the expanding reservoir behind the Garrison Dam—Lake Sakakawea—as a water monster with tentacles spreading across the reservation.[53]

The prairielands on top offered little protection against the elements, and little sustenance for humans, animals, or gardens. With the loss of riparian valley lands, tribal members could no longer access the same levels

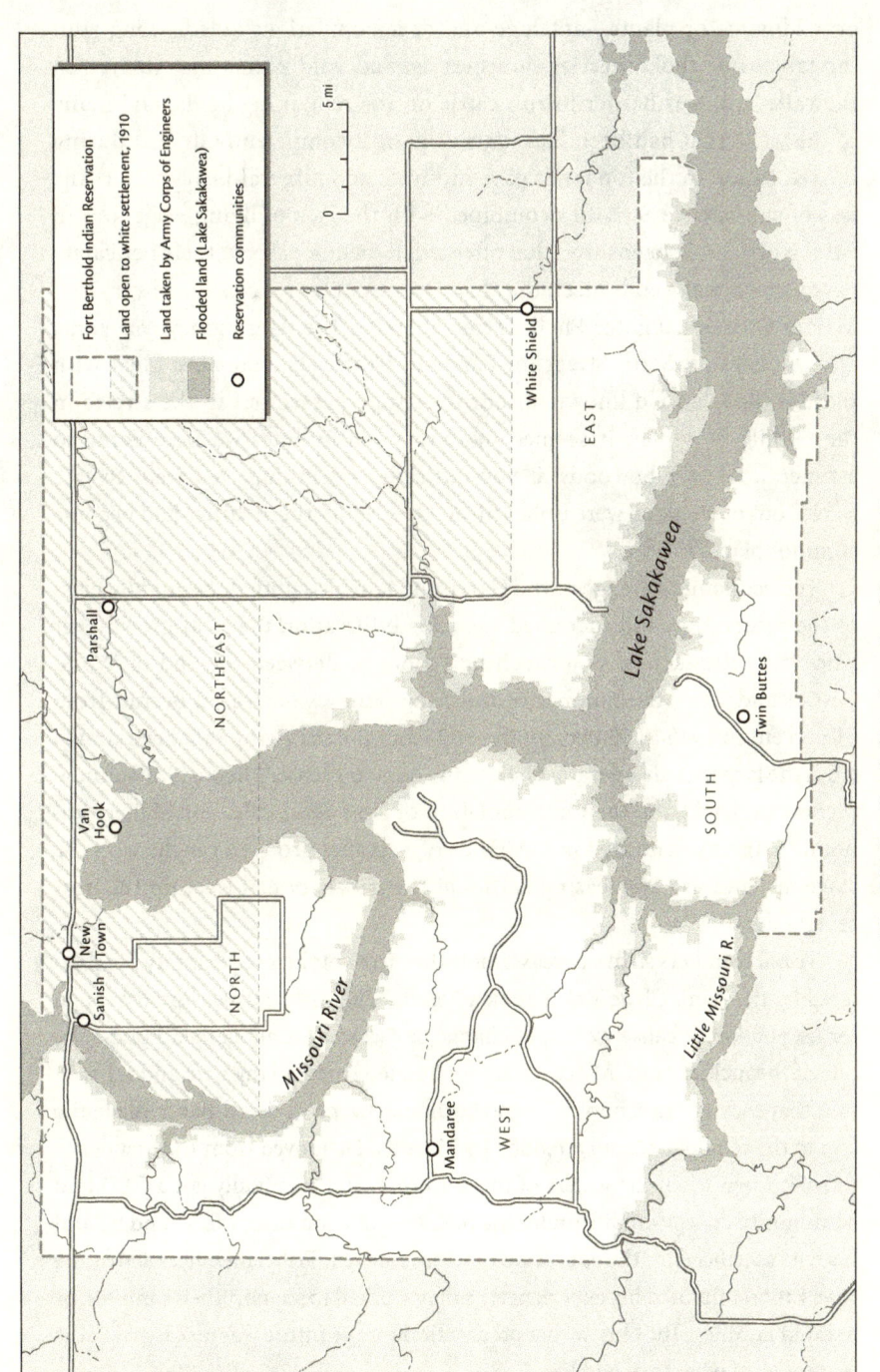

Map 5.2. Fort Berthold in the wake of Garrison Dam

of wild game or plants—antelope and deer populations faded, along with the tangles of chokecherries, Juneberries, and wild plums that thrived in the valleys. It was harder to run cattle on the remaining lands, and many of the wells that had been lackadaisically or incompetently drilled during the relocation to the top lands gave minimal and mineral-heavy water. The loss of subsistence activities combined with the lack of living-wage jobs in rural North Dakota ensured that after tribal members spent their per capita payments to make ends meet, they had few resources for continued survival. Martin Cross's daughter Phyllis remembered, "The dam money was gone, and the bars on Main Street [in Parshall, North Dakota] were filled with Indians. People we'd known all our lives were passed out in the streets in the middle of winter. It seemed like every ten minutes we were going to a funeral.... In Elbowoods, if you got caught drinking, you went to jail. Babies out of wedlock were unheard-of. Overnight, these things had become commonplace."[54]

The economic damage of the Garrison Dam also gutted the middle class of the reservation and increased the class bifurcation that had grown ever since the introduction of a ranching economy. Between the end of World War II and 1960, the number of ranching families decreased overall from 61 percent in 1945 to 30 percent in 1960—but the surviving ranchers, drawn from the larger-scale operators before the dam, increased their overall annual income derived from their accumulation of land and cattle. The higher economic gains concentrated in the hands of a smaller group of ranchers set the stage for land use and leasing battles at the tribal council level for the next several decades.[55]

Tribal members strove to reassemble the pieces of their community life shattered by the dam. Clyde Baker remembered, "The early '50s was pretty rough for us, you know, cause we had to change our way of life altogether. I guess I'm one of the luckier ones. My children, we had ten children my wife and I, I seen to it that they got to school, to a good school." Every weekend Baker made the trip to the religious school attended by his sons. He moved from Independence to New Town when the waters of the dam rose, and eventually got a GED and community college credits under his belt. He got a job in an office, and he and his wife sacrificed for the education of their children. Tribal members across the reservation mirrored his experience, as they worked to support their families, or to build families. They knew that preparation for the future was just as crucial as memories of what they had lost.[56]

This represents one of the central lessons of what happened at Fort Berthold—that our communities and families grow from and are sustained by the land, the places and spaces and territories we marked, worked, populated with stories, planted, and loved. The beautiful practices that make a place a home—from welcome-home dances for servicemen and women, to grandmothers and aunties drying corn—emerge from our landscapes and a deep engagement with our past. But their meaning becomes most powerful when applied and used in the present and the future. As Dreke Irwin explained, "Before we were flooded out, everybody was used to it, grew up and took things for granted that it wasn't gonna ever change. And all of a sudden, everybody had to move. I guess what land you have, you have to make the best of it, to bring up your family."[57]

As the rising waters of Lake Sakakawea submerged the heart of the Fort Berthold landscape, community members dealt with increased political turmoil, narrowed economic choices, the confusion of relocating families and communities, and the emotional demands that accompanied saying goodbye to your home forever. Increased political, class, and race divisions attended this loss of the heart of the Fort Berthold landscape, work practices, and social life, and community members feared the end of their entire way of life. As the BIA exercised vast administrative powers over land transactions and settlement on the residual lands, the tribal council turned to the control over tribal compensation monies to express authority—even as it undermined its own authority through vicious infighting.

Despite the turmoil, community members found ways to say goodbye to their beloved river valley. Their community farewells emphasized the reiteration of community pasts—perhaps because the places that helped tell these stories would soon be underwater. Individual goodbyes focused on place and landscape—a visit to a birthplace, photographs, or even a drive to the edge of Lake Sakakawea to mourn them in later years. Finally, for the people who lived through it, the move to the prairie became defined by what was lost—fertile land, good water, tribal language, cultural knowledge, and the transmission of community and family histories.

Tribal communities mounted a defense when the workings of the federal government endangered things precious to them. When the federal government stole the edges of tribal territories during the late nineteenth and early twentieth centuries, a sense of sovereign territoriality resulted. When the federal government submerged the very heart of the reservation, tribal members struggled to ensure a future for their families and the entire community. Fort Berthold community members mobilized the tools developed through the early twentieth century—sovereign territoriality, indigenous citizenship, and the struggle to exert legitimate political authority both inside and outside the community—not only to fight the Garrison Dam, but to rebuild after the resulting reservoir submerged their lands.

Conclusion

After the relocation from the river valley, the tribe distributed remaining tribal compensation monies per capita. Between 1950 and the spring of 1955, the federal government distributed approximately $4.5 million of the $12.5 million in compensation money per capita, in dribbles of five hundred or a thousand dollars. Because the federal government distributed a little over $3 million to individuals who lost lands in the taken area, by 1956 less than $4.5 million of the compensation money remained. The "No" faction, still in power after delaying the elections due to the chaotic move from the bottomlands, advocated for yet another per capita distribution of all remaining compensation money. After successful lobby for legislation to distribute the rest of the money, the No faction oversaw a $1,343 distribution of the remaining funds to each individual tribal member in 1957. A large portion of these last distributions evaporated: 68 percent went to nondurable goods and services, and 12 percent went to debts.[1]

One cannot help but think back to the plan for the tribal compensation money proposed by the "Yes" faction. In the summer of 1950, Carl Whitman had traveled from community meeting to community meeting, to explain the plan and convince his political opposition that it would provide a better hope for the future. In June of that year, at a community meeting in Nishu, Whitman focused his remarks to an influential elder in the community, Frank Heart. The meeting lasted hours—it started just before four in the afternoon and ended at nine o'clock. Heart, who spoke little English and required translation into Arikara by tribal judge Peter Beauchamp, planned to leave the meeting after a speech in favor of a per capita distribution of compensation money. Before Heart left, Whitman asked Beauchamp to translate a short statement into Arikara. Whitman explained his stance. "This is our father's land—tribal land," he said, "I wish it to continue so."

In 3 years time, the Garrison Dam takes away some of our land—takes the deer, the berries, and so on, and in place we get 12 million and what's left. According to the bill, that will be divided and given to the people who lose lands and improvements. We don't know whether anything will be left.

I personally feel, if anything is left of tribal resources—it will be money. By our forefathers leaving the land intact, we of late years enjoyed its benefits. Those who are here after us want to have those resources after the water comes. All we have to offer is to offer money for their use. If our fathers had divided the tribal assets—we wouldn't have any tribal property to enjoy now. That's why we the council—and we are positive a lot of people feel the same—feel we should preserve this money for future generations.

This plan had been characterized by the No faction as reenacting the worst controls of the Bureau of Indian Affairs for the benefit of the top of the reservation class structure. These criticisms may have been warranted; we will never know. Regardless, the $12.5 million in cash offered by the federal government in exchange for hundreds of years of history, the heart of the tribal land base, and the future stability of the Fort Berthold communities would still be inadequate. From the meeting notes, Whitman's words changed the minds of the people who attended the meeting, but of course not everyone on the reservation attended these long meetings in small spaces, in which proceedings had to be translated into at least one tribal language for the elders who spoke little English.[2]

Carl Whitman and members of the Yes faction still served on the council by the time the final per capita was distributed, but during the two-year delay of the 1956 election, these members remained outnumbered. The translation of land into money into empty pockets became as inevitable as the Garrison Dam. Political control of the council flip-flopped between Cross and Whitman, even after there was no money to fight over. Tribal members learned how to live on the prairie, setting up windbreaks and persistently planting their grandmothers' seeds in gardens of a less fertile soil. Children left the reservation for boarding schools because their parents struggled in the new economy, and some families relocated to urban centers for the same reason. But they all tended to return, cycling back and forth as they sought economic opportunity, an education, or both. The Fort Berthold economy transitioned from one largely based on agriculture and ranching to one based on unemployment. Men and women found office jobs, or they didn't. Rates of welfare rose, as did rates of alcoholism and violent death. Language transmission rates fell dramatically.[3]

Change brewed across the nation. The civil rights movement labored to awaken the conscience of a country. The Cold War ensured that the men—and some women—of the Three Tribes would continue to fight and die for the country that stole their land, first in Korea, then in Vietnam. Tribes terminated by the federal government suffered before fighting their way back to stability. And young Native activists such as those in the National Indian Youth Council began to exchange old ideas that sounded new coming from their mouths. They talked about stolen lands and children, or about the rights indigenous people retained after they signed treaties. They talked about the racism and violence of border towns that sometimes produced the opposite of its intended effect, such as when young activist Clyde Warrior proudly claimed, "The sewage of Europe doesn't run in these veins."[4]

Many assiduously sought to right the wrongs of the past. The sons of two opposing factions on Fort Berthold—Raymond Cross and Hans Walker Jr.—both attended law school and worked to establish new rules for what constituted "just compensation for lands taken." Others just as determinedly worked for a better future, becoming teachers and social workers and nurses—and mothers and fathers who ensured that their children knew and valued their tribal histories.

Three decades after the implementation of the Garrison Dam, then–tribal councilwoman Marie Wells testified before a committee to assess the true costs of the dam as to how the profound shift in the landscape changed how tribal members lived and survived:

> We lived in a beautiful place where we were all together, and people danced and sang the old songs. We picked wild grapes, chokecherries, bull berries, wild plums, buffalo berries, juneberries—those were the ones that came down first—and we dug the wild turnips and dried them for the winter. My mother and grandmother dried the berries for pemmican and corn balls, the buffalo berries made good jam and jelly, and the old people pounded the chokecherries and dried them like burgers and saved them for the winter. The berries were good for us, for our kidneys and hearts and our blood, but they are all gone and now we have heart disease and kidney disease, and our blood is bad with diabetes.[5]

The loss of the bottomlands curtailed the way Fort Berthold tribal members moved through the landscape, cultivated and harvested its resources, and sustained their bodies and their families. Wells gave this 1986 testimony to the Garrison Unit Joint Tribal Advisory Committee (JTAC), charged by the US Senate with the identification and quantification of the true losses suffered by the Three Affiliated Tribes caused by the Garrison Dam.

The testimonies given to the JTAC would, over the next six years, slowly and painfully turn into the recognition and compensation of the losses suffered due to the Garrison Dam and the illegal 1949 congressional act that forced the Three Tribes to accept pennies for their beloved homelands. A joint Senate and the House committee awarded the Three Tribes $149.2 million. The influx of resources allowed the tribal government to implement new programs and plan for longer-term economic stability. But it also led to bloated salaries for tribal council members, an intensification of the spoils system based on family relationships, and the advent of "ghost workers"—employees hired through nepotism who drew salaries but rarely showed up to work. This tendency would only exacerbate with the rapid shift to a boom time economy during the Bakken oil boom in the 2000s as Fort Berthold participated in fracking the Bakken oil field.[6]

Fort Berthold and its history is unique, but the challenges it faced are common. Eminent domain takings happened to many Indian communities in the name of "the public good"—reservation lands sacrificed to dams, bomb testing, uranium mining, and corporate pollution—and each of those communities mobilized all their resources, all their ideas, all their people to fight them.[7] They used new ideas alongside old ones, as had Carl Whitman, who reinterpreted tradition for a modern context and advocated for the long-term health of his tribes. They used their political wiles like Martin Cross, who fought for the disempowered in his community. They used whatever nooks and crannies they could find in the structures of a dominating sovereignty to assert their own—their own right to self-rule, their own right to manage and defend their territories, their own right to control their resources, and their own indigenous citizenship. These histories of twentieth-century Native America are complicated and beautiful and tragic and imperfect. Sometimes it is hard to make sense of them, or to find moral purchase in the stories of the individuals who lived them.

This is what happened at Fort Berthold.

Tribal notions of place in a beloved river valley served as a foundation from which community members could counter and at times co-opt federal spatial projects—whether these projects included mapping the Missouri or allotting lands. But as tribes and the federal government used and understood technologies of sovereignty—both treaties and executive orders—tribal defense of their remaining territories became shaped and structured not only by the community meanings ascribed to place but also by the government-to-government relationship enacted via treaty and land negotiations. When the federal government continued to take bites both large and small of tribal landholdings, the tribes at Fort Berthold developed sovereign territoriality to defend their land base. This constitutes the first unintended effect of the exercise of federal sovereign power.

The second unintended effect resulted from the Indian Reorganization Act, which gave tribes the space necessary to remake tribal authority in ways that both fit community needs and outwardly satisfied the requirements of what the federal government considered legitimate authority within Indian country. As the Three Affiliated Tribes exercised the power to manage their land base and membership, the practice and contestation of that management created opportunities for tribal members to claim and exercise indigenous citizenship. This indigenous citizenship grew from the soil of tribal territories and a defense of the tribal land base, but also claimed and strategically mobilized the rights of US citizenship to ensure the future of the community. Once a space had been cleared for the exercise and definition of tribal authority, its practice spread like vines along the ground.

As one of the foundational concepts of modern sovereign power, the definition and practice of citizenship bears special attention. At Fort Berthold during World War II, tribal members embodied and practiced indigenous citizenship and patriotism through dance, song, and labor. As tribal members used their bodies to index and perform indigenous notions of place, they co-opted powerful nationalistic narratives surrounding military service, national production, and individual consumption—even while their practice of these concepts was structured by a tribal-centric version of both. These practices illuminate a line of meaning drawn from tribal landscapes to community members and their embodiment of place to form a radically indigenous patriotism and citizenship.

When the construction of the Garrison Dam forced tribal and federal sovereignties into conflict over the notion of the public good, tribal members used their practice of indigenous citizenship claims in defense of tribal territories facing inundation. These claims were based on treaty history and the recent gains in the federal-tribal relationship given strength by the Indian Reorganization Act. The mobilization of treaty rights in conjunction with the rights of patriotic citizens serves as one of the key elements in the foundation of modern tribal sovereignty—a sovereignty that sees no paradox between exercising treaty rights and simultaneously claiming the liberties of US citizenship.

The flooding from the Garrison Dam caused deep turmoil. The radical change in tribal territories created an opening for the local Bureau of Indian Affairs to exert wide leverage over tribal lands and territories and usurp tribal authority. Tribal leadership norms devolved as robust battles to define legitimate authority morphed into vicious battles over control of compensation money. The devolution of tribal authority cast its citizenry adrift to survive the disarray associated with the flooding of the heart of its landscape and its own relocation to what constituted a foreign environment. To cope, both individuals and communities developed ways to say goodbye to their beloved bottomlands—goodbyes that centered around the recognition and celebration of the places that sustained their personal and community histories. A continued faith in the futurity of Fort Berthold as a community mediated the loss of faith in tribal authority, expressed through the persistent efforts to cultivate economic and educational opportunities for the next generation. Federal power gutted the heart of the landscape, but previous practices developed to sustain community identity—community celebrations and accompanying cultural and kinship labor—helped Fort Berthold communities weather the chaos.

Clearly, the federal taking of tribal land for the Garrison Dam via eminent domain for the "public good" did not include Native people in its conception of "the public." The notion of the public good also undergirds sovereign legitimate authority—the agreement that the concentration of managerial and juridical power in the hands of a few is justified for the good of the public represented by that sovereign. The conflicting definitions of public good most often brings tribal sovereignties and US federal sovereignty into battle, and the exclusion of Native peoples from the public good remains one of the enduring conflicts that structures US sovereignty. The fascist political theorist Carl Schmitt posited the formulation of modern international law as a reaction to the need for the systematic development of the rights of European sovereignties after the discovery of the New World—that "other" land that needed to be defined, marked, measured, owned. US sovereignty developed and continues to develop dialogically in this vein—with the "other" being at various times the Native peoples, English, French, Russians, and Spanish; Native nations (again) during westward expansion; Pacific takings or interventions such as Hawaii, Guam, Samoa, and the Philippines; interventions in Cuba, Puerto Rico, Argentina, Bolivia,

Brazil, Chile, the Dominican Republic, Ecuador, Guatemala, Haiti, Nicaragua, and Panama; strong-arm economic intervention in Japan, China, and Korea or military operations in Vietnam, Cambodia, and Laos; and a toxic mélange of regime change and military interventions in Syria, Egypt, Iran, Iraq, Libya, Kuwait, and Afghanistan. Our institutions and leaders forged US sovereignty not only through the legal and political actions of the powerful, but by positing it against and negotiating with tribal and other indigenous sovereignties.

Neither tribal sovereignty *nor* US sovereignty are ahistorical, or legal abstractions. We constantly negotiate, contest, shore up, or find our sovereignty diminished. If sovereignty seems amorphous as a concept, as a practice and lived reality it is historical, earthy, and built on the actions and interventions of people and institutions. Battles over land, water, and resources comprise most of these conflicts between federal and tribal sovereignties because these things constitute the "territory" required to maintain a working sovereign body. The story of US sovereignty cannot be understood or told in isolation from its attempts to nullify tribal sovereignties, in this century or in past ones. The indigenous lands loved and nurtured by our community members are always its starting point.

Epilogue

Many people helped drive and support this project. At the same time, one individual stands out above and beyond everyone else for her insight, wisdom, and connection to the events and historical perspectives included in this book. I've been reluctant to center her because I know she would be annoyed at me for doing so. I, like other researchers, asked her for interviews about the events in this book numerous times, and she always just smiled and suggested four other people that I should try to interview first—there were always four other people.

When she did get recognized, it exasperated her. I visited Washington, DC, with her in 2006: I needed to complete research at the National Archives, and she had been invited to a national Native journalism organization honoring of Hank Adams. We met in Washington and knocked around together, visiting the National Archives and monuments. At the event honoring Mr. Adams, after he received his award and as he gave his speech, he looked out over the audience and saw my aunt—Tillie Walker—and deviated from his planned text. He said that the organization should give the award to other people, and if the organizers listened to him, they should give the award next year to Tillie Walker.

I nudged her and said, "Did you hear that?" She shrugged. Never one to take a hint, I nudged her again, "Did you hear what he said about you?" She looked at me with one of her quick, piercing glances that meant that you were either going to get some truth dropped on you or that she was tricking you, but you were also kinda in on the joke. "I can't hear anything," she claimed. As we left the event, Mr. Adams made a beeline to her and greeted her warmly.

This moment continues to shape my understandings of twentieth-century Native history. The recognized visionary, Hank Adams, deserved and received acclaim for the work he did on behalf of Native communities—his tireless activism, his brilliance that wedded community engagement to national consciousness via fish-in protests, his long work and advocacy to build a better future for Native peoples. Simultaneously, he knew Native women who also deserved recognition, and in a moment that defines his own generosity and humility he advocated for them.[1]

Twentieth-century Native American history—like histories of most other eras—tends to focus on the charismatic male leader to the detriment of his sisters, aunties, grandmas, and daughters who also fought and worked for their people. But whereas we can blame non-Native chroniclers for their gendered blinders in earlier centuries, contemporary historians have only ourselves to blame for our seeming inability to center the vital leadership and work provided by Native women in our fight for self-determination and a viable future. Both the white gaze and the Native gaze tends to romanticize the male leader—usually performed in the twentieth century (and the twenty-first) by an Indian man who enjoys the power of long braids and a military style jacket, or a big belt buckle and a cowboy hat. His activist public rhetoric—drawn at least half the time from the insights and analyses of the powerful Native women who raised him, fed him, at times coddled him, and sometimes cussed him out—rarely matches a private commitment to the best and most generous practices toward women of the men in his ancestral line.[2]

This epilogue attempts to shed light on an influential female leader in the Red Power era. It is also part of an argument that while the tragedy of the Garrison Dam never should have happened, it is not the tragic last chapter of declension narrative. As Cheyenne communities say, a nation is not defeated until the hearts of its women are on the ground, and Auntie Tillie's life proves that our communities were not, and are not, defeated. In fact, the gut-punch of injustice and destruction she experienced at Fort Berthold as a teenager drove Auntie Tillie's work and accomplishments. She used her strong, living, beating heart to battle and puncture egos, expose inequities, and laugh with friends and relatives and the students she mentored.[3]

Many Red Power activists experienced similar injustices in the post–World War II right turn in Indian affairs. They saw their parents and grandparents fight the land, water, and resource takings of a new, carelessly cruel world power. They saw the racism weathered by their beloved elders in border-town communities and Bureau of Indian Affairs offices. They experienced how cheaply non-Native communities considered their lives and the lives of their relatives and clan relations. Tillie Walker, Clyde Warrior, Mel Thom, Hank Adams, and countless others came from reservation communities that each fought their own battles with the federal government or neighboring white communities—struggles that centered around tribal landscapes, places, territories, and spaces. Sometimes tribal communities won those battles; more often, they lost—or were remunerated for their loss with inadequate compensation monies. But they were all struggles for dirt. For water. For fish or wild game. Or for the right to control or halt the extraction of coal, oil, gas, or uranium from the tribal land base. And because of their own bravery and the mentorship of people like Auntie Tillie, they changed Native America and our country.

I hope that the other people who knew and loved and respected Auntie Tillie will recognize her in the following few pages. I hope readers who were not lucky enough to know her recognize their own beloved relatives in this description. I did not get enough time with her—nobody did—and I still miss her every day. How short-sighted and thoughtless I was when I was younger! I thought everyone who guided and supported me would always be here, and that I had my whole life to spend with them. Too focused on myself and my own needs, insecurities, and plans, I did not slow down to appreciate my aunt when I was lucky enough to have her here. So, in the following pages, please slow down with me. Take your time, and let's take this time together, to talk about my Auntie Tillie.

Home

Auntie Tillie was born July 11, 1928, during the last gasp of the reservation era and on the cusp of federal recognition of the rights of tribal self-determination. Her father, Hans Walker Sr., was a respected community member and served on the newly organized tribal council formed after the Indian Reorganization Act. The Fort Berthold community also held deep respect for her mother, Mercy Baker Walker, whose Mandan grandparents had raised her after her mother died when she was a tiny girl. Because Auntie Tillie's mom was raised by grandparents who were likely born before 1850, Grandma Mercy and her children had access to unusually deep traditional knowledge even for the period.[4]

Auntie's family was loving and traditional, and she and her siblings grew up speaking Hidatsa, English, and a bit of Mandan. Auntie Tillie's Hidatsa name was Hishua Adesh, or Peppermint Sprout. Grandma Mercy spoke all three languages and her first language was Mandan, but they probably defaulted to Hidatsa in the home because Grandpa Hans didn't speak Mandan. They lived in an extended log house in a protected setting in the pre-Garrison town of Independence. My aunt Patricia Baker-Benally (Mandan, Hidatsa, Blackfeet), who grew up near their home, described it as "always a very busy place." She elaborated, "You were either picking juneberries, or you were going out to plum, or they were butchering, or they were collecting eggs, or they were filling the water barrels. I think there was a natural spring there. You had to hand carry and put it in the barrels. Then of course, the cleaning of the kerosene lights." When Auntie Tillie passed away, her younger sister Reba told me that Auntie Tillie "was incredibly independent, even when we were little."[5]

Both parents supported the unique personalities of their children—each of whom went on to dedicate their lives to being the type of bedrock community members that support and uplift Native America. Auntie's oldest brother, Melvin, earned his master's in social work and returned home to Fort Berthold to support his community. Their brother Hans Jr. earned a law degree and went on to become a legal giant in federal Indian law. Their youngest sister, Reba, became a nurse and dedicated her career to improving health outcomes as a nurse and later as a healthcare administrator. Growing up, Auntie and her siblings were embedded in a close-knit network of blood and clan relations that both supported them and expected much from them.

Figure 7.1. Tillie Walker in 1947. Courtesy of Reid Walker.

During Tillie's adolescence as World War II raged, both Hans Jr. and Melvin served in the armed forces, while their younger sisters helped their parents keep their ranch operating. Auntie Tillie spent the ages of twelve to seventeen drawn into the same welcome-home dances and pitching in to do the work required to keep the home front operating as described in chapter 3. Just as she hit the age when most youth expand their awareness beyond their immediate surroundings to understand larger social structures, Auntie witnessed her parents, relatives, and community members battle against the implementation of the Garrison Dam as documented in chapter 4, forced to relocate from the communities in which she had grown up. After she left for college, during trips home she witnessed the community chaos and mourning described in chapter 5.

The individual who emerged from these experiences was dedicated to family and community, engaging, brave, hardworking, and independent. She was also the opposite of self-promoting—vastly out of step with the later era of Red Power activism embodied by charismatic male leaders who sought microphones and cameras to curate their media image. "She did a lot of amazing things. She was really amazing, but she wouldn't talk about herself," her younger sister Karol Parker (Mandan, Hidatsa) explained. "It was like pulling teeth—but you know that. Trying to get her to talk about herself, she would not do it for *nothing*. She would just make a face like, 'What are you trying to do?' Or she'd turn away or she'd even walk away, I think, going to her kitchen to do something. She didn't want to talk about herself. I think it was just that kind of sense of being humble, maybe self-effacing, that she grew up with."[6] Mandan and Hidatsa cultural values emphasize the shoddiness of "bragging" or talking about yourself—the idea being that if you are doing good things, community members will see it, recognize it, and recognize you for it without you having to promote yourself.

And far from being downtrodden from her ground-level experience with federal injustice at Fort Berthold, Auntie Tillie was bright, passionate, and always active. Parker remembered Auntie Tillie's personality as one that drew people to her—"It was just a real, I don't really know how to describe it, a *sparkly* personality. People were always just wanting to be with her, go with her places. She was a lot of fun." Bruce Davies (Lakota), a mentee, collaborator, and friend, remembered her as "always really cheerful and bright and teasing."[7] Davies documented the nicknames she had for "some of the people she liked best. She called Vine Deloria [Jr.] 'V. D.' and Hank Adams 'Hanky Panky.'"[8]

Davies described Tillie's ability to navigate in two cultures as a personal and intellectual anomaly even for the time. "To me what was most impressive was that she was a college-educated, professional woman, but at home, she would speak Hidatsa with her mother," Davies explained. Charles Cambridge (Diné), who worked with Auntie as one of the board members of an education-funding organization for Native youth known as United Scholarship Service, Inc., also recognized the importance of her activist intellect: "See, one thing about what Tillie, Clyde Warrior, and the folks, all of us, we had this idea of what is possible. Tillie didn't go through the workshops and stuff like that, but she had enough of her own intellect that she could see possibilities."[9]

As a young adult, Auntie Tillie completed her BA in business administration at the University of Nebraska, having also completed work at Haskell Indian Nations University and Willamette University. She told me once that when she was about to leave for college, another community member approached her dad, Hans Sr., and implied that it was a waste of money and resources to send a girl to college. "What did he say?" I asked. Auntie shrugged and smiled, saying, "I don't know, but he came home and told us and laughed about it." Her parents supported her academics, but Auntie Tillie completed her bachelor's degree during the forced removal from the river valley, and times were tough. Her sister Reba related that as a college student she worked to fund her education and took on jobs that ranged from driving a pea truck to working for the Nebraska legislature. After graduation, Auntie and two of her friends traveled by train to Philadelphia to look for work. She didn't have a job or a place to live, but she contacted the Quaker organization known as the American Friends Service Committee and asked for a job, and they hired her. This position would lead to her work organizing the United Scholarship Service.[10]

United Scholarship Service

Auntie Tillie's parents were deeply involved in the Congregationalist church at Fort Berthold, and she had grown up in a family as conversant with Hidatsa hymns as they were with Mandan medicine bundles—likely part of the reason Auntie approached the American Friends Service Committee for employment. I am unclear about the range of her work before the establishment of the United Scholarship Service, but part of her work included administrative support for the summer Workshops on American Indian Affairs conceptualized and instituted by Sol Tax, his students Bob Thomas (Cherokee), Robert Reitz, and Al Wahrhaftig, and Murray and Rosalie Wax.[11]

The summer workshops—described and situated expertly by other historians so I will only summarize them here—transformed the political possibilities imagined by Native youth. McNickle convened his first two-week workshop in Utah in 1951 and would eventually leave the BIA to further develop the workshops and aim them at Native college students. The workshops moved from Utah to Estes Park, then Colorado Springs. Eventually the University of Colorado–Boulder housed the project, which had become a six-week program that presented Native history, anthropological theory, and the experiences of policy practitioners as a foundation to encourage students to make a structural analysis of federal Indian policy, law, and economic inequity. Charles Cambridge asserts that "the Workshops changed Indian politics forever." Cambridge coordinated later iterations of the workshops in the 1960s, and attested to the ripple effect of the consciousness raising that occurred at the workshops as the participants returned to their home communities and began to participate in tribal politics. Cambridge acknowledged that the workshops could also be difficult for participants: "Your range of what truth is expands multiple, multiple, multiple times. Through the workshops and stuff like that the Indian person, we gave him a stubbornness. The girls and the guys, they got pissed."[12]

D'Arcy McNickle (Flathead) lent expertise and helped corral funding for the workshops from places like the Indian Rights Association and the Association on American Indian Affairs. Rev. Galen Weaver of the Board of Home Missions of the Congregationalist Church also ensured funding, and he may have instigated Auntie Tillie's involvement in the workshop logistics. One exchange sifted from the Sol Tax Papers describes a situation in which both Tax and Weaver felt the need to investigate and defend against accusations from a United Church of Christ Office of Communication reporter. The reporter hoped to present a white savior feel-good story to church members but found it impossible after she saw, in her words, that instructors encouraged students to "wallow" in "bitterness."[13] The reporter, Marjorie Hyer, provided an unintentionally hilarious account of the 1957 workshop:

> I was disturbed also by Mr. Thomas' concept of the Christian churches. While the matter was not brought up very often in my presence, enough was said about it from time to time to indicate that his conception of the Christian Church is that it is an appurtenance of the white man's culture which has served in the past, and continues to serve to subjugate the Indian. Even those church people who are interested in Indian problems, he feels, are completely naïve and have been made captive of the Bureau of Indian Affairs' point of view. The Bureau of Indian Affairs,

Mr. Thomas seems to feel, is most of what's wrong with the Indians—that and the fact that the white man came to America. As a matter of fact, when I asked him what he felt was the solution to the problem of the Indian, he said, "The only real answer is for the white man to go back to where he came from." And then laughed and said, "But, of course, that isn't going to happen."[14]

Hyer's account provoked a series of letters between Weaver and Tax, in which Weaver asked Tax to investigate, and Tax agreed to do so forthwith, adding, "and I withhold judgment completely until I learn more. Doubtless you are doing the same!"[15] A week later, after a trip to Colorado Springs, Tax sent a missive to Weaver that concluded that Hyer's report was all "misinterpretation" that "reflects weaknesses not in the Workshop but in the reporter."[16] At the tail end of this minor flurry of correspondence, Tax sent a letter to Auntie Tillie, apparently to share a report of the 1956 workshop and promising the imminent arrival of a report of the 1957 workshop written by Bob Thomas. As the fragmentary letter indicates the need to secure regular funding for the workshop, either Auntie Tillie or Weaver may have sought the reports to provide ammunition for increased or sustained funding from the Congregationalist Church. Later documentation by Rosalie Wax that summarized the workshops held from 1956 through 1960 indicated that Auntie Tillie played a directional role in the early workshops through her work with the American Friends Service Committee.[17]

The work Auntie Tillie accomplished with Weaver and other religious leadership was apparently impressive enough for them to tap her to lead a new, collaborative venture—the United Scholarship Service (USS). The Board for Home Missions of the United Church of Christ and the Association on American Indian Affairs organized the USS in the fall of 1960 to combine administration for scholarship opportunities for Native and Mexican American youth. A few months later, the National Council of the Protestant Episcopal Church also became a sponsor.[18] Charles Cambridge related, "There's a rumor that Vine was the first director of USS, but if he was there, it must have been for a couple of days [chuckles]." A former board member, Cambridge described the racial power dynamics navigated by Auntie Tillie: "Tillie was under these white people, the priests, and ministers. They ran their churches, foundations, and they were a wealthy group." Auntie requested that both Cambridge and Richard Nichols (Santa Clara Pueblo) be placed on the board of trustees, which would change the tenor of the organization.[19]

Figure 7.2. Tillie Walker ca. 1960. Courtesy of Reid Walker

The *Denver Post* covered the establishment of the USS in a December 1960 article titled "Indian Scholarships Promoted," which named "Miss Tillie Walker" as the director of the organization and publicized the forty-five thousand dollars in scholarship monies she would administer: "Through solicitations by Miss Walker and other representatives of the organization, it is hoped the sum can be increased substantially before the next year of school."[20] As field director, Auntie Tillie traveled across the western United States. The USS's 1962 annual report described, "Her travels have taken her to schools and colleges in many parts of the West. She has visited with students in their home communities, encouraging their interest in continuing education, and giving invaluable guidance and counsel." Cambridge notes that during this era, Native students had few scholarship resources available to them. "There were probably only about a dozen groups that were offering small scholarships to Indian students. Tribes were not offering college scholarships, so USS became a big source of scholarships for students."[21]

Davies was thirteen when he met Auntie Tillie while attending a summer program at Dartmouth organized by the A Better Chance (ABC) scholarship program. The program prepared Native American, African American, and Puerto Rican students to transition into elite East Coast boarding schools. Until age eleven Davies lived in Rapid City, South Dakota with his family, which originated from the Wamblee district on Pine Ridge, after which his family moved to Denver. Vine Deloria Jr., whose father Vine Deloria Sr. was a minister in the Episcopal Church, recruited Davies to participate in the United Scholarship Service, which placed him in Phillips Academy in Andover, Massachusetts. Davies met Auntie Tillie at the ABC summer program after Vine Deloria Jr. switched jobs to serve as executive director of the National Congress of American Indians (NCAI). Davies reflected, "My first impression of her was, what was she doing dealing with us kids? We were a bunch of ragamuffin kids, and she was this beautiful, refined, elegant adult lady, and here she was coming out to see us."[22]

My mother, Karol Parker, was a USS student, recruited by Auntie Tillie. She remembered,

> I was just standing around with some of my friends at a [powwow] dance, out in the dark [laughs] and somehow she found me. I don't know how she knew. She was just that kind of person. She could just find anybody [laughs] and then she would talk to you like you just saw her yesterday or like you already knew each other. She so she was like, "Hey!"—she just hit me like that—"you better go to that school!" she said. She started giving me heck. I knew she was teasing, but it was just my first encounter and I looked, and I didn't even know who she was.[23]

My mom had been attending BIA boarding schools since she was eight years old, going home in the summers but spending the school year in Wahpeton, South Dakota. She was a baby when the Corps of Engineers flooded the bottomlands, and because of the economic crisis caused by the Garrison Dam, the lack of resources, and the family's remote location on their allotment twenty miles outside of the newly created village of Mandaree, my grandmother felt her education would be better and access more reliable in a BIA boarding school.

In the intervening years, my mom had adjusted to BIA boarding school, making friends and excelling academically. She told me, "I really didn't want to go [to an East Coast boarding school with USS funding] because I was really planning to go to [Flandreau Indian School]. Silly me, but it's where my friends were." My mom is innately a strong-willed person—a characteristic honed by surviving in a boarding school from the age of eight—but she didn't stand a chance against my grandma and my auntie, two relentless Mandan/Hidatsa women. She related, "Between the two of them, I don't know what they said to each other, but they both presented, 'do this and get a good education, and you go to a BIA school that's not a good education, you're not going to be challenged and it's going to be a waste.'" Laughing, she told me, "I didn't know what all they said to me, but I knew I had to do it."[24]

In retrospect, Davies believes that Auntie Tillie intended to develop the youth "as a natural resource." He explained, "Her idea was that she was going to take us, and use us, or mold us to become the next generation of professionals, and educators, and scholars, and we would end up running Indian Country. She saw us as a natural resource, and she put a lot of effort into trying to keep us happy and keep us at school." When Davies was older, Auntie Tillie explained to him that she had attended a conference on Indian education at which a supposed ally had said that Indian education should focus on vocational employment because Native people were good with their hands. Davies later wrote, "Tillie disagreed. She thought Indians should also be lawyers, doctors and engineers." Cambridge remembered that during this era, the belief that Native people should focus only on vocational training was "deeply ingrained" even within tribal communities. "The few college-trained Indians usually worked for the BIA and they worked to keep the vocation-only mental template in place. Battling these Indians and White people was one of the unwritten policies of USS."[25]

Auntie Tillie gathered USS students placed in East Coast boarding schools for Thanksgiving break retreats, as most students lacked resources to travel home. She organized retreats to Boston, Washington, DC, and other larger cities in the East to give the students time with peers, and with her mentorship. Davies reflected, "I think she saw all of us as her children—she never married and had kids—so I think a lot of her motherly instincts went into taking care of us. I think she watched out for us and tried to give us support, financial and otherwise, whenever we needed it." Navigating the provision of student support and seeking funding could be complicated. Davies remembered, "At that first gathering some wealthy Episcopalian philanthropists sponsored a dinner. They used it as an occasion to reenact the first Thanksgiving meal. The students starred as the Wampanoags and the philanthropists as the pilgrims. Being young, this did not seem surreal to me. I accepted the event as a normal occurrence. But Tillie thought otherwise. She took control over the Thanksgiving retreats. In the following years they were small, closed events for students only." Auntie Tillie would bring powwow and round dance records to the student retreats with her, and the combination of connecting with other Native students and their home cultures helped develop comfort and community for the entire group.[26]

Davies identifies a transformative impact for Indian Country at large in Auntie Tillie's work mentoring and supporting students. He observed,

> She was really sharp and very intelligent and very sophisticated. If you underestimated her, it was at your own peril because I think she was very strong-willed and had a strong purpose. She really succeeded at everything she did. United Scholarship Service, she ran that for a long—ten, twenty years without any problems. She ended up putting about one-hundred, two-hundred kids out there into college and into professional jobs. . . . She educated a whole generation of Indian kids. I think that the people who during the '60s and '70s revolutionized Indian Affairs were mostly people that she educated or sent off to school.[27]

During the first half of the 1960s, Auntie also built friendships and connections with the leaders of the burgeoning Red Power movement—young men whom historians have written about like Hank Adams, Bob Dumont, Mel Thom, Clyde Warrior, but also young women like Della Hopper, Angela Russell, and Della Williams, whom academic historians have neglected. She collaborated with the National Indian Youth Council (NIYC) on its quarterly publication of *Americans Before Columbus*, and in 1964 the Association on American Indian Affairs withdrew as a sponsoring organization—replaced by the NIYC.[28] A later USS annual report narrated the sponsorship shift and the NIYC as "a less affluent group but one representing the new generation of Indian young people." A dribble of articles in the *Denver Post* during this period document the grant work accomplished by the USS, as well as speaking engagements Auntie Tillie did with various community groups.[29] Auntie must have been shaping and expanding the work of the USS in response to the rise of Red Power activism, as well as reshaping her role. By October 1965—under the title at which I imagine Auntie Tillie laughing, "Tillie Walker Gets Job"—the *Denver Post* reported that she was named executive director of the USS.[30]

By this point, the USS office "served as a gathering place when meetings brought NIYC members to Denver," and Auntie Tillie's public statements became more activist.[31] For example, a letter to the editor regarding a racist headline run by the *Denver Post* called into question the biased use of the term "redskin" and "Indian Fighters" by the newspaper. Multiple Native women including Auntie Tillie and her sister Reba signed the letter, under the name "Daughters of Indian Uprisings, 1492 Chapter."[32] In a news story from 1968,

Auntie spoke out in a direct critique of the BIA: "Everyone believes the Bureau of Indian Affairs takes care of the Indian kids, but it doesn't in so many cases." She also critiqued the educational structures: "The attitude of teachers and school systems is frequently such that no faith is shown in the promising young people of minority groups."[33]

Perhaps she was radicalized through her association with the NIYC; perhaps she was part of the reason NIYC members had been radicalized, given her administrative work with the summer Workshops on American Indian Affairs; perhaps it was only at this point that broader society could recognize a long-simmering radicalism in Native communities. Cambridge remembers Auntie as "a homegrown activist. The rest of us point to the AID workshops as the beginning of our awareness and growth into activism. Tillie within her work with the American Friends Service Committee (AFSC) created an awareness of fairness, service, peace, and justice." In an oral history interview with Daniel Cobb, Auntie Tillie explained, "With those young people, the realization of what happened to their ancestors just, you know, it was hard. I mean, I have the same kind of feelings, because they took everything from us here—us people who lived along the Missouri River for centuries and centuries. Suddenly it's all gone and our whole way of life had to be changed." In the same passage, Cobb quotes her critique of the power structure of the time, in which the NCAI and the National Tribal Chairmen's Association were hailed by the establishment as the "legitimate" voice of Indian Country: "It was the government that created tribal councils for God's sakes." Tillie went on to explain that in the NIYC, "Those young people knew that. I felt they had a better understanding than the elected officials had in terms of what was happening to Indian people. And they said it, you know. They were young and they could say it."[34]

The Red Power activist generation had witnessed and experienced the hardships and injustice of the post–World War II conservative shift in Indian affairs. They not only experienced the land takings and floodings, the terminations and relocations, but they also saw their parents and grandparents fight to mitigate the damage. Some, like my Auntie Tillie, worked to support others to fight the injustice they identified in the world around them. The USS served as one venue for Auntie Tillie to create change, and she used all her organizational talents to identify and support promising students as well as to increase the ripple effect of community action. Her natural charisma helped, as the work required commitment and energy. In a *Denver Post* article, Auntie Tillie explained, "We have found out that unless you get out and talk to the families and then follow through with second or third contacts, nothing happens.... We want to find out what is available for these young people, let them know about it, and encourage them to go after it."[35]

By this point, USS work included student outreach, recruitment, and advocacy. Staff helped students apply to college and secure financial aid and encouraged students to persist with their schooling. The USS administered scholarships at the secondary, undergraduate, and graduate levels, and expanded to include Talent Search fieldworkers, who focused on community outreach and identification of promising Native youth in Harlem, Montana; Rapid City, South Dakota; Denver; and Chicago.[36] The USS grew in other ways. The secondary student support program organized to form "the Organization of Native American Students (ONAS) using the Thanksgiving Conference in 1968 as an organization meeting."[37] The USS organized a "Summer Student Project" that placed its students in community-based projects on the Navajo Nation and in Rapid City, South Dakota, and Havre, Montana. It also assumed administration of a Washington Indian Intern project that placed students in federal internships in Washington, DC, for summer college credit. A former and returning USS student, Duane Bird Bear (Mandan, Hidatsa), served as the "Robert F. Kennedy Memorial Fellow for [the] 1969–70 academic year" and planned to meet with college groups to provide "support for student-initiated programs, including Indian Studies."[38] And finally, the staff of four in the main USS office published a newsletter for its students, the *United Scholarship Service News*, which documented projects and highlighted areas of investigation and concern.[39]

Most significantly, however, the USS transitioned from being funded and beholden to white philanthropy to being an all-indigenous board that represented "directly the interests of the Indian and Mexican American communities." Charles Cambridge recollected that when he and Richard Nichols, two young NIYC leaders who were former USS students and the Native representatives to the board of trustees, served on the USS Board, "it was not workable, totally not workable." Cambridge, Nichols, and Auntie Tillie began to strategize how to ask the philanthropists to resign from the board and rebuild it to reflect the communities it served—but without losing their financial support.

"Tillie had an interesting way of rolling her eyes, looking at the ceiling," Cambridge recalled. The trio considered playing on the white guilt of the philanthropists, and their discussion "became a funny session with serious moments. I wanted Richard to tell a story of how he was beaten by the Pueblo village priest. Tillie was rolling her eyes constantly. The guilty approach of 'parents must let their children go' actually did work." The board responded with deep emotion when Cambridge and Nichols presented the idea at an hours-long board meeting at the Olin Hotel in Denver: "You can't believe the shock, the total devastation of these white people that were super liberals helping the poor Indians, giving an awful lot of money to these Indians because they ran different organizations too, but because they were funding USS, they put themselves on the board." After arguing about the motion for three hours, "They finally asked Richard and I to leave the meeting. They kicked the Indians out of the meeting [laughs]. Yes, they kicked the Indians out of the meeting. That was so funny."[40]

The all-white portion of the USS board ended up meeting for another hour while Cambridge, Nichols, and Auntie Tillie waited in the hotel bar. Eventually, the other board members asked Cambridge and Nichols to return to the meeting room. The main concern of the white portion of the USS board was that Native people "weren't capable." Cambridge remembered,

> They started negotiating. "How do we know that you guys know what you're doing?" It became an issue: Were we capable of doing this? Were Indians capable of running an organization? My point was, well, failure is part of the learning process, failure is a great learning experience, and if you can accept failure, then you can almost do anything.... Then finally, I think it was a Methodist minister, he said, "Okay, we'll all resign and we will continue the funding for another year, and then we'll meet again."[41]

The transition immediately shifted USS work and priorities.[42] Bob Dumont, the new USS board chair and longtime collaborator with Auntie Tillie from the summer Workshops on American Indian Affairs, wrote in his first message, "Schools for American Indian and Mexican American communities have traditionally been a 'commodity' doled out to communities much as food 'commodities' are distributed." The following year's annual report included a section titled "Look to the Future" that stated, "The past ten years have taught us that the 'trickle down' effect of providing excellent educational opportunities for talented individual Indian young people is not sufficient to change the structure of Indian communities and the Indian educational system which keep most Indian people apathetic, powerless, and in poverty." Rather, the report asserted, "U.S.S. has always seen its job as developing Indian leadership. There is now a broad enough base of college-educated

Indian leadership so that we can think beyond the college degree to a broader concept of education."⁴³

Poor People's Campaign

The Southern Christian Leadership Conference (SCLC) and Dr. Martin Luther King Jr. began to plan the Poor People's Campaign in November 1967, conceptualizing it as a massive movement to demonstrate the united economic interests and needs of poor people across the nation. They hoped and worked to create a protest that would spur both Congress and the executive branch to take policy action to provide more economic stability for the poorest people in the country. At the time—and to this day—Native Americans represented the lowest per capita income of all the racial/ethnic groups in the United States. In other words, on average we are financially the poorest of the poor. The SCLC sought organizers in many communities across the nation and presented their plans to the Joint Action Strategy Committee of the United Church of Christ. Auntie Tillie was very active on that national committee, and in the months after the presentation she committed to serving on the steering committee for the Poor People's Campaign and began outreach to her network.⁴⁴

Cambridge remembered that in the lead-up to the Poor People's Campaign, "most of the work [for the Native contingent] was done by the USS office and it was difficult. Arrangements [were made] for buses to leave Seattle and Los Angeles with Indians, and the buses would pick up Indians along the way. The buses joined in Denver and after one day, the buses left for Washington, DC. I believe we had a total of six buses and they traveled for nearly a week. Meal stops, white bigots, and other problems created a lot of memories." Most impressive to teenage me was that Auntie met Dr. King in person at planning meetings. Most impressive to middle-aged me is that Auntie took a host of Fort Berthold elders with her to Resurrection City. Elders like Mattie Grinnell, George Crow Flies High, councilwoman Rosie Crow Flies High, and my grandma Myra Baker Snow had lived lives of economic need that they transcended not only because they had a surfeit of determination and ingenuity—but because they knew they could depend on the land and its bounty, and they were "rich in intimate relatives." Auntie made sure those elders were with her in Resurrection City because they knew economic poverty and had survived even the Garrison Dam because of the web of family and clan relationships and generosities and responsibilities that had sustained the Three Tribes throughout disease, wars, droughts, and land takings.⁴⁵

The collective determination of that group of rabble-rousers added to the energy of Resurrection City. They marched and sang and connected with other activists from across the country. They demonstrated at the Supreme Court, and when the doors were locked against them, people like Rosie Crow Flies High banged against the doors shouting, "Let us in!"[46] Jerome Vanderburg (Salish), Victor Charlo (Salish), Bob Dumont (Assiniboine), and Mel Thom (Paiute) met nightly with Auntie and elders like Andrew Dreadfulwater (Cherokee), Al Bridges (Nisqually), and Martha Grass (Ponca) who were interested in planning strategy. Hank Adams and other Washington State tribal activists participated and brought publicity to their assertion of treaty fishing rights, which spurred the Justice Department to agree to review the prosecutions of tribal fisherman to identify whether Washington State had violated any federal or constitutional principles.[47]

Native America hardly agreed on participation in the Poor People's Campaign. In his manifesto *Custer Died for Your Sins*, Vine Deloria Jr. would justify his criticism of Natives who participated, dedicating an entire chapter to delineate the differences between the goals of Native and Black activism—part of which documented an incisive distinction, part of which played into anti-Black racism still rampant in Indian Country. And during the organizing for the Poor People's Campaign, often tribal councils and the National Congress of American Indians refused to participate—despite the dire poverty of nearly all tribal communities during this era. One contemporary chronicler reflected, "Tribal governments chose not to participate, perhaps because the BIA butters their bread. The National Congress of American Indians also stayed out. They sympathized with the Poor People's Campaign and felt that conditions justified the protest, but they were fearful that there might be violence. Shades of Chief Joseph!" The same chronicler also noted that "an Indian woman" at a meeting with then secretary of the interior Stewart Udall "invited him 'to come and live on my 320 acres and live on the 50 cents an acre for a year's grazing lease. Then your people can tell us how much we have to lose by joining the Poor People's Campaign.'"[48]

During the testimony described above and attributed to "an Indian woman," Auntie Tillie rejected the limitations of the white gaze and white assumptions. Her speech repeatedly derided the paternalistic messages delivered by white bureaucrats associated with the Bureau of Indian Affairs: "One of my uncles told me the Superintendent of the Reservation told him there was too much to lose. 'Indians don't act like that. Indians don't do things like that.'" These messages assumed a limited repertoire on the part of tribal activists and tribal members and were an attempt to exacerbate and play upon racial divisions between Native Americans and African Americans. Auntie Tillie firmly rejected that division, asserting, "They mean that Indians don't work with Negroes in this country. That is racism. And I am angry.... I said I was involved in the Poor People's Campaign because Indian people are poor and the poor know no color." She ended her statement with an assertion that rejected the efforts of non-Natives and Natives alike who might attempt to silence or ignore her: "And don't tell me that I am a non-reservation Indian and I can't speak. Because my family lived in the Missouri Valley long before Columbus ever set his feet on these shores [applause and standing ovation]."[49]

I love that speech not only because Auntie was fired up and speaking truth to power but also because she defiantly rejected the limitations others tried to place on her and Native people more generally. Her reference to the thousands of years of history her community and ancestors had in the Missouri River valley not only claimed her deeper, truer right to be heard, but contrasted our community's connection to the superficial temporal connection most other Americans held with this land.

Daniel Cobb, one of the best historians of twentieth-century Native America, asserts, "The devastating impact the construction of the Garrison Dam had on Fort Berthold served as one of the impetuses for her activism, and residents in that community turned out in large numbers for the campaign."[50] Intuitively, I believe Cobb is right—Auntie's defiance of white paternalism emerged from firsthand knowledge from the fight against the dam that compliance is dangerous. But I also think the defiance and strength to speak truth to power, even if you are the only one standing, came from deep community connection, love for community, and love for our tribal lands. Auntie defied the limits of the white imagination because she knew and grew up in a Hidatsa and Mandan reality.

The energy and power of participation in the Poor People's Campaign rippled throughout Indian Country, but also specifically on Fort Berthold. Campaign participants faced backlash, particularly from the tribal council. "They couldn't understand why we would go and march with Blacks," my mother, Karol Parker recalled. "They couldn't understand that we would march at all, for anything.... They thought it was crazy and it was really outside the bounds of what was acceptable." The backlash was also rooted in anti-Black racism: "It was some racist stuff, too. It got personal."[51] But the experience of protesting in unity with powerful, articulate activists from across the country—Native advocates like Martha Grass, in addition to Black and Chicanx organizers—shifted participants' frame of reference after they returned from Washington, DC. Upon return, tribal members took participatory democracy on the reservation further, such as successfully protesting a proposal to allow a company to strip-mine the eastern portion of the reservation.[52]

A demonstration against the local BIA seemed like a challenge to the power structure of the reservation. As a teenager who had just returned from the Poor People's Campaign, my mom remembered the resulting protest and the testimony from campaign participant George Crow Flies High:

> I remember George Crow Flies High got up, there was a chalkboard there, and it was all in Hidatsa—total Hidatsa, no English at all—he was drawing, and he drew this land map, and it just got smaller and smaller and smaller. Pretty soon it was just this little, tiny thing. But it was really effective. First of all, it was visual, and it stuck in my head after how many years, but it was really effective because it showed how over the years we had been losing so much of our land as a resource, and it didn't seem like there was any help from the BIA to protect it. It really didn't seem the tribal council was either. I think they felt that, and maybe that's why they got defensive.

These protests also led to shifts in the tribal council—Rosie Crow Flies High was the first woman elected to the tribal council in 1964, but she continued to serve and was eventually elected tribal chairwoman in 1972–73 and 1974–78. My own grandma, Myra Baker Snow, ran for council after returning from the Poor People's Campaign, and won to serve from 1970–72 and 1973–78. On council my grandma addressed issues like Native rancher access to FHA funding and controversial issues such as the practice of tribal members leasing grazing land from the tribe only to sublease it to non-Native ranchers, who overstocked the acreage and let their cattle eat the prairie to the dirt.[53]

The return home after the Poor People's Campaign spurred change on the reservation, but also in the projects in which Auntie Tillie invested. In addition to remaking the USS into a fully Native organization, she deployed the activist training from the campaign in Denver.

Littleton

If historians mention the Littleton, Colorado, occupation today, they most often group it with protests and takeovers beginning with Alcatraz, ending with

Wounded Knee, and including Seattle, Chicago, Fort Lawton, Ellis Island, and the Trail of Broken Treaties. Bruce Davies, one of the key organizers of the Littleton BIA takeover, wrote, "One fact that stands out, as I ponder Littleton, was the small number of participants in these early protests. There were at most fifty demonstrators who participated in the Littleton protest. They were mostly USS students, USS staff, and friends and relatives." Davies compared that number to the seventy-eight protestors who occupied Alcatraz, or the relatively small numbers of tribal members who began the fish-ins. He concluded, "In those early days small numbers caused big changes."[54]

Arguably, despite relatively less media coverage, the Littleton protests effected further-reaching change for Native America than even the most famous occupations like Alcatraz or Wounded Knee. The Alcatraz and Wounded Knee occupations raised public awareness and continue to inspire activists today, but the Littleton occupation directly changed implementation of BIA policy and gave legal teeth to Indian preference. The Littleton occupation and picketing in 1970 instigated a chain of events that led to the 1974 Supreme Court decision *Morton v. Mancari*, which confirmed the legality of BIA hiring and promotion preferences for members of federally recognized tribes. The unanimous decision asserted, "The preference, as applied, is granted to Indians not as a discrete racial group, but rather, as members of quasi-sovereign tribal entities whose lives and activities are governed by the BIA in a unique fashion"—and is one of the cornerstones of federal Indian law that supports legislation like the Indian Child Welfare Act (ICWA) and undergirds executive standards that recognize tribal sovereignty to this day.[55]

At age nineteen, Davies led the protest organizing. On break from his first year at Wesleyan, he was hanging out at the USS offices when the topic of the ongoing discrimination at the Littleton BIA came up—and he suggested a protest. Davies remembered, "Everyone thought that was a good idea. They said, 'If you go ahead and get other people to buy into it, we'll join in too.' So, I went to the local Indian organizations and got them all to support it." Auntie Tillie's experiences at the Poor People's Campaign may have played a part in their collective decision to move forward with the protest. Davies concluded, "I'm sure she had told us—I don't remember, but she probably told us about her experiences in those demonstrations. That's probably what prompted me to think that we should try demonstrations here."[56]

Although the 1934 passage of the Indian Reorganization Act established Indian preference in hiring, non-Natives in the BIA reinterpreted the law to maintain a status quo in which tribal members filled entry-level positions and non-Natives dominated supervisory and policy-making positions. Auntie Tillie knew several Native employees at the Littleton BIA site who had experienced racial discrimination in hiring or promotion despite the national policy of Indian preference. A March 12, 1970, press release issued by the NIYC contained a description of the complaints by tribal members employed at the Littleton BIA, known as the Littleton Twelve. In addition to conflicts of sick and annual leave inequities between tribal and non-Native employees, the press release asserted,

> The complainants assert that the BIA Littleton Plant Management Engineering Center is run like a private refuge where non-Indian employees can draw enormous salaries and gain unreasonable privileges while paying only lip-service to their duty to the impoverished Indian people it serves, and to the qualified Indians it employs. . . .
>
> The complainants further assert that the office is not only ineffective but has a lackadaisical contempt both of its Indian employees and of its Indian clients. But its Indian employees and clients are linked in a continuing pattern of abuse, contempt, discrimination, and financial mismanagement woven by the BIA. . . .
>
> The Complaint also alleges that job descriptions are rewritten for Anglos so that they can be qualified while the letter of the law is applied to Indians.[57]

Four days later, the entire USS office was picketing outside the Littleton BIA with community allies. Of the thirty to forty participants, Davies estimated that about half knew each other from being in the USS orbit: "Most of those were people who knew Tillie or were United Scholarship students." The other half came from the larger Denver Native community and wanted to support the action. Davies also remembered, "Most of the chanting was being led by Tillie and [Patricia Baker-Benally]. Because of their experience with the Poor People's Campaign, they knew all these songs, and chants, and cheers. They were the ones who were teaching us how to do that stuff."[58]

Davies recalled the details of the protest in matter-of-fact tones: "It was the picket line originally. We did that for a few days, and then we decided to go in and take over the office because they weren't responding to us. We just went in and took it over, and they vacated." Leaders of the nascent American Indian

Figure 7.3. Protesting the Littleton BIA. *Left to right*: unknown protester, Tillie Walker, Patricia Baker-Benally, and Lynda Bernal. Getty Images.

Movement (AIM) like Vernon Bellecourt participated at the time of takeover. Davies remembered that as they were about to occupy the building after the few days of picketing, "Suddenly, Vernon and his brother showed up there with about four, or five, or six real husky ex-con-looking guys and told the BIA, in their interest, to vacate the premises. The BIA guys took off. They didn't really threaten violence, but they looked pretty scary." Davies believes that at the time of the protest, Vernon Bellecourt had been working as a bookkeeper in Denver. And despite Vernon's brother Clyde seeking press coverage from the protest, claiming that he was "in Denver to advise the Indians as to how best to reform—but not destroy—the bureau,"[59] neither Bellecourt stayed around for the actual occupation and the rest of the picketing. Davies remembered about the Bellecourts, "Then they left. I don't know what happened to them after that."[60]

The protest began on March 16 when the demonstrators started picketing and BIA employees called the police to remove them. The March 17 edition of the *Denver Post* covered the protests along with a photograph of Auntie Tillie, my Auntie Pattie, and another former USS student and current USS staff member, Lynda Bernal. The caption read, "The women were loudest in voicing their displeasure at BIA management."

The accompanying article related, "Tillie Walker, a Mandan, called the Washington BIA office and demanded to speak with Commissioner Louis R. Bruce. Bruce was out of the office, however, and she talked with another BIA official, Lyman Babby."[61] Louis Bruce, the commissioner of Indian affairs appointed by President Richard Nixon, represented somewhat of a lightning rod for the protest. The protestors burned him in effigy on March 20, and they demanded his removal with the justification, "The Republican Administration has been most concerned they chose an American Indian who was a Republican and have chosen for us a man who has no concern for the welfare of Indians." Beyond the Republican cronyism they felt he represented, the protesters believed that he was out of touch with the needs of Native people across the country. A *New York Times* interview quoted Auntie Tillie: "He's supposed to be an Indian, but he came to Washington from Greenwich Village.... When you've grown up like a white person and have never been part of an Indian community, you don't seem to really care."[62]

According to the protestors' chronology, on March 18 the pickets began at 11:30 a.m., and by 4:30 p.m. the occupation of the building began. Documents from the activists identified the occupying protestors as Bruce [Davies] (Sioux), Pat Baker (Blackfeet), Lynda Bernal (Taos Pueblo), James Jones Jr. (Cherokee), John Gill (Sioux), Rick Buckanaga (Sioux), Virginia Reeves (Diné), Duane Bird Bear (Hidatsa), Linda Benson (Diné), Harry Buckanaga (Sioux), Madelyn Boyer (Shoshone-Bannock).[63] Davies remembers the occupation as orderly:

> We pretty much tried to keep from damaging or messing with anything. The only thing we did that was odd was that we answered the phones. People would call in, and we'd answer the phone, and we'd talk to other BIA people telling them what's going on. Amongst the BIA people, they all got interested in it, so we were getting a lot of phone calls from all over the country.... We'd say hello, and they'd say, "Is Joe there?" We'd say, "No, we took over. We're protestors. We're in charge now" [chuckles].[64]

By March 19 the *Denver Post* reported that the BIA had sent an investigator to Denver to document and consider the protestors' accusations, which not only included the complaints lodged by the Littleton Twelve, but also accusations of BIA financial mismanagement by the protesters.[65] Their remediation demands included full implementation of Indian preference in hiring, as well as a guarantee for cross-training and/or promotion for tribal members within one year of hiring; training programs and a time table for full employment of Indians; the establishment of an intra-agency review board to adjudicate fair treatment of Native employees; the removal of BIA area offices, which they characterized as administrative bloat; and the specific removal of Louis Bruce and the non-Native Littleton employees accused of discriminatory practices. Finally, the protestors demanded that the BIA contract with Indian organizations and agencies in urban areas to provide services, and that the BIA provide "$50,000 to investigate the Bureau of Indian Affairs Adult Vocational Training Program and the Relocation Program. The emphasis on these programs in BIA have caused hardships on Indian people and must be rectified."[66]

On March 20, the BIA investigator—Barney Old Coyote (Crow), who worked as an assistant area director at the Sacramento office—arrived. The protestors' chronology narrated his arrival:

> 8:00 p.m. By darkness, Barney Old Coyote . . . come to relay the message that Commissioner Bruce is arriving in Denver and is willing to meet with representatives that evening if possible. The Indian people inform Mr. Old Coyote that they have been waiting since Monday to hear from the Commissioner, that they are tired, and that they definitely will not see him at his convenience that evening. Further inform Mr. Old Coyote that Commissioner must meet with the people at large, meeting set for 10:00 a.m.[67]

Within a few days, Old Coyote would be detailed to the Littleton office to act in place of the Littleton non-Native employees accused of discrimination, as Commissioner Bruce put them on leave in response to the demands of protestors. Old Coyote attempted to restore negotiations and order but ended up inflaming the ire of protestors when on March 24 he met the local urban Indian organization in Denver, the White Buffalo Council, and along with assuring them that his primary purpose at Littleton was "to maintain the operation of the Plant," he also characterized the occupying activists as "manipulating the press."[68] The following day, Old Coyote told the *Denver Post* that "he believes the demonstrators have made their point and that it is no longer necessary for them to protest in order to get an audience with federal officials."[69] And near the end of the occupation on March 29, Old Coyote also taped a local radio talk show with another BIA employee, and "declared local demonstrators to be 'youngsters' and notes that the Reservation Indians have not been consulted. Implies that all Denver Indians have never set foot on reservation land." The protestors documented their riposte: "Both he and [fellow BIA employee] Mr. Freeman neglect to mention that no Reservation Indians were consulted about Relocation and AVT [adult vocational training]."[70]

Commissioner Bruce did arrive on March 21 to negotiate with the occupiers at what they now termed the "Indians for National Liberation Building," and acceded to some of their demands (although not the one that called for him to be removed as commissioner). During the negotiations, he declared that there would be no arrests, but at 4:15 p.m. the police entered the building and arrested nine people: James Jones Jr., Linda Benson, Richard Buckanaga, Lynda Bernal, Virginia Reeves, Madelyn Boyer, John Gill, Duane Bird Bear, and Patricia Baker. They had to spend the weekend in jail and were arraigned on March 23 with a trial set for June 22. Their fellow protesters gathered to show support at the courthouse, and then proceeded back to the BIA building, where six more people occupied the building. Brenda Mitchell, Geraldine Shangreau, Bruce Davies, Gerald Gill, Brenda Cuthair, and Harry Buckanaga were arrested and carried out of the building by 7:30 p.m.[71]

Over the next week, the police arrested more protesters, but the media coverage ebbed. The internal documentation by the activists proves more interesting than the *Denver Post* coverage. For example, on March 26 the chronology notes, "Stare-in, Part II. James Jones excels once more." The following day, amid continuing negotiations during which Auntie Tillie, Bob Dumont, Duane Bird Bear, and Gerald Wilkinson declared they would not leave the building until they heard from the secretary of the interior, the protestors' chronology documented that at 4:30 p.m. that "the word 'dialogue' has been uttered by one member of the BIA 43 times since 11:00 a.m." After that the *Denver Post* largely ceased to cover the occupation, although it did last until April 1, when the commissioner of Indian affairs declared the Littleton building to be closed to everyone.[72]

The protest had ended, but the battle was far from over. Bruce Davies returned to Wesleyan and his college studies, but Auntie Tillie approached Harris Sherman to litigate on behalf of the Littleton Twelve. And after the Littleton protest, the commissioner of Indian affairs made policy changes affirming the principle of Indian preference not just in hiring but also in promotion. This seeming expansion of the practice of Indian preference led three non-Native BIA employees to file a class-action lawsuit claiming that Indian preference violated their civil rights by discriminating based on race, in violation of the 1972 Equal Employment Opportunity Act and the 1964 Civil Rights Act. The US District Court for New Mexico agreed with the non-Native employees and decided that the Indian preference portion of the IRA was implicitly repealed by the 1972 act. But Harris Sherman and Harry Sachse eventually won an appeal of the New Mexico district court decision in front of the US Supreme Court, successfully arguing that not only was implicit repeal an inappropriate standard to apply, but that Indian preference in the BIA and Indian Health Service did not constitute a racial preference, but a political one, based on the nation-to-nation relationship between the federal government and tribal governments.[73]

Sherman and Auntie Tillie would collaborate several more times during the 1970s, such as on a case to preserve tuition-free status for Native students at Fort Lewis College per its status as a land-grant institution. Later, Sherman would serve Colorado as the executive director of the Department of Natural Resources and the Obama administration as an undersecretary for the Department of Agriculture. While Bruce Davies was in law school at the University of Denver, Sherman gave a lecture and remembered Davies from the Littleton protest. "[Sherman] remembered me and asked me, 'How is Superwoman? That's my nickname for Tillie.'"[74]

The USS in the 1970s

The USS assumed a more structural approach to its work in its next decade. By the time of the Littleton protest, the USS employed nine staff members and found funding for summer internships and school-year fellows. Former students who became well-respected leaders in Indian Country cycled through the USS offices as interns or fellows or served on its board of directors. My uncle Alan Parker (Cree), Gloria Emerson (Diné), Charles Geboe (Sioux), Duane Bird Bear, Celine Buckanaga (Sioux), Della Williams (Papago), Roger Buffalohead (Ponca), Charles Cambridge, Bruce Davies, and Tillie's longtime collaborator Bob Dumont all contributed to the intellectual and activist community at the USS. A list of "distinguished USS alumni" from the 1970–72 Biennial Report included Anne Rainer (Taos Pueblo), Phillip Sam Deloria (Lakota), Lorraine Misiaszek (Colville), Sydney Beane (Dakota), Benjamin Hanley (Diné), Cecilia Kitto Wilch (Dakota), Frederick Baker (Mandan, Hidatsa), Billy Mills (Lakota), Roger Buffalohead (Ponca), Lee Cook (Ojibwe), Yvonne Knight (Ponca), Wayne Evans (Lakota), Edward Lonefight (Mandan),

Pete Azure (Tsimshian), George Crossland (Osage), and Eloise Dennison DeGroat (Diné), among others.[75]

The 1972 annual report included a letter from the executive director that summarized the massive shift in Native higher education since Auntie Tillie had entered college: "In the early 1950's there were only 400 Native American college students, by 1970 the number had grown to more than 20,000 Native American students in college. The majority of these students need total or almost total financial aid in order to survive in college." But the USS budget was shrinking, both due to rampant inflation and to the relatively fewer philanthropic donations available to Native organizations as the new Red Power media experts in the American Indian Movement achieved ascendancy. Charles Cambridge recalled, "A lot of Indian organizations, if you look at the time that Tillie left USS, the funding for Indian programs just fell through the floor. Money was not around as much and the American Indian Movement, being the sexy . . . politically correct movement. It showed Indians as warriors [laughs]. It fulfilled every white fantasy of an Indian [chuckles]."[76] And while the USS still ran summer internships for its students, in an economically difficult time Auntie Tillie's focus began to shift away from philanthropic donations toward the relatively plush budgets under- or poorly utilized by the BIA.

The USS had worked closely with the BIA scholarship program for a decade, as the USS helped students braid their scholarship dollars with funding from additional sources. In a 1970 letter Auntie Tillie wrote to Franklin Johnson in the Office of Indian Education, she reminded him,

> As you are probably aware 1300 Indian students did not receive Bureau of Indian Affairs grants this past year, although they were eligible. Over the years we have worked closely with the Bureau scholarship program and we have continually stressed the fact that intensive long range planning must be done in this area. It is not simply a matter of handing out funds, but it requires matching educational opportunities and training to the development of Indian communities. The Bureau has refused to structure their scholarship program to meet this need.[77]

In the proposal submitted with the letter to Johnson, the USS also identified mismanagement of funding in the BIA job placement and adult vocational training (AVT) programs, which received $15.6 million and $25 million respectively in fiscal year 1971. The proposal compared that amount to the $3.8 million allocated for BIA college scholarships, and asked, "Is the $40 million appropriated in a sensible manner?"

The proposal described a $400,000 grant given to a vocational training school in Denver, noting, "It is only coincidental that the director of the school is a good friend of Rep. Ben Reifel of South Dakota and Mr. Reifel happened to sponsor and push through this appropriation." That $400,000 grant funded fifty Native students to begin the drafting program, but attrition was high—only twenty-six students remained in the program. "At this rate, each student was given an $8,000 grant for vocational training. This is in addition to the living stipends provided for each participant by the BIA. The average grant for a college student is $868.00 a year." It seems likely that USS staff and Auntie Tillie imagined what they could do for a much wider group of students with a grant of that size—if only the federal structures that doled out the funding had chosen to deploy it in an evidence-based way, rather than to have been guided by cronyism.

Some of the frustration with the mismanagement of Native higher education monies or BIA mismanagement in general may have been funneled into an occasional zine called *Guts and Tripe* published by "the Coalition of American Indian Citizens." The publication's Rhetoric Department listed Auntie Tillie, Patricia Baker, Lynda Bernal, Robert V. Dumont Jr., and Melvin D. Thom. "BULLshit" titled the first interior page of the zine, which included an explanation of why the publication was named *Guts and Tripe*. The Rhetoric Department wrote, "Each week brings new problems in Indian affairs, we continually learn of rip offs of Indian monies by organizations and persons who have no interest or concern for Indian people, and the situation at home remains the same.... 9/10s of the talk (discussions, conferences, meetings, reports, etc.) one hears in Indian affairs is pure BULLSHIT. We feel we have to get at origins, where it is manufactured."[78]

The 1972 issue took aim at the installation of BIA leadership removed from the tribal experience:

> Urban Indians now dominate the Indian scene, i.e. Lee Cook, Chippewa from Minneapolis, former member of the BIA "New Team," is president of the National Congress of American Indians; Louis R. Bruce, Mohawk-Sioux from Greenwich Village, New York, still holds the title of Commissioner of Indian Affairs; Ernest Stevens, Oneida from Los Angeles, Director of BIA Economic Development; Sandy McNabb, who is frantically searching for his Indian background from Long Island, New York, is Director of the Office of Engineering & Construction in BIA.

But the 1972 issue truly focused on "the contract for $225,000 being promoted in BIA for the new law school with Edgar Cahn, of OUR BROTHER'S KEEPER fame, is establishing at Antioch College, Ohio, with a $1 million grant from [the Office of Economic Opportunity]. The $225,000 BIA contract will be for 20–25 Indian students accepted this fall at Cahn's law school" and "will deprive another 200 Indian students from going to college this fall." The remainder of the issue consisted of a parody of reportage that pilloried BIA bureaucrats who were obsessed with taking down "Wilma" (likely Wilma Mankiller) and seeing her behind every dispute, but who were unable to provide a definition for the Nixon administration's new policy of tribal self-determination. In one section a "Bureaucrat" defined self-determination as when "impartial whites run Indian affairs. What kind of operation do you think we would have if we allowed Indians to handle their own affairs." But it also lampooned Indian militants:

> INDIAN MILITANT I will fight to the death for a college in Ohio's right to work in Indian affairs. That's what Indian self-determination is all about, isn't it? I mean if our friends can't work with us, tell us what to do, where to go, how to act, how will we know? . . . We already showed how we operate when we endorsed "Our Keeper's Brother" without reading it. If you think that we're going to let you make us consider abstract things like policies and programs, you're crazy. We've got to keep on those airplanes, man. Right on.

The issue also snarked, "INDIAN SELF-DETERMINATION is laying down your life for a white friend to run Indian affairs."[79]

In 1970 the BIA funneled its education dollars to the entity that became the American Indian Graduate Center (AIGC) and combined with a decline in private donors the USS found it harder to raise money. Auntie Tillie left the USS sometime after 1974 to do fieldwork for a University of Denver Indian child welfare study and continued her national work in the United Church of Christ. By 1976 she moved back to Fort Berthold, likely partially to provide support for her mother, Mercy, who was entering her mid-seventies.

Tribal Council/JTAC

At home, Auntie continued her activism—this time by following in her father's footsteps and running for tribal council. Fort Berthold voters elected her to council from 1978 to 1982 to serve as secretary; from 1982 to 1986 as vice chair;

and from 1986 to 1988 as a councilwoman. She returned to a vastly changed community. My mother recalled,

> When she came back from Denver, she was just shocked at how things had just spread out. The relationships of the families were not as close as they once were, and it was moving down a different track. . . . She had been away right after that time at college, and then working away. When she came back, she saw how things had changed—which, to me, it was just kind of, "This is the way it is." To her, she was comparing it with what she knew.[80]

In her time on tribal council, Auntie Tillie, councilwoman Marie Wells, tribal chairwoman Alyce Spotted Bear, and tribal attorney Ray Cross—a former USS student—worked to represent and gain compensation for the true cost the Garrison Dam had on our communities. When an announcement went out in 1984 that the North Dakota State Water Commission would hold hearings on the impact of the project on North Dakota communities, Spotted Bear directed Cross to attend the hearings in the hopes that the Three Affiliated Tribes would be first to benefit from any additional compensation. Auntie Tillie attended the hearings due to her own interest, and when she saw the state commission refuse to entertain Cross's testimony, she centered the hearings on the tribal council agenda the next day. Although Cross thought the insertion of tribal testimonies into the hearings unlikely, Auntie Tillie and Wells refused to let the issue die. In Paul VanDevelder's account of the time, Spotted Bear attested, "Marie and Tillie were tight. Once they'd made up their minds, you couldn't get a knife blade between them." VanDevelder recounted Auntie Tillie's argument:

> Let us never forget the people in these three tribes whose lives were destroyed by the Garrison Dam. We all know people who are still living with the horror of dislocation and disintegration in their families and communities. I say the dead have a right to be heard. I believe we have a moral obligation to make certain that no opportunity is missed to set this right. Raymond is probably right. We probably won't get to first base. But we'll never know if we don't try.[81]

Cross, Spotted Bear, Wells, and Auntie Tillie negotiated state and national politics with the outcome of a Joint Tribal Advisory Committee (JTAC) formed specifically to center tribal experiences and losses on the Pick-Sloan Plan. By February 1986, JTAC held hearings at Fort Berthold that lasted two days before a packed audience. Emerson Murry, the non-Native chairman of the committee, later said, "I have to say those two days in New Town were as deeply moving as anything I've ever experienced. I've been on a lot of commissions, and I have never heard more authentic testimony." Marie Wells gave moving testimony on the impact of the Garrison Dam, and the JTAC's completed report eventually resulted in an additional $143 million in compensation for the land takings associated with the dam.[82]

I didn't know most of this before I wrote this epilogue, because I became close to Auntie Tillie a decade or so after her advocacy regarding JTAC. My mom sent me to stay with Auntie Tillie out in Independence in high school, and I was awkward and shy. I never asked her enough questions or listened enough. In time we grew close and had fun tooling around the northern plains together—stopping at the little drive-ins that don't seem to exist anymore for a fresh hamburger and (her favorite) a hot fudge sundae. She was funny and insightful and wise and forgiving. I helped her dry corn and thresh beans and plant gardens. She knew everybody, and even the white people in the area had nothing but respect for her—unusual during that time and to this day in North Dakota. She would rope me into random projects like decorating egg-shaped cakes for a bake sale with her fellow instigator Celeste Witham (who made the most delicious yeast rolls I've ever eaten) or making endless Christmas cookies to send out to family. She would take me to visit her hilarious and formidable buddy Wanda Fox or cook up fried chicken and potato salad to meet Rosemarie Mandan for a picnic in the badlands. Rosemarie, who gave an interview for this project that more than any other made pre–Garrison Dam Fort Berthold visceral for me, was as kind as she was strong—perhaps a shared trait among Mandan, Hidatsa, and Arikara women. Many of the people I interviewed for this book first knew me as the awkward teenager hanging around with Auntie Tillie. When I was in graduate school and beginning work on this project, I traveled home to stay with Auntie as often as possible. She helped me contact interviewees and cooked meals of corn soup, frybread, berry pudding, and mint tea or coffee to bring with me for the interview—part of the Mandan and Hidatsa protocol when you ask someone for a favor. She taught and supported me beyond what one can expect in the non-Native world. It was just who she was.

The memories of my interviewees convey all these facets of Auntie—humor, patience, energy, care. Bruce Davies remembered her telling him, "A newspaper article described me as a tribal elder and my brother, Hans, wouldn't let me forget it. He said "Gee, I wish I could be a tribal elder."[83] My mom remembered Auntie unwearyingly helping her understand Hidatsa relationship structures, how much closer we are to each other than are those in Euro-American norms, and the right way to treat your relatives: "That was one of the most important things that she conveyed to me, was just how closely related we are.... I think that's probably the greatest gift, to have [Mandan-Hidatsa relationship norms] conveyed to me and done in a way where she didn't get impatient. She was just real tolerant." My aunt Patricia Baker-Benally agreed:

> She had a great deal of empathy for people, but she also had a very fearless, purposeful movement within her own self; I never got the sense that she ever turned back or looked back. She had a great, great deal of empathy for people, but it was never anything she ever flaunted. It was a quiet regard for that person that she carried. I really believe that quiet regard was a traditional relationship that was part of her being.

Auntie Pattie remembered attending Dr. King's funeral with Auntie Tillie. Because of her work on the Poor People's Campaign, Auntie Tillie received passes allowing her and one other person to attend the funeral services inside Ebeneezer Baptist Church. On the morning of the service, Auntie Tillie and Auntie Patty stood near the entrance to the church and watched as world leaders entered the building. An African American couple stood near them, and Auntie Tillie turned to them and asked them if they were members of the congregation. They were, but due to limited space they did not have the passes granting entrance to the funeral services. Auntie Patty remembered, "She handed her two passes, which was in form of a telegram, to them so that they could attend. That was the kind of person she was." Later, Auntie Patty remembered, "When she passed, the first thing that came to me is my North Star just dimmed."[84]

Many of these memories hold an unusual clarity. In the moment, we were unaware that these would become what we thought of to remember the essence of Auntie. My mom remembered helping Auntie shell corn for drying out in Independence:

> It's like one of those memories that is just like, it's crystal clear in my mind. We had tarps spread out on the ground and we were sitting on the ground shelling. We didn't shell corn right away; we were just cooking it and then we'd spread it out and it'd cool off and then we're eating at

the same time [laughs]. That was done at Independence in front of Aunt Mercy's house. The sky was so clear and then the sunset—it was just a beautiful evening and the memory of it is just so clear and colorful in my mind.

Bruce Davies remembered a calm, comfortable evening he and a girlfriend spent with Auntie Tillie and Grandma Mercy: "I remember the smell of food cooking in the kitchen while we sat on the sofa in the living room. Mercy was knitting and would occasionally make a low-voiced comment to Tillie in Indian and Tillie would reply. Maternal warmth blended with the soft evening lighting and the cozy atmosphere to suggest a nostalgic memory of a possible alternative childhood."[85]

Davies also remembered her parting gift to him when he visited her in North Dakota. He recalled, "She gave me a bag of dried corn that she had grown in her garden and instructed me on how to prepare corn soup. The corn was a variety that the river Indians had grown prior to European contact. She was trying to preserve this old line of corn in her flourishing garden."[86] Auntie did this is so many ways—preserving, cultivating, and passing on the human truths of our indigenous ways.

Auntie Tillie intuitively knew that these were the tools, weapons, and sustenance we could deploy in our battles against the abuses and injustices wrought by settler colonialism—our relationships with each other, being good relatives to each other, laughing, puncturing large egos through humor and humility, working even when we get tired, building connections across differences, and cultivating our youth. None of these things can be done in front of a camera or documented for a report, and rarely do they leave definitive evidence in archives. But they are the foundation of indigenous survival. And they are the reason that this book and twentieth-century Native history is not a tragedy, even though tragic events and processes continue to occur to Native peoples throughout the hemisphere. Ihgaa, maacigidaac. Thank you, Auntie, for everything you taught us.

Notes

Introduction

1. Robert Merrill, "Mrs. Wilde," June 14, 1950, Sol Tax—Fort Berthold Action Anthropology Project, National Anthropological Archives, Smithsonian Institute (hereafter Tax Anthropology Project).

2. "Indians with 'Heavy Hearts' Cede Lands," *Minot Daily News*, May 24, 1948.

3. Wolfe, *Settler Colonialism and the Transformation of Anthropology*; Krasner, "Sovereignty: Political," 14706–9; Foucault, *Security, Territory, Population*, 296; Nelson, *Sovereignty and the Limits of the Liberal Imagination*, 77–146; Elshtain, *Sovereignty*; Lupel, *Globalization and Popular Sovereignty*, 12–18; Hardt and Negri, *Empire*; Elmer, *On Lingering and Being Last*, 3–5.

4. Alfred, *Peace, Power, Righteousness*; Coffey and Tsosie, "Rethinking the Tribal Sovereignty Doctrine"; Smith, "U.S. Empire and the War against Native Sovereignty," 177–91; Wolfe, "Settler Colonialism and the Elimination of the Native"; Krasner, "Sovereignty: Political"; Bruyneel, *Third Space of Sovereignty*; Wolfe, "After the Frontier"; Coulthard, *Red Skin, White Masks*; Moreton-Robinson, *White Possessive*.

5. Elshtain, *Sovereignty*; Nelson, *Sovereignty and the Limits of the Liberal Imagination*, 77, 146; Lupel, *Globalization and Popular Sovereignty*, 12; Schrijer, *Sovereignty over Natural Resources*, 1997; Wolfe, "Settler Colonialism and the Elimination of the Native."

6. Dennison, "Stitching Osage Governance into the Future," 2013; Denetdale, "Value of Oral History."

7. Chakrabarty, *Provincializing Europe*, 3–46; Elmer, *On Lingering and Being Last*, 133–45; Anderson, "Preemption, Precaution, Preparedness," 777–98; Baldwin, "Whiteness and Futurity," 172–87.

8. Parker, "Photographing the Places of Citizenship," 57–86.

9. Patai, "U.S. Academics and Third World Women," 138–44; Waziyatawin, "Power of the Spoken Word," 104; Shuman, *Other People's Stories*, 5; Anderson and Jack, "Learning to Listen," 138; Waziyatawin, *Remember This!*, 38; Freund, "Towards an Ethics of Silence?"; Jessee, "Limits of Oral History"; Sheftel and Zembrzycki, "Who's Afraid of Oral History?"

10. Waziyatawin, "Grandmother to Granddaughter," 34–5; Denetdale, "Value of Oral History"; Trimble, Quinlan, and Sommer, *American Indian Oral History Manual*; Mahuika, *Rethinking Oral History and Tradition*.

11. Shuman, *Other People's Stories*, 3–4.
12. Deloria, introduction to *Speaking of Indians*, xix.
13. Waziyatawin, "Power of the Spoken Word," 105–6.
14. This respect is also based in my interactions with Native community educators. Michelle Pasena (Hopi), who worked at the American Indian Graduate Center (AIGC), explains that Natives educated in western academic institutions must realize that Native communities are filled with elders and community members who have PhDs in language, traditional culture, traditional religion, and other specialties, and that we should enter Native communities with the humility that this realization produces. Gramsci, "Intellectuals," 6–23.
15. Anderson and Jack, "Learning to Listen," 20–22.
16. Rabinow, "Anthropological Observation and Self-Formation," 108–9; Borland, "'That's Not What I Said,'" 73.
17. White, "Using the Past," 222–23.
18. Wilson, *Buffalo Bird Woman's Garden*.
19. Tuck and Gaztambide-Fernández, "Curriculum, Replacement, and Settler Futurity," 72–89.

Chapter 1

1. Thiessen, Wood, and Jones, "Sitting Rabbit 1907 Map," 145–67; Warhus, *Another America*, 43–52.
2. VanDevelder, *Coyote Warrior*, 59.
3. Cronon, *Nature's Metropolis*; Basso, *Wisdom Sits in Places*; Casey, "How to Get from Space to Place"; Scott, *Seeing like a State*. Maher, *Nature's New Deal*, defines landscape as nonhuman nature altered by human labor. As such, it serves as the nexus of interactions between society and the natural environment. Landscape can represent place, but it is also the canvas upon which states and large structures enact expressions of their governance. Seamon, *Life Takes Place*.
4. Pierce, Martin, and Murphy, "Relational Place-Making," 2011.
5. Thiessen, Wood, and Jones, "Sitting Rabbit 1907 Map," 145–67; Reitz field notes, 1951, Tax Anthropology Project.
6. Basso, *Wisdom Sits in Places*; Casey, "How to Get from Space to Place."
7. De Certeau, *Practice of Everyday Life*; Basso, *Wisdom Sits in Places*; Casey, "How to Get from Space to Place"; Kivelson, *Cartographies of Tsardom*.
8. Wood, *Interpretation of Mandan Culture History*, 4–9; Manning, *Grassland*, 40–41.
9. Wood, *Interpretation of Mandan Culture History*, 7; Manning, *Grassland*, 39–40.
10. Sherow, *Grasslands of the United States*, 1–28.
11. Wedel, *Prehistoric Man on the Great Plains*, 158–60; Manning, *Grassland*, 68; Wood, *Interpretation of Mandan Culture History*, 7–8.
12. Wood, *Interpretation of Mandan Culture History*, 4–9.
13. Wood, 4–9; Manning, *Grassland*, 15–16.
14. Missouri River Natural Resources Committee and US Geological Survey, *Missouri River Environmental Assessment Program*; Manning, *Grassland*, chap. 4; Waldram, *As Long as the Rivers Run*, 5.

15. Wood, *Origins of the Hidatsa Indians*, 27–42; Bowers, *Hidatsa*, 297–307.

16. Reitz, June 12, 1952, 3, Tax Anthropology Project; Myra Snow, interview by Eric Wolf, June 25, 1990.

17. Sherow, *Grasslands of the United States*, 25–27; Wood, *Interpretation of Mandan Culture History*, 14–20.

18. Wood, 14–20.

19. Wood, 20–21; Wilson, *Buffalo Bird Woman's Garden*; VanDevelder, *Coyote Warrior*, 22–3.

20. Hanson, *Hidatsa Culture Change*, 71–89; Sherow, *Grasslands of the United States*, 42–65; Hämäläinen, "Rise and Fall of Plains Indian Horse Cultures," 833–62; Calloway, *One Vast Winter Count*.

21. Sherow, *Grasslands of the United States*, 42, 45.

22. Calloway, *One Vast Winter* Count; McLaughlin, "Nation, Tribe, and Class," 101–38.

23. Calloway, *One Vast Winter Count*; Mancall, *American Encounters*; Manning, *Grassland*, 68.

24. Lefebvre, *Production of Space*.

25. Lewis, *Cartographic Encounters*; Kivelson, *Cartographies of Tsardom*; Short, *Cartographic Encounters*, 2009; Lennox, *Homelands and Empires*; Ojala and Nordin, "Mapping Land and People in the North"; Rose-Redwood et al., "Decolonizing the Map."

26. Scott, *Seeing like a State*.

27. Thiessen, Wood, and Jones, "Sitting Rabbit 1907 Map," 147; US Geological Survey, Biological Resources Division, "Missouri River Commission Maps."

28. Pauls, "Place of Space," 74–6.

29. Manning, *Grassland*, 69; Calloway, *One Vast Winter Count*; Eva Case, "Fort Berthold History," Harold W. Case Papers, North Dakota State Historical Society Archives (hereafter Case Papers); Sacagawea Project Board, *Our Story of Eagle Woman*.

30. Smith, *Like-a-Fishhook Village and Fort Berthold*, 4; VanDevelder, *Coyote Warrior*, 58–9; Fenn, *Encounters at the Heart of the World*.

31. Rosemarie Mandan, interview by the author, October 21, 2009; Emmarine Chase, interview by Eric Wolf, June 20, 1990; Snow interview; VanDevelder, *Coyote Warrior*, 59.

32. Hanson, *Hidatsa Culture Change*, 107–23; Meyer, *Village Indians*, 94–100; VanDevelder, *Coyote Warrior*, 60; Barthelemy, "Hushgah Adiish the Badlands Lodge."

33. Meyer, *Village Indians*, 100–101; Hannah, "Analysis of the Assimilation of White Culture by Hidatsa Indians," 57–58.

34. Meyer, *Village Indians*, 124–25; Smith, "U.S. Empire and the War against Native Sovereignty," 178. For a more contemporary example of how the spaces and places of domestic life can reflect larger community political and economic shifts, see Cattelino, "Florida Seminole Housing and the Social Meaning of Sovereignty," 699–736. See also Pauls, "Place of Space," 74–76.

35. Meyer, *Village Indians*, 125; Smith, "U.S. Empire and the War against Native Sovereignty," 179; Matthews, *Ethnography and Philology*, 11–12.

36. Thiessen, Wood, and Jones, "Sitting Rabbit 1907 Map," 152–53, 160–61.

37. Orin G. Libby to Sitting Rabbit, February 26, 1906; and C. L. Hall to O. G. Libby, [March] 27, 1906, both in Orin Grant Libby Papers, North Dakota State Historical Society Archives (hereafter Libby Papers).

38. Orin G. Libby to Sitting Rabbit, September 3, 1906, Libby Papers. In addition to his racism toward Sitting Rabbit, in 1915 Libby wrote of Arikara tribal member Red Star—whom he wanted to bring to the "Custer battlefield"—that he wanted some sort of authority over him because "there is likely to be a good deal of liquor in circulation," and "we cannot wait for him to straggle in at any time that suits him." O. G. Libby to Fort Berthold Superintendent E. W. Jermark, June 17, 1915, Fort Berthold Agency, National Archives and Records Administration, Kansas City, MO (hereafter Kansas City NARA).

39. Cronon, *Changes in the Land*.

40. Meyer, *Village Indians*, 103; VanDevelder, *Coyote Warrior*, 60–61.

41. Meyer, *Village Indians*, 118–21. "When the men go off hunting, the women cannot work in the cornfields without being raped and murdered by the Sioux" (VanDevelder, *Coyote Warrior*, 60). By 1870 treaty-making had been discontinued, so the establishment of reservations—or their modification via taking land—were negotiated locally before being sent to the executive branch to be issued as an executive order.

42. Meyer, *Village Indians*, 123–24.

43. Meyer, 113–14. The original territory as defined by the 1851 Ft. Laramie Treaty was more than twelve million acres.

44. Case, "Fort Berthold History"; VanDevelder, *Coyote Warrior*, 77.

45. Maaxiiriwiash, quoted in Wilson, *Waheenee*, 176.

46. Meyer, *Village Indians*, 134–49. The Arikaras tended to locate themselves toward the eastern side of the reservation; the Mandans, south and west of the Missouri; and the Hidatsas, in many locations but especially near Elbowoods.

47. Meyer, 149–55. Fort Berthold Indian Agent Thomas Richards to the Commissioner of Indian Affairs, February 9, 1900, Fort Berthold Agency, Kansas City NARA. McLaughlin, "Nation, Tribe, and Class," 107.

48. Sack, *Human Territoriality*, 19. See "Tribe" in Smelser and Baltes, *International Encyclopedia of the Social and Behavioral Sciences*, 15906.

49. 1899 Annual Report; and Fort Berthold Indian Agent Thomas Richards to the Commissioner of Indian Affairs, December 23, 1899, both in Fort Berthold Agency, Kansas City NARA.

50. Meyer, *Village Indians*, 155–65.

51. Meyer, 158. Local superintendent of Indian Affairs E. W. Jermark did not attempt to rule with an iron fist as did, for example, the local Indian agent at Standing Rock, but tribal members did have to petition him for permission to hold social dances. In one letter from Jermark granting permission for a Fourth of July dance to be held in the Shell Creek district, he banned tribal members from giving away "articles of an expensive nature" but did allow tribal members to give away "presents of the usual nature, including calicos, mocassins [sic], pipes and feathers." He also banned the participation of "boys under the age of twenty-five years." E. W. Jermark to Whom It May Concern, June 29, 1915, Fort Berthold Agency, Kansas City NARA.

52. Parman, "Indian and the Civilian Conservation Corps," 39–40; Meyer, *Village Indians*, 16.

53. Meyer, *Village Indians*, 186–89; VanDevelder, *Coyote Warrior*, 91.

54. Cross, "'Twice-Born' from the Waters"; Meyer, *Village Indians*, 190–95; VanDevelder, *Coyote Warrior*, 91. Oral history interviewee Alameda Baker (b. January 2, 1924)

recounted in 1997 how she was born to a large family that included two brothers and six sisters. After attending school in Elbowoods, when she was ten years old her parents decided to send her to a girls' school in Bismarck—her tenth year coinciding with one of the worst drought years on the northern plains. Alameda Baker, interview by the author, August 29, 1997. See Child, *Boarding School Seasons* for similar stories of economics influencing decision making around education.

55. Dreke Irwin, interview by the author, October 20, 2009; Mandan interview.

56. Chase interview; Cecelia Brown, interview by Eric Wolf, July 17, 1990.

57. Gilman and Schneider, *Way to Independence*, 223, 225, 250–51; Tillie Walker, interview by the author, September 29, 2009. Regarding language use, many oral history interviewees recount growing up speaking their tribal language, learning English upon entering school, but continuing to use tribal languages at home or in the community. Edwin Benson, interview by the author, August 1997. Some interviewees may not have spoken tribal languages at home—especially if their parents had gone off-reservation for schooling—but their parents would "talk Indian" to each other to communicate. Alameda Baker interview; Edwin Benson, interview by the author, July 26, 2013; Fred Baker, interview by the author, August 7, 2013; Barbara Roy, Aurelia Gillette, and Florence Gillette-Brady, interview by the author, August 7, 2013.

58. Sitting Rabbit (Little Owl) appears in Harold Case's account of Chief Sitting Crow's life. "In the fall [of 1883] [Sitting]Crow together with Bears Ghost, Spotted Bear, Young Buffalo, Little Owl, Young Wolf, Frank Packinaw, Last in Line, Spotted Eagle, and several others went to the Yellowstone to hunt eagles." The young men encountered some white men who tried to alternately steal and trade for their wagon, after which several of them pray and fast to encourage luck in their hunting. Rev. Harold Case was particularly proud of the conversions of Sitting Crow and Sitting Rabbit/Little Owl. He wrote, "The meetings this fall were in memory of Shoont Hanska, whose picture now hangs in the church, and of Little Owl and Sitting Crow, who once tortured themselves in the Sun Dance, but now are officers in the church, rejoicing in the knowledge of the true God." "Where Once Sun Dancers Whirled, They Came to Worship God—1925," Case Papers.

Chapter 2

1. Hudson, "Bridge Called Four Bears." Hudson lists the tribal leaders who spoke: Drags Wolf, Bull Head (Ben Benson), Lean Bear, Wolf Lies Down, Little Owl, White Buffalo (Robert Lincoln), Sitting Crow, and Louis Baker served as interpreter. "Three of the elders in ceremonial regalia, Ft. Berthold Reservation, ND," 00041-04863, Reverend Harold W. Case Photograph Collection, in Case Papers. Harold Case remembered the drought of 1934 thusly: "We remembered, too, the skeleton of a horse lying out on 'the North Dakota desert,' dried skin stretched taut across whitened bones and drawn back from the teeth in a ghastly grin; I mentally labeled it, 'the ghost of '34, or the spirit of the drought.'" "Two Across the River," Case Papers.

2. Petition dated February 2, 1933, Case Papers; "Dedication of the Four Bears Bridge, June 16, 1934, Elbowoods, ND," Case Photograph Collection, Case Papers.

3. "Facts about the proposed Elbowoods Bridge," Elbowoods Bridge Association, reproduced in Hudson's, "Bridge Called Four Bears."

4. Native and rural southern and western community interactions with New Deal programs illustrate similar dynamics of economically disempowered communities seizing the economic and political opportunities presented by such programs to realize local priorities with federal monies. For more examples in Native America, see Morgan, "Constructions and Contestations of the Authoritative Voice," 56–83; and Osburn, "'In a name of justice and fairness.'" For more on rural southern and western communities, see Cannon, "Power Relations," 133–60; Maher, "'Crazy Quilt Farming on Round Land,'" 319–39; and Schulman, *From Cotton Belt to Sunbelt*, 3–134.

5. Joseph Harris to William Beyer, 1936, Fort Berthold Indian Agency, Kansas City NARA.

6. Krasner, "Sovereignty: Political," 14706–9; Lyons, *X-Marks*, 2010; Fleischmann, Van Styvendale, and McCarroll, *Narratives of Citizenship*.

7. Troutman, "Citizenship of Dance," 91; Rusco, *Fateful Time*. Rusco also reminds us that the 1884 Supreme Court decision *Elk v. Wilkins* confirmed that the Fourteenth Amendment did not apply to Native Americans because they were not yet subject to the jurisdiction of the national government. For more on Eastman's views on citizenship, see Carlson, "'Indian for a While,'" 604–25; and Bruyneel, "Challenging American Boundaries," 33.

8. Bruyneel, "Challenging American Boundaries," 30–43; Rosier, *Serving Their Country*, 25–36; Vigil, *Indigenous Intellectuals*.

9. Bruyneel, "Challenging American Boundaries"; Troutman, "Citizenship of Dance," 97–103.

10. Bruyneel, "Challenging American Boundaries"; Tani, "States' Rights, Welfare Rights, and the 'Indian Problem.'"

11. Bruyneel, "Challenging American Boundaries," 30–43. For a classic community-based analysis of political activism and tribal belonging in a Northern Plains community, see Hoxie, *Parading through* History, 295–348; Isin, "Socius of Citizenship"; Fleischmann, Van Styvendale, and McCarroll, *Narratives of Citizenship*; and Tani, "States' Rights, Welfare Rights, and the "Indian Problem.'"

12. For more on Americanization efforts and citizenship in the early twentieth century, see Sanchez, *Becoming Mexican American*; Shah, *Contagious Divides*; Erman, "Puerto Rico and the Promise of United States Citizenship"; Stange, "Pittsburgh Survey"; and Cousins, "Citizenship and Selfhood," 99–105. An example of the racial discrimination from the time involving Hans Walker Sr. was related in a public speech made by Tony Moran at a Mandaree Powwow in the early 2000s. Moran remembered hearing that prominent Three Affiliated Tribes community leaders had been targeted for police harassment. In the story, Hans Walker Sr. was sentenced to community service picking up trash by the side of the road for having a broken taillight on his car—despite the minor nature of the infraction and Walker's position as an upstanding community leader. For the strategic deployment of US citizenship, see Troutman, *Indian Blues*, 49–61.

13. Kelly, "Indian Reorganization Act," 291–312; Koppes, "From New Deal to Termination," 543–66; Philp, "Termination," 165–80; Washburn, "Fifty-Year Perspective on the Indian Reorganization Act," 279–89; Biolsi, "IRA and the Politics of Acculturation," 656–59. For more on Collier and his land-related activism before entering the Bureau of Indian Affairs, see Rosier, *Serving Their Country*, 55–69. For more on Collier's pre-BIA activism and the creation of the IRA, see Prucha, *Great Father*, 940–44, 957–63.

For Collier's press release on the IRA, see "Memorandum for the press regarding the Indian Reorganization Act," February 13, 1934, Fort Berthold Indian Agency, Kansas City NARA.

14. Biolsi, "'Indian Self-Government,'" 23–28; Rusco, *Fateful Time*; Economic and Social Survey, 1934, Fort Berthold Indian Agency, Kansas City NARA.

15. Prucha, *Great Father*, 958–59; Questions on the Wheeler-Howard Bill, Elbowoods, September 30, 1934, Fort Berthold Indian Agency, Kansas City NARA.

16. Rosier, *Serving Their Country*, 36; Meyer, *Village Indians*, 160–64. Between 1890 and 1934, the federal government stole 6,867,423 acres of the Three Tribes' land. The first, largest cession was a result of an 1880 executive order that took tribal lands and granted them to the Northern Pacific Railroad. The second in 1891 resulted from Dawes; the Dawes cession took 20 percent of post-1880 executive order land base, or 228,168 acres.

17. Meyer, *Village Indians*, 195–97; Petition for Incorporation, Fort Berthold Indian Agency, Kansas City NARA; Certification of Charter, Fort Berthold Indian Agency, National Archives and Records Administration, Washington, DC (hereafter NARA). Norcini, "Political Process of Factionalism and Self-Governance," 544–90, documents such a politicization process embedded in the new IRA technologies of suffrage at Santa Clara. Weisiger, "Gendered Injustice," 437–55, explains the politicization of the Navajos as they organized against the IRA in response to Collier's Navajo Livestock Reduction program.

18. Report on Organization Work at Fort Berthold, Fieldworker Holtz to Commissioner of Indian Affairs John Collier, November 16, 1935, Fort Berthold Indian Agency, NARA.

19. Report on Organization Work at Fort Berthold.

20. Let Ballots Be Mailed, Fort Berthold Indian Agency, Kansas City NARA.

21. Three Affiliated Tribes Constitution and By-Laws, Fort Berthold Indian Agency, NARA.

22. *Taken Lands* offers the notion of "indigenous citizenship" as an alternative to characterizations of indigenous negotiations of nation-state citizenship rights and indigenous land and resource claims as "ambivalent," "strategic," "differentiated," or "hybrid." Many of these terms are used to describe the same dynamic, but this project finds aspects of these various terminologies problematic—though they do describe situations similar to what was happening at Fort Berthold. For an example of "hybrid citizenship," see Troutman, *Indian Blues* and "Citizenship of Dance." Rosier uses the term "hybrid patriotism" in *Serving Their Country*. For an exploration of "ambivalent citizenship," see Bruyneel, "Challenging American Boundaries." Biolsi's article "Imagined Geographies" characterizes indigenous insistence for the "right to be Indian and American at the same time" alternately as cultural or dual citizenship that exists within "a hybrid political space in which the simultaneous existence of two nations in the same physical space is naturalized" (252). Blackburn, "Differentiating Indigenous Citizenship," refers to a similar dynamic among the present-day Nisga'a tribe in Canada as "differentiated" citizenship.

23. Powell, Seminar Discussion, Committee on Institutional Cooperation-American Indian Studies Seminar. Hoxie provides a carefully considered and resonant explanation of the dynamics of forming tribal and US sovereignty in his chapter "Missing the Point" in *Beyond Red Power*.

24. Three Affiliated Tribes Constitution and By-Laws.

25. Minutes of the Fort Berthold Business Council, November 2, 1935, Fort Berthold Indian Agency, Kansas City NARA.

26. Telegram reporting results of constitutional ratification vote, Fort Berthold Indian Agent William Beyer to Commissioner of Indian Affairs John Collier, May 19, 1936, Fort Berthold Indian Agency, NARA.

27. Community voting results on the adoption of the IRA constitution and bylaws, May 15, 1936, Fort Berthold Indian Agency, Kansas City NARA. Three Affiliated Tribes constitution and bylaw voting results, Fort Berthold Indian Agency, NARA. The Shell Creek dissenters largely consisted of a band of the Hidatsas known as the Xo'shga (Euro-American observers referred to them as the "irreconcilables" or "seceders") after the band followed tribal leader Crow Flies High in 1870 to live off the reservation at Fort Buford. The Xo'shga remained off the reservation until 1894, when armed guard returned them to Fort Berthold. Matzko, *Reconstructing Fort Union*, 23–24; Meyer, *Village Indians*,138–40; Barthelemy, "Hushgah Adiish the Badlands Lodge."

28. For the Mekeel-Collier exchange, see Mekeel, "Appraisal of the Indian Reorganization Act," 209–17; and Collier, "Collier Replies to Mekeel," 422–26. Kelly, "Indian Reorganization Act," 291–312; Koppes "From New Deal to Termination," 543–66; Philp, "Termination," 165–80; Washburn, "Fifty-Year Perspective on the Indian Reorganization Act," 279–89; Biolsi "IRA and the Politics of Acculturation," 656–59; Morgan, "Constructions and Contestations of the Authoritative Voice," 56–83; Norcini, "Political Process of Factionalism and Self-Governance," 544–90; Weisiger, "Gendered Injustice," 437–55; Osburn, "'In a name of justice and fairness,'" 69.

29. Special Meeting of the Fort Berthold Tribal Business Council, March 18, 1937, Fort Berthold Indian Agency, Kansas City NARA.

30. Minutes of the Business Council, November 28, 1934, Fort Berthold Indian Agency, Kansas City NARA.

31. Rev. Harold Case characterized community sentiment at Fort Berthold in paternalistic but telling prose: "Self-government! We've heard it and talked, it will almost be a relief to have it. The Indians so little understand, most of them think it is something the gov't is going to hand them on a silver platter. They are not sure what, but anything with $10,000,000 attached to it is something, and something that will give them more land. A few older ones think it will bring back the old Indian ways, perhaps even the buffalo! Of course none want to give up their cars, eye glasses or false teeth, but it would be grand to have buffalo to hunt again." Correspondence, 1930–1939, Case Papers.

32. Response to Collier's Questionnaire on Tribal Organization, Fort Berthold Indian Agent William Beyer to Commissioner of Indian Affairs John Collier, July 27, 1934, Fort Berthold 066–9582, NARA.

33. Superintendent William Beyer to Commissioner of Indian Affairs John Collier, July 7, 1936, Fort Berthold Indian Agency, Kansas City NARA; William Zimmerman, Assistant Commissioner of Indian Affairs to William Beyer, Fort Berthold Agency Superintendent, July 28, 1936, Fort Berthold 066–9582, NARA.

34. Tribal Business Council election results, September 1, 1936, Fort Berthold 066–9582, NARA; 021 Wheeler Howard Act 1936–37, Fort Berthold Indian Agency, Kansas City NARA.

35. "Patent fee lands" denote lands owned by individuals—meaning that they were neither communally held by the tribe nor held in trust by the US government. Meyer, *Village Indians*, 170–76. Minutes of a meeting of the Tribal Business Committee, May 25, 1934; and *Fort Berthold Bulletin*, August 1938, both in Fort Berthold Indian Agency, Kansas City NARA. An example of the complexity of land statuses on Fort Berthold can be found in Township Maps, Fort Berthold Indian Agency, Kansas City NARA.

36. Reservation Brand Book, 1936, Fort Berthold Indian Agency, Kansas City NARA. The October 27, 1936, conference at Devils Lake was reported in the *Fort Berthold Bulletin*, November 20, 1936, Fort Berthold Indian Agency, Kansas City NARA.

37. Minutes and Resolutions Tribal Business Committee, 1934–37; and Letter regarding tribal acquisition of allotted lands, Superintendent William Beyer to Commissioner of Indian Affairs John Collier, January 27, 1938, both in Fort Berthold Indian Agency, Kansas City NARA.

38. Minutes and Resolutions Tribal Business Committee, 1934–37.

39. Regular Meeting of the Fort Berthold Tribal Business Council, August 12, 1937, Elbowoods, North Dakota; and Millie Anderson, Little Missouri/Red Butte District, Economic and Social Survey 1934, both in Fort Berthold Indian Agency, Kansas City NARA.

40. Hidatsa narratives based on oral histories and DNA testing contest the accepted narrative about Cagáagawia. Sacagawea Project Board, *Our Story of Eagle Woman, Sacagawea*.

41. Doerfler, *Those Who Belong*. Meyer, *Village Indians*, 200–202, describes a one-third increase in population between 1906 and 1932, and an additional 36 percent growth from 1932 to1946.

42. Doerfler, *Those Who Belong*.

43. The political rights of US citizenship were always explicitly tied to economic expectations. For example, in the nineteenth century through the 1920s, only Indians who were considered "productive" and "industrious" enough to manage their lands could gain the rights of citizens (Dawes Act); women were excluded from citizenship partly based on their disassociation from the public sphere of wage labor; African Americans were confined to the lower rungs of the economic ladder and denied the full rights of citizenship (Jim Crow); and immigrants could gain citizenship through being engaged with wage labor or productively using western lands (Homestead Act).

44. Minutes of the Fort Berthold Tribal Business Council Meeting, January 14, 1937, Fort Berthold Indian Agency, Kansas City NARA. Information on the clan structure from corrections from Walker interview.

45. McLaughlin, "Nation, Tribe, and Class," 107–8; Norcini, "Political Process of Factionalism and Self-Governance," 544–90.

46. For example, see the Letter of Complaints regarding Indian Judge Daniel Wolf, August 31, 1935, Fort Berthold 066–9582, NARA.

47. Petition for Reelection (no date), Fort Berthold 066–9582, NARA. Additional names attached to the petition can be found in Indian Reorganization Act, Fort Berthold Indian Agency, Kansas City NARA.

48. Voter registration lists can be found in IRA, Fort Berthold Indian Agency, Kansas City NARA. One such list is in Reitz field notes, Tax Anthropology Project.

49. June 16, 1936, Resolution against the IRA government at Fort Berthold, Fort Berthold 066-9582, NARA; F. H. Daiker, Assistant to the Commissioner of Indian Affairs to Frank Heart, Floyd Montclair, Philip Atkins, and Walter S. Face, June 24, 1936; and William Beyer, Fort Berthold Superintendent to John Collier, Commissioner of Indian Affairs, July 3, 1936, both in Fort Berthold Indian Agency, Kansas City NARA.

50. Fort Berthold Superintendent William Beyer to Commissioner of Indian Affairs John Collier, June 29, 1936, Fort Berthold Indian Agency, Kansas City NARA.

51. The Tribal Business Council election results for Shell Creek were as follows: Drags Wolf received fifty-five votes; Mark Mahto, forty votes; Robert Dancing Bull, forty votes; Leo Young Wolf, thirty-five votes; Charles Fox, nineteen votes; Michael Mason, nineteen votes.

52. In response to the accusations, Drags Wolf assured the new council that he did not circulate information on the Charles Fox candidacy, and in fact he had "cast one vote for Charles Fox." Beyer had little patience for either Mahto or Montclair, describing Mahto as "inclined to do everything he can to obstruct progress toward reorganization, especially on this reservation." Montclair, he wrote, was "a chronic troublemaker. He appears frequently in the Indian Court. At one time he was ordered off the reservation, I understand by complaints raised by his fellow tribesmen. His mentality is far below normal." Fort Berthold Superintendent William Beyer to Commissioner of Indian Affairs John Collier, September 18, 1936, Fort Berthold 066-9582, NARA. Petition, Floyd Montclair to Commissioner of Indian Affairs John Collier and Secretary of the Interior Harold Ickes, September 15, 1936, Fort Berthold 066-9582, NARA; *Fort Berthold Service Bulletin*, December 19, 1936, Fort Berthold Indian Agency, Kansas City NARA.

53. Vaughn, *Encyclopedia of American Journalism*, 323. For an example of the anti-IRA bent of *Indian Truth*, see Sniffen, "Navajo 'Self-Government'"; and Letter from Three Affiliated Tribes Tribal Business Council to M. K. Sniffen, via John Collier, July 1937; 021 IRA, Box 263, Fort Berthold Indian Agency, Kansas City NARA.

54. Three Affiliated Tribes Tribal Business Council Secretary Peter Beauchamp to Commissioner of Indian Affairs John Collier, August 11, 1938; and Fort Berthold Superintendent William Beyer to Commissioner of Indian Affairs John Collier, May 8, 1940, both in Fort Berthold 066-9582, NARA.

55. Fort Berthold Superintendent William Beyer to Commissioner of Indian Affairs John Collier, February 2, 1937; Memorial on the formation of Fort Berthold Americans, by Oscar Burr, Chair, February 2, 1941; Three Affiliated Tribes Tribal Business Council Resolution, March 13, 1941; Fort Berthold Superintendent William Beyer to Commissioner of Indian Affairs John Collier, May 1, 1941; and Assistant to Commissioner of Indian Affairs J. C. McCaskill to Fort Berthold Superintendent William Beyer, June 18, 1941; all in Fort Berthold 066-9582, NARA. *Fort Berthold Service Bulletin*, May 1941, Fort Berthold Indian Agency, Kansas City NARA.

56. *Fort Berthold Bulletin*, May 20, 1939; and Jackson Dancing Bull to North Dakota Senator William Langer, September 11, 1942, both in Fort Berthold 066-9582, NARA.

57. *Fort Berthold Bulletin*, March 1941, Fort Berthold Indian Agency, Kansas City NARA.

58. Floyd Montclair to Senator William Langer, September 20, 1942; and Assistant Commissioner of Indian Affairs William Zimmerman to Senator William Langer,

regarding the Jackson Dancing Bull complaint, November 2, 1942, both in Fort Berthold 066-9582, NARA; McLaughlin, "Nation, Tribe, and Class," 110.

Chapter 3

1. Lyda Bearstail, interview by the author, October 16, 2006. In other communities, such groups had similarly playful names, such as the "MacArthur Society" in Lucky Mound in which Rosemarie Mandan's mother and aunties participated. Mandan interview.

2. Clyde Baker, interview by Eric Wolf, July 17, 1990; Troutman, *Indian Blues*, 10-31.

3. Resolution Further Opposing Garrison Dam, April 24, 1945, Fort Berthold Indian Agency, Kansas City NARA; Mandan interview.

4. Walker interview; Mandan interview; Bearstail interview. Bearstail: "Then they'd put money in a pot.... [S]omebody would make a fancy cake and they'd feed the soldier and they'd give him money and they'd dance with him and that's how they honored them and helped them." Walker interview. The dance halls are also mentioned in Pete Coffey Sr., interview by Eric Wolf, 1990; and Clyde Baker interview. Baker remembered, "They used to have these honor dances for everyone that went in the service. They honored him, that's when they danced at night, not during the day like they do now. They danced at night ... they'd honor them, give them money, a few dollars. But them days you didn't see no shawl dancers, women shawl dancers. All you saw was men dancing. Unless a man's honor song was sung and his mother and his family, immediate family would get up and help him dance, that's the only time you saw women dance. There was no shawl dancing like that.... Every segment had a hall in them days, every segment."

5. For more on Northern Plains singing style, see Troutman, *Indian Blues*; Browner, *Heartbeat of the People*; and Browner, "Acoustic Geography of Intertribal Pow-wow Songs."

6. Mandan interview; Gail Baker, interview by the author, October 22, 2009.

7. Walker interview. Walker said that this must have been around the beginning of when they used *mashee* (white) words, i.e. English. Browner, "Acoustic Geography of Intertribal Pow-wow Songs." See Ellis, *Dancing People* 117, for another, more popularized example of this fusion of Native song form and American wartime lyric via a forty-nine song: "Oh my dearest, / Uncle Sam is calling me. / I must go. / Will you wait for me my dear? / Don't you worry, don't you cry." At Fort Berthold, many interviewees remember a much wider range of types of songs. I asked Rosemarie Mandan what the lyrics of doorway songs were like. She recounted, "My girlfriend, her husband is no good, took off [laughs]. They were teasing, funny songs, but really *nice!*" I asked if they were pretty, to which she replied, "Yes, *pretty* songs, yes.... They say that when they went around [and sang] those doorway songs, they could really come up with one *right* in front of [the tent], especially if they knew who was in there, they could come up with one good right now. Cause I remember one that was crazy, it says, 'My girlfriend is in there'—cause this person was married to a non-Indian—'smelling like a white man' [both laugh]. So now you kinda get the idea" (Mandan interview).

8. Coffey interview, track 3.

9. Ellis, "'There Is No Doubt,'" 543-69; Roach, *Cities of the Dead*, 26; Axtmann, "Dance: Celebration and Resistance," 97.

10. Bearstail interview.

11. Walker interview, 2009; Fred Baker interview.

12. Bearstail interview; Mintz and Du Bois, "Anthropology of Food and Eating," 99–119; Merrill, "Fort Berthold Relocation Problems (preliminary draft)," 27, Sol Tax Papers, Special Collections Research Center, University of Chicago Library (hereafter Sol Tax Papers).

13. Walker interview; Bearstail interview; Coffey interview.

14. Walker interview; Fred Baker interview.

15. As Rosemarie Mandan remembered—about her own welcome-home dance after serving during peacetime as one of the few women in the armed forces in the early 1950s—"You remember that when you get back, [from] out there. I even remember, how when they bring you in, I had my grandpa Chubby Fox, and Albert Fox were the ones that brought me in, so its really interesting how you remember. I remember those guys, and they were teasing me, and talking. . . . I even remember them singing 'Till We Meet Again' [laughs]. It sticks in your head!" (Mandan interview).

16. Brubaker and Cooper, "Beyond 'Identity,'" 1–47; Anderson, *Imagined Communities*; Lyons, *X-Marks*, chap. 4; Renato and Flores, "Identity, Conflict and Evolving Latino Communities"; Sassen, *Globalization and Its Discontents*; Isin, "Conclusion: The Socius of Citizenship"; Vom Hau and Wilde, "'We have always lived here'"; Clarke et al., *Disputing Citizenship*.

17. Bearstail interview, 2006.

18. Gail Baker interview, 2009.

19. Irwin interview.

20. Fred Baker interview; Mandan interview; Benson interview, 2013.

21. Basso, *Wisdom Sits in Places*, 7. Photographs, Fort Berthold Agency, Kansas City NARA. When I asked Rosemarie Mandan what she thought of her brothers going off to fight, she reflected, "Oh it was awful! Because of the hardship at home. To begin with, we had to do men's [work]. I was a teenage—not even a teenager. We had to do men's work, and help my mother get horses, put harnesses on the horses, cause everything back then was with teams. And then we even helped cut hay. I remember that one summer my mother and I cut hay, stack it and all of that; oh yeah, it was hard. And we still had to have gardens, they used to have what they called community gardens, that was by the river by my Grandma Youngbird's place. . . . And that was another thing, we used to have to go take care of the community gardens" (Mandan interview). VanDevelder, *Coyote Warrior*, 93.

22. For more on Indian citizenship and work, especially agricultural work, see Hoxie, *Final Promise*. *Fort Berthold Bulletin*, February 1942, Fort Berthold Agency, Kansas City NARA; Phillips, *This Land, This Nation*. Another example of Fort Berthold Indian Office narratives of patriotic productivity again comes from the April 1941 *Fort Berthold Bulletin*: "What I Should Do: 1. Realize that I am a citizen, and that the battle of life is mine, just as much as it is to every other citizen. 2. I should plan to work to provide the necessities of life for myself and loved ones. 3. I must grow to realize and understand that true freedom and independence can be attained only by myself—that it is up to me to provide for my needs in life and not lean on the other fellow . . . 8. In short, I must make myself understand that true independence and self respect comes only by doing all in my power to support myself instead of depending on the Relief Department."

23. *Fort Berthold Bulletin*, January 1942, Fort Berthold Agency, Kansas City NARA. Another example of the confluence of food production as patriotism in the WWII context reads, "Welfare News: . . . As a group, Indian people are very patriotic and loyal to their country. They have raised a large amount of money for the Red Cross, they have sent their young men to fight in large numbers. But it is just as important that the people at home work hard and long to produce food for themselves. The slogan 'Food will win the war' should be the battlecry of our people. Today a 'loafer' is a 'slacker.' Remember that!" *Fort Berthold Bulletin*, April 1942, Fort Berthold Indian Agency, Kansas City NARA.

24. *Fort Berthold Bulletin*, April 1942. Higher beef prices and federal subsidies raised Fort Berthold income from cattle sales by more than 1,000 percent during World War II, according to McLaughlin, "Nation, Tribe, and Class," 111.

25. Fred Baker interview.

26. Cohen, *Making a New Deal*; Cohen *Consumer's Republic*; Schulman, *From Cotton Belt to Sunbelt*; Cronon, *Nature's Metropolis*; Needham, *Power Lines*.

27. Phillips, *This Land, This Nation*.

28. McLaughlin, "Nation, Tribe, and Class," 112.

29. VanDevelder, *Coyote Warrior*, 112; *Fort Berthold Bulletin*, September 1941, Fort Berthold Agency, Kansas City NARA; Phillips, *This Land, This Nation*, 219–27.

30. *Fort Berthold Bulletin*, September 1941. Tribal governments were also determined to "do their part" for the war effort, and several used tribal funds to buy thousands of dollars' worth of bonds, while others allowed the United States to delay payments from litigated land cases that had been decided in favor of the tribe. Bernstein, *American Indians and World War II*, 68; Boime, "Waving the Red Flag and Reconstituting Old Glory," 3–25.

31. *Fort Berthold Bulletin*, February 1942; and Box 298, Lease records, 1938 crop acreage allotments, 1942–1945, both in Fort Berthold Agency, Kansas City NARA.

32. Bernstein, *American Indians and World War II*, 66–67.

33. Bernstein, 91; Special Meeting of the Fort Berthold Tribal Business Council, March 18, 1937, Fort Berthold Indian Agency, Kansas City NARA.

34. For an interesting discussion of the cultural imperative toward generosity, see Ellis, *Dancing People*, 44–45.

35. Schmittou and Logan, "Fluidity of Meaning," 589–90; Resolution Further Opposing Garrison Dam.

36. Bernstein, *American Indians and World War II*, 35, 44–45, 54.

37. *Fort Berthold Bulletin*, January 1942 (Civilian Conservation Corps–Indian Division Notes written by Ben Goodbird, Enrollee Camp Assistant); Schmittou and Logan, "Fluidity of Meaning," 590; Philip Deloria, *Indians in Unexpected Places*, 136–82.

38. *Fort Berthold Bulletin*, January 1942 (CCC-ID Notes written by Ben Goodbird), Fort Berthold Agency, Kansas City NARA.

39. Emery Goodbird Sr., interview by Eric Wolf, 1990. Goodbird recalled, "Before we went, my mother, Ellen Blackhawk Goodbird, always got the older people—at that time they had a lot of medicine, the older people had a lot of medicine—so before I went they either gave me a plume or either gave me how to paint my face or how to use anything that was there because they didn't have no paint there, mud or anything. That was for our safety. In them days we went through a ceremony. They tell you what you can do, and this one lady, was Rachel Wolf, and she said, 'my grandchild' she said 'I'll paint your nose; and

don't be scared because you're not going to be wounded, or you'll come home.' And so I did that a couple times." Mr. Goodbird served many tours of service in Korea and Vietnam, and as of the time of the interview, he still hadn't received discharge papers from active service. Although Mr. Goodbird served in Korea and Vietnam, and not World War II, the cultural practice was common during the Second World War as well.

40. Mandan interview; Irwin interview; Benson interview, 2013.

41. Coffey interview. Coffey went on to say, "It's amazing how many powwow songs there is. Like I said years ago there'd be only one group of singers there and they'll sing all night long until the wee hours and never sing the same song twice. And I admire these singing groups. There's a lot of hidden talent there, to remember those songs. You take the Baker boys, the Mandaree Singers, especially Billy, boy he's got a good memory." Thad Mason quote from Gail Baker interview.

42. Low and Lawrence-Zúñiga, *Anthropology of Space and Place*, 1–30; Basso, *Wisdom Sits in Places*, 7; Coffey interview.

43. Browner, *Heartbeat of the People* 73–4; Bernstein, *American Indians and World War II*, 9.

44. Bearstail interview.

45. Lefebvre's *Production of Space* describes the importance of accumulation and its inherent violence as the foundations of the realization of state sovereignty.

46. Irwin interview; Gail Baker interview. Gail Baker said after the interview that Nick Knight and Marvin Paint heard someone singing the song behind enemy lines and came back and wanted to have it translated into Hidatsa. An online account relates: "During World War Two, Nick (Knight) Fox was standing guard near a fox hole. The sound of the wind brought the melody of the flag song to him. Davis Painte had a similar experience. When they returned home after the war in 1946 the Arikara singers at Nishu added the words to the melody" (Louis Garcia, "A Message from Garcia: The Arikara Flag Song," *Devil's Lake (ND) Daily Journal*, November 28, 2023, https://www.devilslakejournal.com/news/3204/a-message-from-garcia-the-arikara-flag-song/). For more information on flag songs, see Ellis, *Dancing People*, 43.

47. Boime, "Waving the Red Flag and Reconstituting Old Glory," 3–25.

48. Schmittou and Logan, "Fluidity of Meaning," 559–604.

49. This dynamic may reflect cultural and temporal specificity. Troutman notes the lyrics of a World War I Lakota flag song: "There is fighting over there / That's where the Lakota boys will go / They say the Americans are saying that." The admittedly small sample size of Troutman's Lakota lyrics prevents generalizations, but none of the military service–related songs he relates refer to home territory or earth as does the Fort Berthold flag song. Victory song example 1: "The Germans made me mad / So not only their land but flag / Are what I made them give me." Victory song example 2: "They are charging from afar [x4] / The Germans retreat crying / The Lakota boys are charging from afar / The Germans retreat crying." Victory song example 3: "German, I have been watching your tracks / Worthless one! / I would have followed you wherever you would have gone!" (Troutman, *Indian Blues*, 54–55).

50. Ellis, "'There Is No Doubt,'" 543–69.

51. VanDevelder, *Coyote Warrior*, 93, 288.

52. VanDevelder, 102; Resolution Opposing Lower Dam, November 15, 1943, Fort Berthold Indian Agency, Kansas City NARA.

Chapter 4

1. George Gillette photograph "Lo, the Poor Indian..."; and *Washington Post*, May 21, 1948, both in Fort Berthold Indian Agency, Kansas City NARA.
2. "Indians with 'Heavy Hearts' Cede Lands to Government; Chairman Expresses Faith in Congress," *Minot (ND) Daily News*, May 24, 1948.
3. McNickle, introduction to *Dams and Other Disasters*.
4. White, *It's Your Misfortune and None of My Own*; Weist, "For the Public Good"; Klein and Zellmer, *Mississippi River Tragedies*.
5. Roy, Gillette, and Gillette-Brady interview.
6. VanDevelder, *Coyote Warrior*, 99–100; Reisner, *Cadillac Desert*; Ridgeway, *Missouri Basin's Pick-Sloan Plan*, 3–7.
7. Ridgeway, *Missouri Basin's Pick-Sloan Plan*, 8–10; VanDevelder, *Coyote Warrior*, 88, 98; Lawson, *Dammed Indians*, 14–29. The five dams and the reservations they affect are the Oahe Dam (Standing Rock and Cheyenne River Reservations); Fort Randall Dam (Yankton Reservation); Big Bend Dam (Crow Creek and Lower Brule Reservations); Garrison Dam (Fort Berthold Reservation); and Gavins Point Dam (Santee Sioux Reservation). Parman, *Indians and the American West*, 111; Berman, *Circle of Goods*, 6; Meyer, *Village Indians*, 211–34; VanDevelder, *Coyote Warrior*, 88, 98–99.
8. Ridgeway, *Missouri Basin's Pick-Sloan Plan*, 212–42; Lawson, *Dammed Indians*, 23–24.
9. Lawson *Dammed Indians*, 19; Ridgeway, *Missouri Basin's Pick-Sloan Plan*, 240–42; VanDevelder, *Coyote Warrior*, 100, 104.
10. Ridgeway, *Missouri Basin's Pick-Sloan Plan*, 20–23.
11. Phillips, *This Land, This Nation*; Schulman, *From Cotton Belt to Sunbelt*; Ridgeway, *Missouri Basin's Pick-Sloan Plan*, 42–60.
12. Phillips, *This Land, This Nation*.
13. Rivers often have nationalist propaganda projected onto them, such as national myths of modernity. Shama, *Landscape and Memory*, 363–64; Ridgeway, *Missouri Basin's Pick-Sloan Plan*, 17–47; Lawson, *Dammed Indians*, 10.
14. Lawson, *Dammed Indians*, 10; Waldram, *As Long as the Rivers Run*, 179–80, 172, 182; Hauptman, *In the Shadow of Kinzua*, chap. 4.
15. Lawson, *Dammed Indians*, 46–59.
16. Mandan interview; Benson interview, 2013.
17. Quoted from 1946 Garrison Dam hearings in "Special Edition: Dealing with the History and Culture of the Tribes," *Mandaree Village Voice*, vol. 2, no. 5 (1994), 5.
18. Resolution Opposing Lower Dam, November 15, 1943, Fort Berthold Indian Agency, Kansas City NARA.
19. Fort Berthold Americans, Inc., Elbowoods, ND, "No 'ISM' but AMERICANISM," Fort Berthold Indian Agency, Kansas City NARA.
20. Resolution Further Opposing Garrison Dam, Fort Berthold Tribal Business Council, April 24, 1945, Fort Berthold Indian Agency, Kansas City NARA; VanDevelder, *Coyote Warrior*, 105.
21. E. Reybold, Lieutenant General, Office of the Chief of Engineers, War Department to North Dakota Representative William Lemke, June 13, 1945, Fort Berthold Indian Agency, Kansas City NARA; VanDevelder, *Coyote Warrior*, 104–6.

22. VanDevelder, *Coyote Warrior*, 115–24; McMillan, *Making Indian Law*, 125–43. Felix Cohen, Associate Solicitor, Department of the Interior, Memorandum for the Senate Committee on Indian Affairs, October 17, 1945; and Three Affiliated Tribes Tribal Council Resolution: To employ an attorney to represent the Three Affiliated Tribes in their opposition to the construction of a dam at Garrison, North Dakota, October 18, 1945, both in Fort Berthold Indian Agency, Kansas City NARA.

23. VanDevelder, *Coyote Warrior*, 120–23; Study and Report on the Various Plans Heretofore Submitted to the Congress in Regard to the Upper Missouri River Basin, March 15, 1946, by Daniel Walser, Fort Berthold Indian Agency, Kansas City NARA.

24. VanDevelder, *Coyote Warrior*, 124–26.

25. VanDevelder, 123–24.

26. Cross, "'Twice-Born' from the Waters," 126; Letter, Martin Cross to A. L. Wathen, Chief Engineer, Office of Indian Affairs, July 8, 1946, Fort Berthold Indian Agency, Kansas City NARA.

27. Girard Davidson, Assistant Secretary of the Interior, to George Gillette, Chairman of the Fort Berthold Tribal Business Committee, November 22, 1946, Fort Berthold Indian Agency, Kansas City NARA.

28. Meeting in the Secretary's Conference Room December 16, 1946, for the purpose of obtaining the views of the three affiliated tribes of the Fort Berthold Reservation on the lieu lands offered by the Secretary of War, Fort Berthold Indian Agency, Kansas City NARA.

29. VanDevelder, *Coyote Warrior*, 127–30.

30. Tribal Business Council Meeting Minutes, September 25, 1947, Tax Anthropology Project. Case served as counsel for many Indian tribes during this period, but his alcoholism hampered the benefits of his idealism and commitment. Lazarus, *Black Hills/White Justice*.

31. Tribal Business Council Meeting Minutes, September 27, 1947, Tax Anthropology Project.

32. Social and Economic Report on the Future of the Fort Berthold Reservation, North Dakota, completed January 15, 1948, Tax Anthropology Project.

33. Merrill fieldnotes, Tax Anthropology Project.

34. Visit with Carl Whitman, Sunday, June 4, 1950, Merrill Field Notes, Tax Anthropology Project Whitman's grandmother raised him as a child, as his father died when he was young and his mother entered a new relationship with a man known as a cattle thief and bootlegger. When Whitman was twelve years old, the local Indian agent described him: "He is now attending one of the reservation schools and promises to become a bright and intelligent man." Letter, Fort Berthold Indian Agent Thomas Richards to Commissioner of Indian Affairs, October 23, 1899, Fort Berthold Agency, Kansas City NARA.

35. Hearing Held Before the Subcommittee on Interior and Insular Affairs, US Senate, April 29, 1949, Sol Tax Papers. Also present in the Sol Tax anthropology papers are numerous assertions from Fort Berthold tribal members (both elected and general community members) that Cross struggled with an alcohol addiction that interfered with his ability to support his large family. Many gossiped that his non-Native wife was the primary caretaker of their five children, and that she had petitioned to receive

Cross's Individual Indian Money (IIM) money directly from the BIA to provide for the family. Regardless of the veracity of this gossip, it indicates a divided and personalized Fort Berthold political scene. Cross's many appearances before Congress during this period illustrate that he truly believed in his advocacy for disenfranchised members of the Three Affiliated Tribes.

36. Hearing Held Before the Subcommittee on Interior and Insular Affairs; and Resolution of Tribal Business Council Concerning Garrison Dam Settlement, March 15, 1950, both in Tax Anthropology Project.

37. Hearings before Indian Affairs Committee, January 17, 1950, Tax Anthropology Project.

38. Nishu District Community Meeting, June 18, 1950, Merrill Field Notes, Tax Anthropology Project.

39. Resolution of Tribal Business Council Concerning Garrison Dam Settlement.

40. Beaver Creek District Community Meeting, June 16, 1950, Merrill Field Notes; and Nishu District Community Meeting, June 18, 1950, both in Tax Anthropology Project.

41. Nishu District Community Meeting, June 18, 1950. Quote regarding signers of the per capita petition from Davis Painte in Nishu Meeting.

42. Carl Whitman, interview by Eric Wolf, 1990. For more on Sol Tax and his students, see Cobb, *Native Activism*, chaps. 2 and 3; Smith, "Political Thought of Sol Tax," 129–170; and Daubenmier, *Meskwaki and Anthropologists*, 2008.

43. Letter, NCAI Acting Secretary Ruth Bronson to Senator Joseph O'Mahoney, December 17, 1949, Tax Anthropology Project.

44. Mandan interview.

45. Mark Mahto, *Fort Berthold Bulletin*, "The Indian Viewpoint," August 9, 1946, Fort Berthold Indian Agency, Kansas City NARA.

46. VanDevelder, *Coyote Warrior*, 124.

47. VanDevelder, 124. Wolf, quoted from 1946 Garrison Dam hearings in "Special Edition," *Mandaree Village Voice*, 5.

48. "Three Affiliated Tribes Seek to Block Construction of Dam," *Minot (ND) Daily News*, September 1946.

49. Nishu District Lieu Lands Meeting Minutes, December 8, 1946, Fort Berthold Indian Agency, Kansas City NARA.

50. Charging Eagle District Lieu Lands Meeting Minutes, December 11, 1946, Fort Berthold Indian Agency, Kansas City NARA.

51. Peter Beauchamp, Merrill Field Notes, Tax Anthropology Project.

52. Shell Creek District Lieu Lands Meeting Minutes, December 9, 1946, Fort Berthold Indian Agency, Kansas City NARA.

53. Nishu District Lieu Lands Meeting Minutes, December 8, 1946; Wright, "Rhetorical Spaces in Memorial Places"; Ruin, "Housing Spirits."

54. Nishu District Lieu Lands Meeting Minutes, December 8, 1946; Lucky Mound District Lieu Lands Meeting Minutes, December 11, 1946, Fort Berthold Indian Agency, Kansas City NARA.

55. Charging Eagle District Lieu Lands Meeting Minutes, December 11, 1946; Rivas-Rodríguez and Olguín, *Latina/os and World War II*; Azuma, "Lure of Military Imperialism"; Krebs, *Fighting for Rights*.

56. These "last arrow" ceremonies, begun in 1916, show the powerful convergence of the definition of the Indian body as it is tied to notions of work, progress, and "industry." Hoxie, *Final Promise*, 180.

57. Both Mrs. Jackson Ripley's and Mrs. Byron Wilde's statements can be found in Nishu District Community Meeting, June 18, 1950.

58. Lucky Mound District Lieu Lands Meeting Minutes, December 11, 1946.

59. Congregationalist Church Committee Meeting, June 11, 1950, Merrill Field Notes, Tax Anthropology Project.

60. Fieldnotes from ballgame, Elbowoods, June 4, 1950; and Robert Merrill to wife, June 4, 1950; both in Merrill Field Notes, Tax Anthropology Project.

61. Fieldnotes from ballgame; Merrill to wife, June 4, 1950.

62. Carl Sylvester, "The Voice of Flood-Threatened Indians," unknown publication date; and Fort Berthold Indian Defense Association, *Indian Tribes Fight Eviction* (Elbowoods, ND: August 1946), both in Fort Berthold Indian Agency, Kansas City NARA.

63. VanDevelder, *Coyote Warrior*, 123–24; Elbowoods meeting with Pick and Aahndahl, May 27, 1946, Fort Berthold Indian Agency, Kansas City NARA.

64. Martin Cross, testimony to Congress, April 30, 1949, Tax Anthropology Project. Charging Eagle District Lieu Lands Meeting Minutes, December 6, 1946; and Nishu District Lieu Lands Meeting Minutes, December 11, 1946, both in Fort Berthold Indian Agency, Kansas City NARA.

65. Carl Sylvester, Elbowoods District, Special Mtg of TBC, B2F7, September 25, 1947, Tax Anthropology Project.

66. Meeting in Assistant Secretary Davidson's office December 23, 1946, for the purpose of obtaining the views of the Three Affiliated Tribes of the Fort Berthold Reservation on the Lieu Lands offered by the Secretary of War, Tax Anthropology Project.

67. Roy, Gillette, and Gillette-Brady interview

Chapter 5

1. Merrill, "Fort Berthold Relocation Problems (preliminary draft)," 50, Sol Tax Papers; Merrill field notes, "Goodbird," 7, Tax Anthropology Project.

2. Merrill, "Fort Berthold Relocation Problems," 50; Merrill field notes, "Goodbird," 7.

3. Merrill field notes, "Mrs. Spotted Wolf," Tax Anthropology Project.

4. Merrill, "Fort Berthold Relocation Problems," 53, 68; Reitz field notes, "Mrs. Duckett," July 9, 1951; and Bruner Field Notes, July 19, 1951, both in Tax Anthropology Project; "August 7, 1950, Monday," Notes, in Testimony during Hearings on H.R. 8411, "Per Capita Payments to Members of the Three Affiliated Tribes, Fort Berthold Reservation," August 7, 1950, Fort Berthold Indian Agency, Kansas City NARA.

5. Memorandum, "Reservation attitude toward relocation," Fort Berthold Superintendent R. W. Quinn to Aberdeen Area Director G. W. Spaulding, never submitted, n.d., Fort Berthold Indian Agency, Kansas City NARA.

6. Reitz field notes, December 6, 1952, 7, Tax Anthropology Project.

7. Memorandum, "Reservation attitude toward relocation." Information on the timeline of the flooding and carrying capacity of the residual reservation from Merrill, "Fort Berthold Relocation Problems," 70–7.

8. Testimony during Hearings on H.R. 8411.
9. Testimony during Hearings on H.R. 8411.
10. Testimony during Hearings on H.R. 8411.
11. Philip Atkins testimony, in Testimony during Hearings on H.R. 8411.
12. William Dean testimony, in Testimony during Hearings on H.R. 8411.
13. Merrill field notes, Tribal Council Meeting, June 1950, Tax Anthropology Project; Memorandum, "Reservation attitude toward relocation."
14. "The Cross drive is intended to unseat the Tribal Council and Cross does not expect to get H.R. 8411 passed," Notes, in Testimony during Hearings on H.R. 8411.
15. Memorandum, "Reservation attitude toward relocation"; J. H. Cooper Aberdeen Area Director to Commissioner of Indian Affairs, May 25, 1952, quoting from a letter from Fort Berthold Superintendent Quinn, Fort Berthold Indian Agency, Kansas City NARA.
16. Bruner field notes, June 20, 1951, Nishu, Tax Anthropology Project.
17. Reitz Field Notes, August 15, 1951, 3–4, Tax Anthropology Project.
18. Reitz field notes, December 6, 1952.
19. Three Affiliated Tribes Business Council Resolution, December 14, 1950, Fort Berthold Indian Agency, Kansas City NARA.
20. Reitz Field Notes, August 14, 1951, Tax Anthropology Project. "Old Mrs. W. spoke at length about how sad it was to have such poor representatives on the council, men who drank all the time, and remarked that she understood that these men had been drunk most of the time they were in Washington, and most of the time while they were in Aberdeen, and Ben corroborated this" (Reitz Field Notes, August 15, 1951, 5).
21. Three Affiliated Tribes Special Meeting Minutes, September 26, 1952, Fort Berthold Indian Agency, Kansas City NARA.
22. Paige Baker Sr., "Observations of a Hillbilly," unpublished editorial, Tax Anthropology Project.
23. Mandan interview.
24. Memorandum, "Reservation attitude toward relocation."
25. Memorandum, "Reservation attitude toward relocation."
26. "Citizens" editorial, *Killdeer (ND) Herald*, January 14, 1952.
27. Memorandum, "Reservation attitude toward relocation."
28. Reitz field notes, October 5, 1951, Tax Anthropology Project.
29. Reitz field notes, October 5, 1951.
30. "Charlie Parshall," in Reitz field notes, October 5, 1951, 508.
31. Reitz field notes, July 9, 1951.
32. Independence District Meeting, December 20, 1950, Fort Berthold Indian Agency, Kansas City NARA.
33. Bruner Field Notes, August 7, 1951, 221, Tax Anthropology Project.
34. Bruner Field Notes, August 1951, 241, Tax Anthropology Project.
35. BIA family classifications and land information, Fort Berthold Indian Agency, North Dakota, Kansas City NARA.
36. Reitz field notes, Tax Anthropology Project.
37. Nishu District Meeting, December 11, 1950, Fort Berthold Indian Agency, Kansas City NARA.
38. Independence District Meeting, December 20, 1950.

39. Independence District Meeting, December 20, 1950.
40. Mandan interview.
41. VanDevelder, *Coyote Warrior*, 139–41.
42. Shell Creek "Farewell to the Valley" program, Sol Tax Papers.
43. Shell Creek "Farewell to the Valley" program.
44. Bruner Field Notes, August 1951, 280.
45. Bruner Field Notes, August 1951, 280.
46. Mandan interview; Mary Elk, interview by the author, October 25, 2009.
47. Irwin interview; Elk interview.
48. VanDevelder, *Coyote Warrior*, 32.
49. Clyde Baker interview; Mandan interview.
50. Cross, "'Twice-Born' from the Waters," 130.
51. Getches, Wilkinson, and Williams, *Cases and Materials on Federal Indian Law*, 204–24; Gail Baker interview; VanDevelder, *Coyote Warrior*, 178.
52. VanDevelder, *Coyote Warrior*, 166.
53. Cross, "'Twice-Born' from the Waters," 129.
54. VanDevelder, *Coyote Warrior*, 172–74.
55. McLaughlin, "Nation, Tribe, and Class," 114–17; McLaughlin, "Politics of Agricultural Decline," 20–22.
56. Clyde Baker interview.
57. Irwin interview.

Conclusion

1. Meyer, *Village Indians*, 232–33.
2. Nishu District Meeting, Sunday, June 18, 1950, Merrill field notes, 3:50–9 p.m., 10–11, Sol Tax—Fort Berthold Action Anthropology Project, NAA-SI.
3. VanDevelder, *Coyote Warrior*,191. By 1982, "The unemployment rate at Fort Berthold had risen to 85 percent. Four out of five school-age children were malnourished. Infant mortality rates were quadruple the national average. Life expectancy for men had dropped below fifty years."
4. Smith and Warrior, *Like a Hurricane*.
5. VanDevelder, *Coyote Warrior*, 216–17.
6. Cross, "'Twice-Born' from the Waters," 134; VanDevelder, *Coyote Warrior*, 238.
7. Rosier, "Dam Building and Treaty Breaking," 345–68; Hauptman, *In the Shadow of Kinzua*, chap. 4; Weist, "For the Public Good"; Bilharz, *Allegany Senecas and Kinzua Dam*; Piasta, "Seneca Resistance"; Preucel and Pecos, "Place: Cochiti Pueblo, Core Values, and Authorized Heritage Discourse," 221–42; Jackson, "Indigenous Peoples and Water Justice."

Epilogue

1. Adams received the third American Indian Visionary Award presented by *Indian Country Today* at the National Press Club in Washington, DC, in 2006. Adams also asserted that Maiselle Bridges (Nisqually), Ramona Bennett (Puyallup), and Suzan Harjo (Cheyenne, Muscogee) should receive the award.

2. Academic production focusing on a single charismatic male leader tends to replicate white tropes that stereotype Native men, from the "medicine man" to the Indian warrior/freedom fighter, to the noble chief—often in hagiographic terms.

3. This epilogue deviates from the usual tone of the historian because it conflicts with the kinship norms Auntie Tillie helped teach me. In our communities, our families are tightly connected. White norms would consider Auntie a distant relative—we are related because my great-great-great grandfather Short Bull is also her great-great grandfather. In the white way, this would make her my "third cousin once removed," which mostly sounds like nonsense to me. In the relationship norms of the Mandans and Hidatsas, Short Bull's daughters from whom we are descended—Sand Snake Woman for Auntie Tillie, Spotted Woman for me—were sisters, which made their sons, Louis Baker Sr. and Percy Baker, brothers. Because Louis and Percy Baker were brothers (cousins according to white norms), their children were also brothers and sisters. Thus, Auntie Tillie's mom Mercy Walker and my grandma Myra Baker Snow were sisters. Because they were sisters in the Mandan/Hidatsa relationship structure, their daughters were also sisters—Auntie Tillie and my mom, Karol Parker. This is why I call her Auntie Tillie in this epilogue, although in the Mandan/Hidatsa way she would also be my mother—because your mother's sisters are also your mothers in our tribal kinship norms.

4. Karol Parker, interview by the author, June 21, 2023.

5. Patricia Baker-Benally, interview by the author, July 30, 2023; Walker obituary, February 7, 2018.

6. Parker interview.

7. Bruce Davies, interview by the author, April 13, 2021.

8. Davies, *Memories of Tillie*.

9. Cambridge, interview by the author, April 6, 2021; Davies interview.

10. Walker obituary; "Tillie Walker Gets Job," *Denver Post*, October 23, 1965, 31.

11. McKenzie-Jones, "Evolving Voices"; Cobb, *Native Activism*.

12. Baker-Benally interview; Cambridge interview; Cambridge follow-up notes. Cambridge's explanation particularly resonates in response to the characterization of the workshops found in "Anthropologists and Other Friends," chap. 4 of Vine Deloria Jr.'s manifesto *Custer Died for Your Sins*. Deloria's chapter paints "young Indians" as the dupes of anthropologists and anthropological knowledge production, and asserts that Native youth attempted to authenticate their Indian identities by becoming alcoholics. As strident, hilarious, and satisfying as Deloria's takedown of anthropologists was, it also reads as cruel in its characterization of the National Indian Youth Council leaders—including Clyde Warrior who died of cirrhosis in 1968—and other youth participants in the summer workshops.

13. Cobb, *Native Activism*; Memorandum, Hyer to Weaver, July 24, 1957, Sol Tax Papers.

14. Memorandum, Hyer to Weaver.

15. Letter, Tax to Weaver, August 8, 1957, Tax Sol Papers.

16. Letter, Tax to Weaver.

17. Letter, Tax to Walker, January 4, 1958, Sol Tax Papers; McKenzie-Jones, "Evolving Voices."

18. United Scholarship Service (hereafter USS), 1962 Annual Report, October 1, 1962, Galen R. Weaver Indian Project, Amistad Research Center, New Orleans, LA.

19. Cambridge interview. The *New York Times* does document Vine Deloria Jr. as a USS "Staff Associate" in "News Notes: Campus and Classroom," *New York Times*, September 6, 1964, E9.

20. Robert Fenwick, "Indian Scholarships Promoted," *Denver Post*, December 14, 1960, 33.

21. Cambridge follow-up notes; USS, 1962 Annual Report. From 1961 to 1962, the USS received over 300 applications for scholarship assistance from Native American and Mexican American students in both secondary and post-secondary schools. It made 196 grants—156 to Native American students for a total funding amount of $49,166 (the equivalent over half a million dollars in 2023), and 40 to Mexican American students for a total funding amount of $12,254 (approximately $125,000 in contemporary value). The Native students mostly came from western states—South Dakota, Oklahoma, North Dakota, New Mexico, Arizona, Washington, Montana, Colorado, and Idaho—although several did live in places like Wisconsin, New York, Missouri, North Carolina, and Michigan. Over half, or 58 percent, came from reservation or predominately Native communities, and 24 percent came from urban areas. The remaining students lived in small, off-reservation or border towns. Surprisingly, Sioux, Hidatsa, Cherokee, Chippewa, Hopi, Oneida, Seneca, Winnebago, and Crow students had the largest tribal representation among the scholars funded. The annual report explained, "The fact that few of these students come from the large Indian populations of the Southwest is in large measure due to the tribal resources available to the Navajo, Apache, and Laguna Pueblo tribes in this area." The report also made clear that the organization's work included aid to students to help them navigate and braid funding. Of the 92 students it funded, only 22.8 percent, or 21 students, received aid solely from USS—the remaining students received aid from one to five other sources.

22. Davies interview.

23. Parker interview.

24. Parker interview.

25. Cambridge follow-up notes; Davies, *Memories of Tillie*.

26. Davies, *Memories of Tillie*; Parker interview.

27. Davies interview.

28. "Education's Importance Is Stressed," *Denver Post*, December 30, 1965, 8; USS Annual Report for 1968–69, National Council on Indian Opportunity Records, National Archives and Records Administration, College Park, MD (hereafter NCIO Records).

29. "$50,000 to Distribute," *Denver Post*, May 3, 1961, 12; "166 Get Grants for Education," *Denver Post*, September 1, 1961, 10; "Women in Religion," *Denver Post*, March 4, 1964, 26; "Foreign Students to Talk," *Denver Post*, August 14, 1965, 23; "Women in Action," *Denver Post*, January 1, 1966, 26; "Scholarships Go to 4 Students," *Denver Post*, July 6, 1966, 124; Carol Wilcox, "Indian Education," *Denver Post*, January 18, 1967, 50.

30. "Tillie Walker Gets Job," 31.

31. Cobb, *Native Activism*, 171.

32. "Open Forum: Headlines," *Denver Post*, April 4, 1966, 19.

33. "HEW Grant to Aid Indian, Spanish-Surnamed Youths," *Denver Post*, March 21, 1968, 31; Bureau of Indian Affairs, "United Scholarship Service Gets Carnegie Grant."

34. Cambridge follow-up notes; Cobb, *Native Activism*, 171–72.

35. "HEW Grant," 31.

36. Robert V. Dumont Jr., "From the Chairman," in USS Annual Report for 1968–69, 18; and USS Annual Report for 1968–69. The USS invested the bulk of the scholarship money in the 150 college-level students—nearly 44 percent, or $44,068 of its $100,453 total scholarship monies ($880,000 in 2023 dollars). Forty-six high school students in private boarding schools received $35,435, or 35 percent of the total scholarship money. Twenty-four graduate students in 1968–69 received the remaining 20 percent of the scholarship budget. The 1968–69 Annual Report also described how USS staff worked as advocates "to challenge the restrictive requirements set by many schools and colleges." The increased complexity of the program meant an intense work schedule. In addition to the four Talent Search fieldworkers, only four staff members kept the USS main office running—the executive director, an associate director, a college counselor, and a secretary. The Talent Search, or recruitment arm, of the organization heightened the complexity and cost of the work. The 1968–69 Annual Report noted, "Talent Search field workers recruit students directly, person to person, and provide follow-up services of a sort we have not been able to provide before. The overall quality of our scholarship programs had undoubtedly improved, as a result. However, the drain on our limited resources has also been marked: Talent Search workers are bringing in a greater number of urgent or emergency needs to our attention than we have dealt with in past years."

37. USS Annual Report for 1968–69, 19. ONAS published a quarterly newsletter, and advocated with the USS to evolve their student placements: "ONAS has enunciated a policy that the pressures on a single Indian student in an independent school are too great for most young people to bear and that any school seriously interested in Indian participation should commit itself to accepting a minimum of two Indian students per year, with an eventual goal of six or more Indian students on campus."

38. USS Annual Report for 1968–69, 20.

39. USS Annual Report for 1968–69, 26.

40. Cambridge interview; Cambridge follow-up notes.

41. Cambridge interview.

42. "Now Independent Agency," *USS News* 1 no. 3 (February 1969), NCIO Records.

43. USS Annual Report for 1969.

44. Baker-Benally interview.

45. Baker-Benally interview; Cobb, *Native Activism*. The phrase "rich in intimate relatives" is from a Fred Hoxie description of Crow relationship structures, similar to Hidatsa and Mandan structures, as the Hidatsas and the Crows originated from the same tribe.

46. Cobb, *Native Activism*, 180.

47. Baker-Benally interview; Cambridge follow-up notes; Theodore Hetzel, "Indian Power at Resurrection City," *Indian Truth*, Fall 1968, 14.

48. Baker-Benally interview; Cobb, *Native Activism*, 169. In Cambridge's follow-up notes, he added, "The Poor People's Campaign is the defining moment for Indian organizations and it was the line drawn in the sand. Clyde Warrior was against Indian participation in the Campaign because Indians had different goals than other minorities. I thought it would be an experiment but after the Campaign, I believed that Clyde was right and Indians should not have joined the Campaign. Clyde was dying and he was not involved in any negotiations with Rev. Martin Luther King. Dr. King needed the Indians

as the showcase of poverty in the United States. He promised funding and we agreed to participate in the campaign."

49. Cobb, *Native Activism*, 147–48.

50. Cobb, *Say We Are Nations*; Cobb, *Native Activism*, 158.

51. Parker interview.

52. Parker interview; Cobb, *Native Activism*, 195.

53. Parker interview.

54. Davies, *Memories of Tillie*.

55. Morton v. Mancari; Santa Clara Pueblo v. Martinez; Indian Child Welfare Act; Presidential Memorandum on Uniform Standards for Tribal Consultation; Haaland v. Brackeen.

56. Davies interview.

57. NIYC Press Release, March 12, 1970, NCIO Records.

58. Davies interview.

59. "Bellecourt: Protest Not Over," *Denver Post*, March 18, 1970, 3.

60. Davies interview.

61. Dennis Mason, "Indians Protest at Littleton BIA Office," *Denver Post*, March 17, 1970, 48.

62. Littleton occupiers demand with signature lines, March 20, 1970, NCIO Records; "Nine Indians Are Jailed after a Four-Day Sit-In at Bureau Office in Colorado," *New York Times*, March 23, 1970, 28.

63. "Press Release, Littleton, Colorado," March 19, 1970, NCIO Records.

64. Davies interview.

65. "Investigator Flying Here to Hear Indian Charges," *Denver Post*, March 19, 1970, 3.

66. Memo to Harrison Loesch, March 19, 1970, NCIO Records.

67. Littleton protest chronology, NCIO Records.

68. Protestor demands, NCIO Records; George Lane, "Protestors Expect Arrest; Indians Continue BIA Center Lock-In," *Denver Post*, March 20, 1970, 35; George Lane, "9 Arrested in Littleton; 3 Officials of BIA Suspended," *Denver Post*, March 22, 1970, 1; "Six More Arrests Made; Officers Use Stretchers to Oust Indians from BIA Office," *Denver Post*, March 24, 1970, 3; Littleton protest chronology.

69. "Indian Dispute; New Office Chief Gives Plans," *Denver Post*, March 25, 1970, 4.

70. Littleton protest chronology.

71. George Lane, "Sit-In at Littleton; Indians' Plan: Outwait U.S.," *Denver Post*, March 21, 1970, 26; Littleton protest chronology; "Nine Indians Plead Innocent, Released," *Denver Post*, March 23, 1970, 14; Telegram to Harrison Loesch, March 21, 1970; and "Indian People Arrested and Jailed," both in NCIO Records.

72. Associated Press, "Indians Attempting to Widen Sit-Ins," *Denver Post*, March 24, 1970, 3; "Picketing Abated; Indians Assured BIA Parley," *Denver Post*, March 28, 1970, 3; "Review of Week's News; The Denver Area; More Arrests," *Denver Post*, March 29, 1970, 3.

73. Mancari v. Morton; Morton v. Mancari.

74. Tahdooahnippah, et al. v. Thimmig, et al.; Fred Brown, "Free-Tuition Bill Gains for Colorado Indians," *Denver Post*, March 16, 1971, 44; "Old Problem of Indian Tuition at Fort Lewis Returns Anew," *Denver Post*, August 16, 1972, 26; Jane Earle, "Indians Hope Litigation at End," *Denver Post*, July 15, 1973, 42; Davies, *Memories of Tillie*; Davies

interview. Davies remains ambivalent about the larger impact of Indian preference: "I'm a little ambivalent because one of the things that I have noticed is the bureaucratization of Indian Country. Bureaucracy seems to be a big part of the culture now."

75. *USS News* 1, no. 6 (November 1969), NCIO Records. Biennial Report of the United Scholarship Service, 1970–1972, Elizabeth C. Rosenthal Collection, University of Oklahoma Libraries.

76. Cambridge interview; Biennial Report of the United Scholarship Service. Between the 1970–71 academic year and the 1971–72 academic year, the number of high school students aided by the USS dropped from 38 to 13—and the scholarship monies disbursed dropped from $75,600 to $36,320. The number of colleges students aided also dropped, from 108 to 77. Graduate funding was the only area that increased, from 12 to 19 students.

77. Letter, Walker to Johnson, May 4, 1970, NCIO Records.

78. *Guts and Tripe, Idle Moon* 1 no. 3 (1972), in Hank Adams Papers, Public Policy Papers, Mudd Manuscript Library, Princeton University.

79. *Guts and Tripe, Idle Moon*; Jane Earle, "Mrs. Harris Caught in Indian Dispute," *Denver Post*, August 5, 1971, 3.

80. Parker interview.

81. VanDevelder, *Coyote Warrior*, 193–98.

82. VanDevelder, 215–18.

83. Davies, *Memories of Tillie*.

84. Baker-Benally interview.

85. Parker interview; Davies, *Memories of Tillie*.

86. Davies, *Memories of Tillie*.

Bibliography

Oral History Interviews

Baker, Alameda. Interview by the author. Video recording. New Town, ND, August 29, 1997.
Baker, Clyde. Interview by Eric Wolf, National Park Service. Tape recording converted to digital audio file. New Town, ND, July 17, 1990.
Baker, Fred. Interview by the author. Digital audio recording. New Town, ND, August 7, 2013.
Baker, Gail. Interview by the author. Digital audio recording. Bakersfield, ND, October 22, 2009.
Baker-Benally, Patricia. Interview by the author. Digital audio recording via phone. July 30, 2023.
Bearstail, Lyda. Interview by the author. Digital audio recording. Mandaree, ND, October 16, 2006.
Benson, Edwin. Interview by the author. Video recording. Twin Buttes, ND, August 1997.
———. Interview by the author. Digital audio recording. Twin Buttes, ND, July 26, 2013.
Brown, Cecelia. Interview by Eric Wolf, National Park Service. Tape recording converted to digital audio file. White Shield, ND, July 17, 1990.
Cambridge, Charles. Interview by the author. Zoom recording. April 6, 2021.
Chase, Emmarine. Interview by Eric Wolf, National Park Service. Tape recording converted to digital audio file. Bear Den Coulee, ND, June 20, 1990.
Coffey, Pete, Sr. Interview by Eric Wolf, National Park Service. Tape recording converted to digital audio file. Location unknown, 1990.
Davies, Bruce. Interview by the author. Zoom recording. April 13, 2021.
Elk, Mary. Interview by the author. Digital audio recording. New Town, ND, October 25, 2009.
Goodbird, Emery, Sr. Interview by Eric Wolf, National Park Service. Tape recording converted to digital audio file. Location unknown, 1990.
Irwin, Dreke. Interview by the author. Digital audio recording. New Town, ND, October 20, 2009.
Mandan, Rosemarie. Interview by the author. Digital audio recording. Bakersfield, ND, October 21, 2009.
Parker, Karol. Interview by the author. Digital audio recording. Bismarck, ND, June 21, 2023.

Roy, Barbara, Aurelia Gillette, and Florence Gillette-Brady. Interview by the author. Digital audio recording. August 7, 2013.
Snow, Myra. Interview by Eric Wolf, National Park Service. Tape recording converted to digital audio file. New Town, ND, June 25, 1990.
Walker, Tillie. Interview by the author. Interview notes. Independence, ND, September 29, 2009.
Whitman, Carl. Interview by Eric Wolf, National Park Service. Tape recording converted to digital audio file. Location unknown, date unknown, 1990.

Archival Sources

Adams, Hank. Papers. 1958–78. Public Policy Papers. Mudd Manuscript Library, Princeton University.
Case, Harold W. Papers. 1864–1989. North Dakota State Historical Society Archives.
Fort Berthold Indian Agency, North Dakota. Records Concerning Indian Organization, RG 75. Records of the Bureau of Indian Affairs. National Archives and Records Administration, Washington, DC.
Fort Berthold Indian Agency, North Dakota. Records of the Bureau of Indian Affairs, RG 75. National Archives and Records Administration–Central Plains Region, Kansas City, MO.
Fort Berthold Project Records. Sol Tax–Fort Berthold Action Anthropology Project (Manuscript 4805). National Anthropological Archives, Smithsonian Institution.
Libby, Orin Grant. Papers. Series 1. Secretary of the State Historical Society of North Dakota, 1905–43. Correspondence: Outgoing Letters, 1905–11. North Dakota State Historical Society Archives.
Missouri River Basin Reports and Related Records. 1946–52. Division of Resources, Branch of Irrigation. RG 75. Records of the Bureau of Indian Affairs. National Archives and Records Administration, Washington, DC.
Records of the National Council on Indian Opportunity. RG 220. National Archives and Records Administration, College Park, MD.
Tax, Sol. Papers. 1923–89. Special Collections Research Center, University of Chicago Library.
United Scholarship Service. Annual Report, October 1, 1962. Galen R. Weaver Indian Project. Box: 1949–64. Series 1. Administrative Records, 1943–69. Amistad Research Center, Tulane University, New Orleans.
——. Annual Report for 1968–69. United Scholarship Service, Inc. Records of the National Council on Indian Opportunity, 1968–74. Pt. 4: S–Z. National Archives and Records Administration, College Park, MD.
——. Biennial Report for 1970–72. Reports. Elizabeth C. Rosenthal Collection. Western History Collections. University of Oklahoma Libraries.

Books, Articles, and Theses

Alfred, Taiaiake. *Peace, Power, and Righteousness: An Indigenous Manifesto*. New York: Oxford University Press, 1999.

Barsh, Russel L. "Progressive-Era Bureaucrats and the Unity of Twentieth Century Federal Indian Policy." *American Indian Quarterly* 15, no. 1 (Winter 1991): 1–18.

Deloria, Vine, Jr. "Federal Policy and the Perennial Question." *American Indian Quarterly* 15, no. 1 (Winter 1991): 19-22.

Boxburger, Daniel L. "Individualism or Tribalism?: The 'Dialectic' of Indian Policy." *American Indian Quarterly* 15, no. 1 (Winter 1991): 29-32.

Hauptman, Laurence M. "A Harbinger of the Indian New Deal." *American Indian Quarterly* 15, no. 1 (Winter 1991): 33-34.

Hoxie, Frederick E. "Shadow and Substance." *American Indian Quarterly* 15, no. 1 (Winter 1991): 35-38.

Clow, Richmond L. "A Hesitant Second." *American Indian Quarterly* 15, no. 1 (Winter 1991): 39-44.

Parman, Donald L. "Probing the Intellectual Quagmire." *American Indian Quarterly* 15, no. 1 (Winter 1991): 45-48.

Rusco, Elmer R. "John Collier: Architect of Sovereignty or Assimilation?" *American Indian Quarterly* 15, no. 1 (Winter 1991): 49-54.

Kelly, Lawrence C. "The Ludington Papers: Overstating the Evidence." *American Indian Quarterly* 15, no. 1 (Winter 1991): 55-58.

Barsh, Russel L. "Are We Stuck in the Slime of History?" *American Indian Quarterly* 15, no. 1 (Winter 1991): 59-64.

Anderson, Ben. "Preemption, Precaution, Preparedness: Anticipatory Action and Future Geographies." *Progress in Human Geography* 34, no. 6 (2010): 777–98.

Anderson, Benedict. *Imagined Communities: Reflections on the Origin and Spread of Nationalism.* New York: Verso, 1991.

Anderson, Kathryn, and Dana Jack. "Learning to Listen: Interview Techniques and Analyses." In *Women's Words: The Feminist Practice of Oral History*, edited by Sherna Berger Gluck and Daphne Patai. New York: Routledge, 1991.

Axtmann, Ann. "Dance: Celebration and Resistance, Native American Indian Intertribal Powwow Performance." PhD diss., New York University, 1999.

Azuma, Eiichiro. "The Lure of Military Imperialism: Race, Martial Citizenship, and Minority American Transnationalism during the Cold War." *Journal of American Ethnic History* 36, no. 2 (2017): 72–82.

Baldwin, Andrew. "Whiteness and Futurity: Towards a Research Agenda." *Progress in Human Geography* 36, no. 2 (2012): 172–87.

Banks, Dennis. *Ojibwa Warrior: Dennis Banks and the Rise of the American Indian Movement.* With contributions by Richard Erdoes. Norman: University of Oklahoma Press, 2004.

Barthelemy, Michael, Jr. "Hushgah Adiish the Badlands Lodge: A Hidatsa Cultural Hub on the Upper-Missouri River in the Late Nineteenth Century." University of New Mexico Digital Repository, 2016. https://digitalrepository.unm.edu/hist_etds/4.

Basso, Keith. *Wisdom Sits in Places: Landscape and Language among the Western Apache.* Albuquerque: University of New Mexico Press, 1996.

Berman, Tressa. *Circle of Goods: Women, Work, and Welfare in a Reservation Community.* Albany: State University of New York Press, 2003.

Bernstein, Alison. *American Indians and World War II: Toward a New Era in Indian Affairs.* Norman: University of Oklahoma Press, 1991.

Bilharz, Joy Ann. *The Allegany Senecas and Kinzua Dam: Forced Relocation through Two Generations*. Lincoln: University of Nebraska Press, 1998.

Billington, David, and Donald Jackson. *Big Dams of the New Deal Era: A Confluence of Engineering and Politics*. Norman: University of Oklahoma Press, 2006.

Biolsi, Thomas. "Imagined Geographies: Sovereignty, Indigenous Space, and American Indian Struggle." *American Ethnologist* 32, no. 2 (May 2005): 239–59.

———. "'Indian Self-Government' as a Technique of Domination." *American Indian Quarterly* 15, no. 1 (Winter 1991): 23–28.

———. "The IRA and the Politics of Acculturation: The Sioux Case." *American Anthropologist*, n.s., 87, no. 3 (September 1985): 656–59.

———. *Organizing the Lakota: The Political Economy of the New Deal on the Pine Ridge and Rosebud Reservations*. Tucson: University of Arizona Press, 1998.

Blackburn, Carole. "Differentiating Indigenous Citizenship: Seeking Multiplicity in Rights, Identity, and Sovereignty in Canada." *American Ethnologist* 36, no. 1 (February 2009): 66–78.

Blansett, Kent. *Journey to Freedom: Richard Oakes, Alcatraz, and the Red Power Movement*. New Haven, CT: Yale University Press, 2018.

Boime, Albert. "Waving the Red Flag and Reconstituting Old Glory." *Smithsonian Studies in American Art* 4, no. 2 (Spring 1990).

Borland, Katherine. "'That's Not What I Said': Interpretive Conflict in Oral Narrative Research." In *Women's Words: The Feminist Practice of Oral History*, edited by Sherna Berger Gluck and Daphne Patai, 63–75. New York: Routledge, 1991.

Bowers, Alfred W. *Mandan Social and Ceremonial Organization*. Chicago: University of Chicago Press, 1950.

———. *Hidatsa Social and Ceremonial Organization*. 1965. Reprint, Lincoln: University of Nebraska Press, 1992.

Browner, Tara. "An Acoustic Geography of Intertribal Pow-wow Songs." In *Music of the First Nations: Tradition and Innovation in Native North America*, edited by Tara Browner, 131–40. Chicago: University of Illinois Press, 2009.

———. *Heartbeat of the People: Music and Dance of the Northern Pow-Wow*. Urbana: University of Illinois Press, 2002.

Brubaker, Rogers, and Frederick Cooper. "Beyond 'Identity.'" *Theory and Society* 29, no. 1 (February 2000): 1–47.

Bruner, Edward. "Primary Group Experience and the Processes of Acculturation." *American Anthropologist*, n.s., 58, no. 4 (August 1956): 605–23.

———. "Two Processes of Change in Mandan-Hidatsa Kinship Terminology." *American Anthropologist*, n.s., 57, no. 4 (August 1955): 840–50.

Bruyneel, Kevin. "Challenging American Boundaries: Indigenous People and the 'Gift' of U.S. Citizenship." *Studies in American Political Development* 18, no. 1 (Spring 2004).

———. *The Third Space of Sovereignty: The Postcolonial Politics of US-Indigenous Relations*. Minneapolis: University of Minnesota Press, 2007.

Calloway, Colin. *One Vast Winter Count: The Native American West before Lewis and Clark*. Lincoln: University of Nebraska Press, 2003.

Cannon, Brian Q. "Power Relations: Western Rural Electric Cooperatives and the New Deal." *Western Historical Quarterly* 31, no. 2 (Summer 2000): 133–60.

Carlson, David J. "'Indian for a While': Charles Eastman's 'Indian Boyhood' and the Discourse of Allotment." *American Indian Quarterly* 25, no. 4 (Fall 2001): 604–25.

Carlson, Leonard. *Indians, Bureaucrats, and Land: The Dawes Act and the Decline of Indian Farming*. Westport, CT: Greenwood Press, 1981.

Casey, Edward. "How to Get from Space to Place in a Fairly Short Stretch of Time: Phenomological Prolegomana." In *Senses of Place*, edited by Steven Feld and Keith Basso. Santa Fe: School of American Research Press, 1996.

Case, Rev. Harold, and Mrs. *100 Years at Ft. Berthold: The History of Fort Berthold Indian Mission 1876–1976*. Self-published, 1977.

Castillo, Victoria. "Indigenous 'Messengers' Petitioning for Justice: Citizenship and Indigenous Rights in Peru, 1900–1945." PhD diss., University of Michigan, 2009.

Cattelino, Jessica. "Florida Seminole Housing and the Social Meaning of Sovereignty." *Comparative Study of Society and History* 48, no. 3 (July 2006).

Chakrabarty, Dipesh. *Provincializing Europe: Postcolonial Thought and Historical Difference*. Princeton, NJ: Princeton University Press, 2000.

Child, Brenda. *Boarding School Seasons: American Indian Families, 1900–1940*. Lincoln: University of Nebraska Press, 2001.

Clarke, John, Kathleen Coll, Evelina Dagnino, and Catherine Neveu, eds. *Disputing Citizenship*. Bristol: Policy Press, 2014.

Clayton, Daniel. *Islands of Truth: The Imperial Fashioning of Vancouver Island*. Vancouver: University of British Columbia Press, 2000.

Cobb, Daniel. *Native Activism in Cold War America: The Struggle for Sovereignty*. Lawrence: University Press of Kansas, 2008.

———, ed. *Say We Are Nations: Documents of Politics and Protest in Indigenous America since 1887*. Chapel Hill: University of North Carolina Press, 2015.

Cobb, Daniel, and Loretta Fowler, eds. *Beyond Red Power: American Indian Politics and Activism Since 1900*. Santa Fe: School for Advanced Research Press, 2007.

Coffey, Wallace, and Rebecca Tsosie. "Rethinking the Tribal Sovereignty Doctrine: Cultural Sovereignty and the Collective Future of Indian Nations." *Stanford Law and Policy Review* 12 (2001): 191.

Cohen, Lizabeth. *A Consumer's Republic: The Politics of Mass Consumption in Postwar America*. New York: Vintage, 2003.

———. *Making a New Deal: Industrial Workers in Chicago, 1919–1939*. New York: Cambridge University Press, 1990.

Collier, John. "Collier Replies to Mekeel." *American Anthropologist* 46, no. 3 (July–September 1944): 422–26.

Coulthard, Glen. *Red Skin, White Masks: Rejecting the Colonial Politics of Recognition*. Minneapolis: University of Minnesota Press, 2014.

Cousins, Robert J. "Citizenship and Selfhood: Negotiating Narratives of National and Personal Identity, 1900–1920." PhD diss., Purdue University, 1997.

Cowger, Thomas. *The National Congress of American Indians: The Founding Years*. Lincoln: University of Nebraska Press, 1999.

Cronon, William. *Changes in the Land: Indians, Colonists, and the Ecology of New England*. New York: Hill and Wang, 1983.

———. *Nature's Metropolis: Chicago and the Great West*. New York: W. W. Norton, 1991.

Cross, Raymond. "'Twice-Born' from the Waters: The Two-Hundred-Year Journey of the Mandan, Hidatsa, and Arikara Indians." In *Lewis and Clark: Legacies, Memories, and New Perspectives*, edited by Kris Fresonke and Mark David Spence. Berkeley: University of California Press, 2004.

Daubenmier, Judith M. *The Meskwaki and Anthropologists: Action Anthropology Reconsidered.* Lincoln: University of Nebraska Press, 2008.

De Certeau, Michel. *The Practice of Everyday Life.* Translated by Steven Rendell. Berkeley: University of California Press, 1984.

Deloria, Philip J. *Indians in Unexpected Places.* Lawrence: University Press of Press, 2004.

Deloria, Vine, Jr. Introduction to *Speaking of Indians*, by Ella Deloria. Lincoln: University of Nebraska Press, 1998.

———. *Red Earth, White Lies: Native Americans and the Myth of Scientific Fact.* New York: Scribner, 1995.

Denetdale, Jennifer Nez. "The Value of Oral History on the Path to Dine/Navajo Sovereignty." In *Diné Perspectives: Revitalizing and Reclaiming Navajo Thought*, edited by Lloyd L. Lee, 68–82. Tucson: University of Arizona Press, 2014.

Dennison, Jean. "Stitching Osage Governance into the Future." *American Indian Culture and Research Journal* 37, no. 2 (2013): 115–28.

Doerfler, Jill. *Those Who Belong: Identity, Family, Blood, and Citizenship among the White Earth Anishinaabeg.* East Lansing: Michigan State University Press, 2015.

Densmore, Frances. *Mandan and Hidatsa Music.* Bureau of American Ethnology Bulletin 80. Washington, DC: Government Printing Office, 1923.

———. "The Songs of Indian Soldiers during the World War." *Musical Quarterly* 20 (1934): 419–25.

Ellis, Clyde. *A Dancing People: Powwow Culture on the Southern Plains.* Lawrence: University Press of Kansas, 2003.

———. "'There Is No Doubt . . . the Dances Should Be Curtailed: Indian Dances and Federal Policy on the Southern Plains, 1880–1930." *Pacific Historical Review* 70, no. 4 (November 2001): 543–69.

Elmer, Johnathan. *On Lingering and Being Last: Race and Sovereignty in the New World.* New York: Fordham University Press, 2008.

Elshtain, Jean Bethke. *Sovereignty: God, State, and Self.* New York: Basic Books, 2008.

Emmerich, Lisa. "'Right in the Midst of My Own People': Native American Women and the Field Matron Program." *American Indian Quarterly* 15 (1991): 201–16.

Erman, Samuel. "Puerto Rico and the Promise of United States Citizenship: Struggles around Status in a New Empire, 1898–1917." PhD diss., University of Michigan–Ann Arbor, 2010.

Fenelon, James, and Mary Louise Defender-Wilson. "Voyage of Domination, 'Purchase' as Conquest, Sakakawea for Savagery: Distorted Icons from Misrepresentations of the Lewis and Clark Expedition." *Wicazo Sa Review* 19 (2004): 85–104.

Fenn, Elizabeth A. *Encounters at the Heart of the World: A History of the Mandan People.* New York: Hill and Wang, 2014.

Fixico, Donald. *Termination and Relocation: Federal Indian Policy, 1945–1960.* Albuquerque: University of New Mexico Press, 1986.

Fleischmann, Aloys N. M., Nancy Van Styvendale, and Cody McCarroll. *Narratives of Citizenship: Indigenous and Diasporic Peoples Unsettle the Nation-State*. Edmonton: University of Alberta Press, 2011.
Foucault, Michel. *Security, Territory, Population: Lectures at the College de France, 1977-78*. Translated by Graham Burchell. New York: Palgrave Macmillan, 2007.
Freund, Alexander. "Towards an Ethics of Silence? Negotiating Off-the-Record Events and Identity in Oral History." In *The Oral History Reader*, edited by Robert Perks and Alistair Thomson, 253-66. New York: Routledge, 2015.
Getches, David H., Charles F. Wilkinson, and Robert A. Williams Jr., eds. *Cases and Materials on Federal Indian Law*. 4th ed. Saint Paul, MN: West Group, 1998.
Gilman, Carolyn, and Mary Jane Schneider. *The Way to Independence: Memories of a Hidatsa Indian Family, 1840-1920*. Saint Paul: Minnesota Historical Society Press, 1987.
Gramsci, Antonio. "The Intellectuals." In *Selections from the Prison Notebooks of Antonio Gramsci*, edited and translated by Quintin Hoare and Geoffrey Nowell Smith, 6-23. New York: International Publishers, 1971.
Greenwald, Emily. *Reconfiguring the Reservation: The Nez Perces, Jicarilla Apaches, and the Dawes Act*. Albuquerque: University of New Mexico Press, 2002.
Gunderson, M. "The Effects of the Garrison Dam on the Community of Elbowoods." Master's thesis, University of North Dakota, 2001.
Guthrie, Chester, and Leo Gerald. "Upper Missouri Agency: An Account of Indian Administration on the Frontier." *Pacific Historical Review* 10 (1941): 47-56.
Hall, Charles Lemon. *The Fort Berthold Mission: Elbowoods, North Dakota*. New York: American Missionary Association, 1923.
Hämäläinen, Pekka. "The Rise and Fall of Plains Indian Horse Cultures." *Journal of American History* 90, no. 3 (2003): 833-62.
Hannah, Paul S. "An Analysis of the Assimilation of White Culture by Hidatsa Indians of North Dakota." Master's thesis, University of North Dakota, 1953.
Hanson, Jeffery. *Hidatsa Culture Change, 1780-1845: A Cultural Ecological Approach*. Lincoln, NE: National Park Service, Midwest Archeological Center, 1983.
Hardt, Michael, and Antonio Negri. *Empire*. Cambridge, MA: Harvard, 2007.
Hauptman, Laurence M. *In the Shadow of Kinzua: The Seneca Nation of Indians since World War II*. Syracuse, NY: Syracuse University Press, 2014.
Hilger, M. Inez. "Some Customs Related to Arikara Indian Child Life." *Primitive Man* 24 (1951): 67-71.
Holston, James. *Insurgent Citizenship: Disjunctions of Democracy and Modernity in Brazil*. Princeton, NJ: Princeton University Press, 2008.
Howard, James. "Butterfly's Mandan Winter Count: 1833-1876." *Ethnohistory* 7 (Winter 1960): 28-43.
Hoxie, Frederick. *A Final Promise: The Campaign to Assimilate the Indians, 1880-1920*. Lincoln: University of Nebraska Press, 1984.
———. "From Prison to Homeland: The Cheyenne River Indian Reservation before WWI." *South Dakota History* 10 (Winter 1979): 1-24.
———. "Missing the Point: Academic Experts and American Indian Politics." In *Beyond Red Power: American Indian Politics and Activism since 1900*, edited by Daniel M. Cobb and Loretta Fowler, 16-32. Santa Fe: School for Advanced Research Press, 2007.

———. *Parading Through History: The Making of the Crow Nation in America, 1805–1935*. New York: Cambridge University Press, 1995.

Isin, Engin F. "Conclusion: The Socius of Citizenship." In *Recasting the Social in Citizenship*, edited by Engin F. Isin, 281–86. Toronto: University of Toronto Press, 2008.

Iverson, Peter. *When Indians Became Cowboys: Native Peoples and Cattle Ranching in the American West*. Norman: University of Oklahoma Press, 1994.

Jackson, Sue. "Indigenous Peoples and Water Justice in a Globalizing World." In *The Oxford Handbook of Water Politics and Policy*, edited by Ken Conca and Erika Weinthal, 120–41. New York: Oxford University Press, 2018.

Jessee, Erin. "The Limits of Oral History: Ethics and Methodology Amid Highly Politicized Research Settings." *Oral History Review* 38, no. 2 (2011): 287–307.

Johansen, E. Bruce, ed. *Native Americans Today: A Biographical Dictionary*. Denver: Greenwood, 2010.

Kelly, Lawrence. *The Assault on Assimilation: John Collier and the Origins of Indian Policy Reform*. Albuquerque: University of New Mexico Press, 1983.

———. "The Indian Reorganization Act: The Dream and the Reality." *Pacific Historical Review* 44 (1975): 291–312.

Kelsey, Robin. "Viewing the Archive: Timothy O'Sullivan's Photographs for the Wheeler Survey, 1871–74." *Art Bulletin* 85, no. 4 (December 2003): 702–23.

Kennard, Edward. "Mandan Grammar." *International Journal of American Linguistics* 9 (1936): 1–43.

Kivelson, Valerie Ann. *Cartographies of Tsardom: The Land and Its Meanings in Seventeenth-Century Russia*. Ithaca: Cornell University Press, 2006.

Klein, Christine, and Sandra Zellmer. *Mississippi River Tragedies a Century of Unnatural Disaster*. New York: New York University Press, 2014.

Koppes, Clayton. "From New Deal to Termination: Liberalism and Indian Policy, 1933–1953." *Pacific Historical Review* 46 (1977): 543–66.

Krasner, S. D. "Sovereignty: Political." In *International Encyclopedia of the Social and Behavioral Sciences*, edited by Neil J. Smelser and Paul B. Baltes, 14706–9. Amsterdam: Elsevier, 2001.

Krebs, Ronald R. *Fighting for Rights: Military Service and the Politics of Citizenship*. Ithaca: Cornell University Press, 2010.

Krech, Shepard. *The Ecological Indian: Myth and History*. New York: Norton, 1999.

Lansing, Michael. "Plains Indian Women and Interracial Marriage in the Upper Missouri Trade, 1804–1868." *Western Historical Quarterly* 31 (2000): 413–33.

Lawson, Michael. *Dammed Indians: The Pick-Sloan Plan and the Missouri River Sioux, 1944–1980*. Norman: University of Oklahoma Press, 1982.

Lazarus, Edward. *Black Hills/White Justice: The Sioux Nation Versus the United States, 1775 to the Present*. Lincoln: University of Nebraska Press, 1999.

Lefebvre, Henri. *The Production of Space*. Translated by Donald Nicholson-Smith. Malden, MA: Blackwell Publishing, 1991.

Lennox, Jeffers. *Homelands and Empires: Indigenous Spaces, Imperial Fictions, and Competition for Territory in Northeastern North America, 1690–1763*. Toronto: University of Toronto Press, 2017.

Lewis, G. Malcolm. *Cartographic Encounters: Perspectives on Native American Mapmaking and Map Use*. Chicago: University of Chicago Press, 1998.

Low, Setha, and Denise Lawrence-Zúñiga, eds. *The Anthropology of Space and Place: Locating Culture*. Malden, MA: Blackwell Publishing, 2003.

Lowie, Robert. *Notes on the Social Organization and Customs of the Mandan, Hidatsa, and Crow Indians*. New York: American Museum of Natural History, 1917.

Lupel, Adam. *Globalization and Popular Sovereignty: Democracy's Transnational Dilemma*. New York: Routledge, 2009.

Lyons, Scott Richard. *X-Marks: Native Signatures of Assent*. Minneapolis: University of Minnesota Press, 2010.

Maher, Neil. "'Crazy Quilt Farming on Round Land': The Great Depression, the Soil Conservation Service, and the Politics of Landscape Change on the Great Plains during the New Deal Era." *Western Historical Quarterly* 31 (2000): 319–39.

——. *Nature's New Deal: The Civilian Conservation Corps and the Roots of the American Environmental Movement*. New York: Oxford University Press, 2007.

Mahuika, Nepia. *Rethinking Oral History and Tradition: An Indigenous Perspective*. New York: Oxford University Press, 2019.

Mancall, Peter. *American Encounters: Natives and Newcomers from European Contact to Indian Removal, 1500–1850*. New York: Routledge, 2000.

Manning, Richard. *Grassland: The History, Biology, Politics, and Promise of the American Prairie*. New York: Penguin, 1995.

Martinez, David. *Life of the Indigenous Mind: Vine Deloria Jr. and the Birth of the Red Power Movement*. Lincoln: University of Nebraska Press, 2019.

Matthews, Washington. "The Earth Lodge in Art." *American Anthropologist* 4 (1902): 1–12.

——. *Ethnography and Philology of the Hidatsa Indians*. Washington, DC: Government Printing Office, 1877.

Matzko, John Austin. *Reconstructing Fort Union*. Lincoln: University of Nebraska Press, 2001.

McKenzie-Jones, Paul. *Clyde Warrior: Tradition, Community, and Red Power*. Norman: University of Oklahoma Press, 2015.

——. "Evolving Voices of Dissent: The Workshops on American Indian Affairs, 1956–1972." *American Indian Quarterly* 38, no. 2 (2014): 207–36.

——. "'We are among the poor, the powerless, the inexperienced and the inarticulate': Clyde Warrior's Campaign for a 'Greater Indian America.'" *American Indian Quarterly* 34, no. 2 (2010): 224–57.

McLaughlin, Castle. "Nation, Tribe, and Class: The Dynamics of Agrarian Transformation on the Fort Berthold Reservation." *American Indian Culture and Research Journal* 22, no. 3 (1998): 101–38.

——. "The Politics of Agricultural Decline on the Fort Berthold Indian Reservation, North Dakota." *Culture and Agriculture* 12, no. 44 (1992): 20–22.

McMillen, Christian. *Making Indian Law: The Hualapai Land Case and the Birth of Ethnohistory*. New Haven, CT: Yale University Press, 2007.

McNickle, D'Arcy. Introduction to *Dams and Other Disasters: A Century of the Army Corps of Engineers in Civil Works*, by Arthur E. Morgan. Boston: P. Sargent, 1971.

Means, Russell. *Where White Men Fear to Tread: The Autobiography of Russell Means*. New York: St. Martin Griffin, 1995.

Mekeel, H. Scudder. "Appraisal of the Indian Reorganization Act." *American Anthropologist* 46, no. 2 (April–June 1944): 209–17.

Meyer, Melissa. *The White Earth Tragedy: Ethnicity and Dispossession at a Minnesota Anishinaabe Reservation, 1889–1920.* Lincoln: University of Nebraska Press, 1994.

Meyer, Roy. *The Village Indians of the Upper Missouri: The Mandans, Hidatsas, and Arikaras.* Lincoln: University of Nebraska Press, 1977.

Mintz, Sidney W., and Christine M. Du Bois. "The Anthropology of Food and Eating." *Annual Review of Anthropology* 31 (2002): 99–119.

Morgan, Mindy. "Constructions and Contestations of the Authoritative Voice: Native American Communities and the Federal Writers' Project, 1935–41." *American Indian Quarterly* 29, nos. 1 and 2 (Winter/Spring 2005): 56–83.

Moreton-Robinson, Aileen. *The White Possessive: Property, Power, and Indigenous Sovereignty.* Minneapolis: University of Minnesota Press, 2015.

Needham, Andrew. *Power Lines: Phoenix and the Making of the Modern Southwest.* Princeton, NJ: Princeton University Press, 2014.

Nelson, Scott G. *Sovereignty and the Limits of the Liberal Imagination.* New York: Routledge, 2010.

Nesper, Larry. *The Walleye War: The Struggle for Ojibwe Spearfishing and Treaty Rights.* Lincoln: University of Nebraska Press, 2002.

Newman, Marshall. "The Blond Mandan: A Critical Review of an Old Problem." *Southwestern Journal of Anthropology* 6, no. 3 (Autumn 1950): 255–72.

Norcini, Marilyn. "The Political Process of Factionalism and Self-Governance at Santa Clara Pueblo, New Mexico." *Proceedings of the American Philosophical Society* 149, no. 4 (December 2005): 544–90.

Ojala, Carl-Gösta, and Jonas Monié Nordin. "Mapping Land and People in the North: Early Modern Colonial Expansion, Exploitation, and Knowledge." *Scandinavian Studies* 91, no. 12 (2019): 98–133.

Osburn, Katherine M. B. "'In a name of justice and fairness': The Mississippi Choctaw Indian Federation versus the BIA, 1934." In *Beyond Red Power: American Indian Politics and Activism Since 1900*, edited by Daniel Cobb and Loretta Fowler, 109–25. Santa Fe: School for Advanced Research Press, 2007.

Parker, Angela. "Photographing the Places of Citizenship: The 1922 Crow Industrial Survey." *Native American and Indigenous Studies* 2, no. 2 (2015): 57–86.

Parman, Donald. "The Indian and the Civilian Conservation Corps." *Pacific Historical Review* 40, no. 1 (February 1971): 39–56.

———. *Indians and the American West in the Twentieth Century.* Bloomington: Indiana University Press, 1994.

———. *The Navajo and the New Deal.* New Haven, CT: Yale University Press, 1976.

Patai, Daphne. "U.S. Academics and Third World Women: Is Ethical Research Possible?" In *Women's Words: The Feminist Practice of Oral History*, edited by Sherna Berger Gluck and Daphne Patai. New York: Routledge, 1991.

Pauls, Elizabeth P. "The Place of Space: Architecture, Landscape, and Social Life." In *Historical Archaeology*, edited by Martin Hall and Stephen Silliman. Malden, MA: Blackwell Publishing, 2006.

Peters, Virginia Bergman. *Women of the Earth Lodges: Tribal Life on the Plains.* Norman: University of Oklahoma Press, 2000.

Phillips, Sarah. *This Land, This Nation: Conservation, Rural America, and the New Deal*. New York: Cambridge University Press, 2007.

Philp, Kenneth. "Termination: A Legacy of the Indian New Deal." *Western Historical Quarterly* 14 (April 1983): 165–80.

Piasta, Urszula. "Seneca Resistance: Surviving the Kinzua Dam." In *American Indians and Popular Culture*, edited by Elizabeth DeLaney Hoffman. Santa Barbara: Praeger, 2012.

Pierce, J., D. G. Martin, and J. T Murphy. "Relational Place-Making: The Networked Politics of Place." *Transactions of the Institute of British Geographers* 36 (2011): 54–70.

Potter, Tracy. *Sheheke: Mandan Indian Diplomat—The Story of White Coyote, Thomas Jefferson, and Lewis and Clark*. Helena, MT: Farcountry Press, 2003.

Powers, Ramon, and James Leiker. "Cholera among the Plains Indians: Perceptions, Causes, Consequences." *Western Historical Quarterly* 29, no. 3 (Fall 1998): 317–40.

Prucha, Francis Paul. *American Indian Treaties: The History of a Political Anomaly*. Berkeley: University of California Press, 1994.

———. *The Great Father: The United States Government and the American Indians*. Lincoln: University of Nebraska Press, 1995.

Pruecel, Robert, and Regis Pecos. "Place: Cochiti Pueblo, Core Values, and Authorized Heritage Discourse." In *Heritage Keywords*, edited by Kathryn Lafrenz Samuels and Trinidad Rico. Boulder: University Press of Colorado, 2015.

Rabinow, Paul. "Anthropological Observation and Self-Formation." In *Subjectivity: Ethnographic Investigations*, edited by Joao Biehl, Byron Good, and Arthur Kleinman, 108–9. Berkeley: University of California Press, 2007.

Reifel, Ben. "The Problem of Relocating Families on the Fort Berthold Indian Reservation." *Journal of Farm Economics* 32 (November 1950): 644–46.

Reisner, Marc. *Cadillac Desert: The American West and Its Disappearing Water*. New York: Viking, 1986.

Renato, Rosaldo, and William Flores. "Identity, Conflict and Evolving Latino Communities: Cultural Citizenship in San Jose." In *Latino Cultural Citizenship: Claiming Identity, Space, and Rights*, edited by William Flores and Rina Benmayor. Boston: Beacon Press, 1997.

Ridgeway, Marian. *The Missouri Basin's Pick-Sloan Plan*. Urbana: University of Illinois Press, 1955.

Rietz, Robert. "Leadership, Initiative, and Economic Progress on an American Indian Reservation." *Economic Development and Cultural Change* 2, no. 1 (April 1953): 60–70.

Rivas-Rodríguez, Maggie, and B. V. Olguín, eds. *Latina/os and World War II: Mobility, Agency, and Ideology*. Austin: University of Texas Press, 2014.

Roach, Joseph. *Cities of the Dead: Circum-Atlantic Performance*. New York: Columbia University Press, 1996.

Rose-Redwood, Reuben, Natchee Blu Barnd, Annita Hetoevėhotohke'E Lucchesi, Sharon Dias, and Wil Patrick. "Decolonizing the Map: Recentering Indigenous Mappings." *Cartographica* 55, no. 3 (2020): 151–62.

Rosier, Paul C. "Dam Building and Treaty Breaking: The Kinzua Dam Controversy, 1936–1958." *Pennsylvania Magazine of History and Biography* 119, no. 4 (October 1995): 345–68.

———. *Serving Their Country: American Indian Politics and Patriotism in the Twentieth Century.* Cambridge, MA: Harvard University Press, 2009.

———. "'They Are Ancestral Homelands': Race, Place, and Politics in Cold War Native America, 1945–1961." *Journal of American History* 92 (2006): 1300–26.

Ruin, Hans. "Housing Spirits: The Grave as an Exemplary Site of Memory." In *Routledge International Handbook of Memory Studies,* edited by Anna Lisa Tota and Trever Hagen, 131–40. New York: Routledge, 2015.

Rusco, Elmer. *A Fateful Time: The Background and Legislative History of the Indian Reorganization Act.* Las Vegas: University of Nevada Press, 2000.

Russell, Brian. "Flooded Lifeways: A Study of the Garrison Dam and Its Environmental Impact upon the Three Affiliated Tribes of the Fort Berthold Indian Reservation." Master's thesis, University of North Dakota, 2000.

Russell, Brian, and D. Jerome Tweton. *Promise of Water: The Legacy of Pick-Sloan and the Irrigation of North Dakota.* Bismarck: North Dakota Humanities Council, 2002.

Sacagawea Project Board. *Our Story of Eagle Woman, Sacagawea: They Got It Wrong.* Orange, CA: Paragon Agency, 2021.

Sack, Robert. *Human Territoriality: Its Theory and History.* Cambridge: Cambridge University Press, 1986.

Sanchez, George J. *Becoming Mexican American: Ethnicity, Culture, and Identity in Chicano Los Angeles, 1900–1945.* New York: Oxford University Press, 1993.

Sandstrom, Tessa. "A Re-Emerging History: History of the Four Bears Bridge and the Lost Communities of North Dakota." Master's thesis, University of North Dakota, 2006.

Sassen, Saskia. *Globalization and Its Discontents: Essays on the New Mobility of People and Money.* New York: New Press, 1998.

Schmittou, Douglas, and Michael Logan. "Fluidity of Meaning: Flag Imagery in Plains Indian Art." *American Indian Quarterly* 26 (2002): 559–604.

Schrijer, Nico. *Sovereignty over Natural Resources: Balancing Rights and Duties.* Cambridge: Cambridge University Press, 1997.

Schulman, Bruce. *From Cotton Belt to Sunbelt: Federal Policy, Economic Development, and the Transformation of the South, 1938–1980.* Durham, NC: Duke University Press, 1994.

Scott, James. *Seeing like a State: How Certain Schemes to Improve the Human Condition Have Failed.* New Haven, CT: Yale University Press, 1999.

Seamon, David. *Life Takes Place: Phenomenology, Lifeworlds, and Place Making.* New York: Routledge, 2018.

Sekula, Allan. "The Body and the Archive." In *The Contest of Meaning: Critical Histories of Photography,* edited by Richard Bolton, 350–61. Cambridge, MA: MIT Press, 1989.

———. "Reading an Archive: Photography between Labor and Capital." In *The Photography Reader,* edited by Liz Wells, 359–60. New York: Routledge, 2003.

Shah, Nyan. *Contagious Divides: Epidemics and Race in San Francisco's Chinatown.* Berkeley: University of California Press, 2001.

Shama, Simon. *Landscape and Memory.* New York: Vintage, 1996.

Sheftel, Anna, and Stacey Zembrzycki. "Who's Afraid of Oral History? Fifty Years of Debates and Anxiety About Ethics." *Oral History Review* 43, no. 2 (2019): 338–66.

Sherow, James E. *The Grasslands of the United States: An Environmental History*. Denver: ABC-CLIO, 2007.
Short, John Rennie. *Cartographic Encounters: Indigenous Peoples and the Exploration of the New World*. London: Reaktion, 2009.
Shuman, Amy. *Other People's Stories: Entitlement Claims and the Critique of Empathy*. Urbana: University of Illinois Press, 2005.
Smelser, Neil J., and Paul B. Baltes, eds. *International Encyclopedia of the Social and Behavioral Sciences*. Oxford: Elsevier, 2001.
Smith, Andrea. "U.S. Empire and the War against Native Sovereignty." In *Conquest: Sexual Violence and American Indian Genocide*, 177–92. Cambridge, MA: South End Press, 2005.
Smith, George Hubert. *Like-A-Fishhook Village and Fort Berthold, Garrison Reservoir, North Dakota*. Anthropological Papers no. 2. Washington, DC: US Department of the Interior, National Park Service, 1972.
Smith, Joshua. "The Political Thought of Sol Tax: The Principles of Non-Assimilation and Self-Government in Action Anthropology." *Histories of Anthropology Annual* 6, no. 1 (2010): 129–70.
Smith, Paul Chaat, and Robert Warrior. *Like a Hurricane: The Indian Movement from Alcatraz to Wounded Knee*. New York: New Press, 1996.
Sniffen, Matthew K., ed. "Navajo 'Self-Government.'" *Indian Truth* 14, no. 5 (May 1937).
Stange, Maren. "The Pittsburgh Survey: Lewis Hine and the Establishment of the Documentary Style." In *Symbols of Ideal Life: Social Documentary Photography in America, 1890–1950*, 47–87. New York: Cambridge University Press, 1992.
Tagg, John. *The Burden of Representation: Essays on Photographies and Histories*. Amherst: University of Massachusetts Press, 1988.
Tani, Karen M. "States' Rights, Welfare Rights, and the 'Indian Problem': Negotiating Citizenship and Sovereignty, 1935–1954." *Law and History Review* 33, no. 1 (2015): 1–40.
Thiessen, Thomas D., W. Raymond Wood, and A. Wesley Jones. "The Sitting Rabbit 1907 Map of the Missouri River in North Dakota." *Plains Anthropologist* 24 (1979): 145–67.
Trennert, Robert. "Educating Indian Girls at Nonreservation Boarding Schools, 1878–1920." *Western Historical Quarterly* 13 (1982): 271–90.
Trimble, Charles E., Mary Kay Quinlan, and Barbara W. Sommer. *The American Indian Oral History Manual: Making Many Voices Heard*. New York: Routledge, 2016.
Troutman, John. "Citizenship of Dance." In *Beyond Red Power: American Indian Politics and Activism since 1900*, edited by Daniel Cobb and Loretta Fowler, 91–108. Santa Fe: School for Advanced Research Press, 2007.
———. *Indian Blues: American Indians and Politics of Music, 1879–1934*. Norman: University of Oklahoma Press, 2009.
Tuck, Eve, and Rubén A. Gaztambide-Fernández. "Curriculum, Replacement, and Settler Futurity." *Journal of Curriculum Theorizing* 29, no. 1 (2013).
Valandra, Edward, and Vine Deloria Jr. *Not without Our Consent: Lakota Resistance to Termination, 1950–1959*. Urbana: University of Illinois Press, 2006.
VanDevelder, Paul. *Coyote Warrior: One Man, Three Tribes, and the Trial That Forged a Nation*. New York: Little, Brown, 2004.

Varsanyi, Monica W. "Interrogating 'Urban Citizenship' vis-à-vis Undocumented Migration." *Citizenship Studies* 10, no. 2 (2006): 229–49.
Vaughn, Stephen L., ed. *Encyclopedia of American Journalism*. New York: Routledge, 2008.
Vigil, Kiara M. *Indigenous Intellectuals: Sovereignty, Citizenship, and the American Imagination, 1880–1930*. Cambridge: Cambridge University Press, 2015.
Vom Hau, Matthias, and Guillermo Wilde. "'We have always lived here': Indigenous Movements, Citizenship and Poverty in Argentina." *Journal of Development Studies* 46, no. 7 (2010): 1283–1303.
Waldram, J. B. *As Long as the Rivers Run: Hydroelectric Development and Native Communities in Western Canada*. Winnipeg: University of Manitoba Press, 1988.
Warhus, Mark. *Another America: Native American Maps and the History of Our Land*. New York: St. Martin's Press, 1997.
Washburn, Wilcomb E. "A Fifty-Year Perspective on the Indian Reorganization Act." *American Anthropologist* 86, no. 2 (June 1984): 279–89.
Wedel, Waldo. *Prehistoric Man on the Great Plains*. Norman: University of Oklahoma Press, 1961.
Weisiger, Marsha. "Gendered Injustice: Navajo Livestock Reduction in the New Deal Era." *Western Historical Quarterly* 38, no. 4 (Winter 2007): 437–55.
Weist, Katherine. "For the Public Good: Native Americans, Hydroelectric Dams, and the Iron Triangle." In *Trusteeship in Change: Toward Tribal Autonomy in Resource Management*, edited by Imre Sutton and Richard L. Clow, 55–72. Boulder: University Press of Colorado, 2001.
Wessel, Thomas. "Agent of Acculturation: Farming on the Northern Plains Reservations, 1880–1910." *Agricultural History* 60, no. 2 (Spring 1986): 233–45.
White, Richard. *It's Your Misfortune and None of My Own: A New History of the American West*. Norman: University of Oklahoma Press, 1993.
——. *Middle Ground: Indians, Empires, and Republics in the Great Lakes Region, 1650–1815*. New York: Cambridge University Press, 1991.
——. "Using the Past: History and Native American Studies." In *Studying Native America: Problems and Prospects*, edited by Russell Thornton, 217–43. Madison: University of Wisconsin Press, 1998.
Wilkins, David. *American Indian Sovereignty and the U.S. Supreme Court: The Masking of Justice*. Austin: University of Texas Press, 1997.
——. *Red Prophet: The Punishing Intellectualism of Vine Deloria, Jr.* Chicago: Fulcrum Publishing, 2018.
Will, George F. "Some Hidatsa and Mandan Tales." *Journal of American Folklore* 25 (1912): 93–94.
Williams, Robert. *The American Indian in Western Legal Thought: The Discourses of Conquest*. New York: Oxford University Press, 1990.
——. *Like a Loaded Weapon: The Rehnquist Court, Indian Rights, and the Legal History of Racism in America*. Minneapolis: University of Minnesota Press, 2005.
Wilson, Angela Cavender (now Waziyatawin). "Grandmother to Granddaughter: Generations of Oral History in a Dakota Family." In *Natives and Academics: Researching and Writing about American Indians*, edited by Devon Mihesuah, 27–36. Lincoln: University of Nebraska Press, 1998.

———. "Power of the Spoken Word: Native Oral Traditions in American Indian History." In *Rethinking American Indian History*, edited by Donald Fixico, 101-16. Albuquerque: University of New Mexico Press, 1997.

———. *Remember This! Dakota Decolonization and the Eli Taylor Narratives*. Lincoln: University of Nebraska Press, 2005.

Wilson, Gilbert. *Agriculture of the Hidatsa Indians: An Indian Interpretation*. Minneapolis: University of Minnesota, 1917.

———. *Buffalo Bird Woman's Garden*. 1917. Reprint, Saint Paul: Minnesota State Historical Society Press, 1987.

———. *Waheenee: An Indian Girl's Story*. New York: American Museum of Natural History, 1921.

Wolfe, Patrick. "After the Frontier: Separation and Absorption in US Indian Policy." *Settler Colonial Studies* 1, no. 1 (2011): 13-51.

———. "Settler Colonialism and the Elimination of the Native." *Journal of Genocide Research* 8, no. 4 (2006): 387-409.

———. *Settler Colonialism and the Transformation of Anthropology: The Politics and Poetics of an Ethnographic Event*. London: Cassell, 1999.

Wood, W. Raymond. *An Interpretation of Mandan Culture History*. Smithsonian Institution, Bureau of American Ethnology Bulletin 198. Washington, DC: Government Printing Office, 1967.

———. *The Origins of the Hidatsa Indians: A Review of Ethnohistorical and Traditional Data*. Lincoln: J&L Reprint Company, 1986.

Wood, W. Raymond, and Thomas D. Thiessen. *Early Fur Trade on the Northern Plains: Canadian Traders among the Mandan and Hidatsa Indians, 1738-1818*. Norman: University of Oklahoma Press, 1985.

Wright, Elizabethada A. "Rhetorical Spaces in Memorial Places: The Cemetery as a Rhetorical Memory Place/Space." *Rhetoric Society Quarterly* 35, no. 4 (2005): 51-81.

Other Sources

Bureau of Indian Affairs. "United Scholarship Service Gets Carnegie Grant." BIA Press Release, May 3, 1967.

Cambridge, Charles. Follow-up notes to oral history interview and Epilogue. February 23, 2024.

Case, Ralph Hoyt. *Fort Berthold Dam Site v. the Garrison Dam Site: Statement of Fact and Law*. N.p., 1947.

Davies, Bruce. *Memories of Tillie*. Self-published, March 2018.

Fort Berthold Indian Defense Association. *Indian Tribes Fight Eviction*. Elbowoods, ND: The Association, 1946.

Haaland v. Brackeen, 599 U.S. ___ (2023).

Harris, Leo. *Water is Coming: Souvenir Garrison Dam Project*. Fargo, ND: Forum Publishing Company, 1949.

Hudson, Marilyn. "A Bridge Called Four Bears." New Town, ND: self-published, 1998.

Mancari v. Morton, 359 F. Supp. 585 (D.N.M. 1973).

Morton v. Mancari, 417 U.S. 535 (1974).

National Endowment for the Humanities. *History of the Upper Great Plains as Recorded by the Participating American Indian Tribes from 1850 to the Present: A Suggested Approach to Showing on Television the Historical Background for Vital Contemporary Plains Indian Issues.* 1970–.

Neal, Bigelow. *The Valley of the Damned.* Garrison, ND: Independent Publishing, 1949.

North Dakota. *Garrison Dam and Reservoir Project.* Bismarck: North Dakota State Department of Public Instruction, 1947.

Peinado, J. Carlos. *Waterbuster.* DVD. Brave Boat Productions, 2006.

Peter Kiewit Sons' Co. *Miracle on the Missouri.* Riverdale, ND: Morrison-Knudsen Company, 1954.

Powell, Malea. Seminar Discussion. Group discussion. Committee on Institutional Cooperation-American Indian Studies Seminar. Michigan State University, Lansing, MI, June 22, 2009.

Presidential Memorandum of November 30, 2022. Memorandum on Uniform Standards for Tribal Consultation. Retrieved from https://www.whitehouse.gov/briefing-room/presidential-actions/2022/11/30/memorandum-on-uniform-standards-for-tribal-consultation/ on July 24, 2023.

Robinson, Sheila. *Taming the Big Muddy: The Story of Garrison Dam.* Garrison, ND: BHG, 1997.

Santa Clara Pueblo v. Martinez, 436 U.S. 49 (1978).

Tahdooahnippah et al. v. Thimmig et al., 481 F.2d 438 (10th Cir. 1973).

US Congress. Indian Child Welfare Act. 1978. Public Law 95-608, 25 USC.

US Geological Survey. Biological Resources Division. "Missouri River Commission Maps." https://www.cerc.usgs.gov/data/1894maps/.

US Senate. *Hearings Before the US Senate Committee on Indian Affairs.* 79th Cong., 1st Sess., October 9, 1945. Washington, DC: Government Printing Office, 1945.

———. *Hearings S. 2480 and S. 2663 Before the Select Committee on Indian Affairs.* 98th Cong., 2d Sess, June 21, 1984. Washington, DC: Government Printing Office, 1984.

Index

1870 executive order, 30, 34, 37
1880 executive order, 31, 34, 37, 219n16

Aberdeen, S.Dak., 151, 158, 231n20
A Better Chance (ABC) program, 188
Adams, Hank, 180–81, 184, 191, 196, 232n1
Agricultural Adjustment Administration (AAA), 92
Agricultural Conservation Program, 92
Alcatraz Island, 198–99
American Friends Service Committee, 185, 187, 192
American Fur Company (Pierre Chouteau, Jr., & Co. after 1838), 23, 26
American Indian Chicago Conference, 128
American Indian Federation, 68, 70
American Indian Graduate Center (AIGC), 208, 214n14
American Indian Movement (AIM), 200–201, 206
American Legion, 68, 70
Anderson, Millie, 61–62, 221n39
Andover, Mass., 189
Antelope Society, 153, 166
Antelope Woman, 161
Antioch College, 208
Arapahos, 20
Arikaras, 9, 17–20, 25–26, 29, 31, 34, 133, 137, 216n46
Army Corps of Engineers, 60, 104, 109–11, 113, 116, 119, 122, 129, 130, 144, 150–51, 161, 163, 169

Assiniboines, 20
Assiniboine Woman, 35, 41
Association on American Indian Affairs, 186–87, 191
Atkins, Edna, 131–32, 134, 138
Atkins, Philip, 59, 65, 147
Atkins, Roy, 95
Awáati (Missouri River), 1, 16–17, 19, 22–24, 34, 37–38, 40, 43, 104, 110, 153, 168
Azure, Pete, 206

Babby, Lyman, 202
Bad Gun, 28
Baker-Benally, Patricia, 182, 200–204, 207, 211
Baker, Billy, 98
Baker, Clyde, 76, 157, 166, 170
Baker, Frederick, 81, 88–89, 205
Baker, Gail, 79, 84–85, 167, 226n46
Baker, James, 59
Baker, John, 95
Baker, Louis, Jr., 95, 217n1, 233n3
Baker, Percy, 233n3
Baker, Paige, Sr., 152
Baker, Theodore, 95
Bakken oil field, 176
Basso, Keith, 12
Bateman, Earl, 107, 118
Bateman, Guy, 95
Bateman, Paul, 95
Beane, Sydney, 205
Bears Arm, 43, 56
Bearstail, Lyda (Black Bear), 74–75, 77–78, 80, 83, 87, 100, 162, 223n4

Beauchamp, Peter, 58–60, 132, 136, 155, 173
Beaver Creek, 37, 54, 59, 65–66, 71, 114, 142, 156, 162
Beitzel, C. H., 118
Bell, Joseph, 96
Bell, William, 157
Bellecourt, Clyde, 201
Bellecourt, Vernon, 201
Benson, Ben, 59
Benson, Edwin, 85, 97, 115
Benson, Linda, 202, 204
Bernal, Lynda, 201–2, 204, 207
Beyer, William R., 45, 51, 66–67, 69–70
Big Bend Dam, 227n7
Bird Bear, Duane, 193, 202, 204
Birdsbill, Lawrence, 74
Bismarck, N.Dak., 28, 109, 217, 222n52
Blackfeet, 20, 58, 182, 202
Black Hawk, 44
Black Hills, 20
Blake, Finley, 78
Bodin, Jean, 3
Boulder, Colo., 186
Boyer, Madelyn, 202, 204
Brady, Florence Gillette, 140
Bridges, Al, 196
Bronson, Ruth, 129
Brophy, William, 116
Brown, Cecelia, 38–39
Brown, Louis, 165
Bruce, Louis R. 202–4, 207
Bruner, Edward, 128, 143, 149, 157, 164
Bruyneel, Kevin, 46
Buckanaga, Celine, 205
Buckanaga, Harry, 202, 204
Buckanaga, Rick, 202, 204
Bucks County, Pa., 45
Buffalohead, W. Roger, 205
Burdick, Quentin, 145, 148
Bureau of Indian Affairs (BIA), 5–6, 135, 196–202, 203–4, 206–8, 218n13, 229n35; and Aberdeen, 151, 158; and activism, 218n13; and administrative battles, 113, 171; Adult Vocational Training Program, 203; agency buildings, 121; and agriculturalists, 157; and anthropologists, 144, 150; and border towns, 181; and boarding schools, 189; Circular 1665, 80; critics of, 48–49, 66, 79, 178, 191, 202, 206; employees, 5–6, 48, 144, 159–60; and Fort Berthold, 57, 64, 68, 71, 91–92, 107, 118, 140; and Interior Department, 127; and landownership, 86; and Missouri River Basin, 158; and Native Americans, 49, 55, 79, 148, 167, 178, 206; and North Dakota, 66, 145; and racism, 146, 181; and reclamation, 156; and relocation policy, 161; Relocation Program, 168, 203; reporting of, 186; and reservations, 167, 174;and Robert Reitz, 128, 164; and Sol Tax, 128; and staff, 123, 158, 168, 178, 196; and surveys, 86; and territorial control, 10; and Three Tribes, 154; and white citizens, 153, 196
Burke Act (1906), 46, 49

Cagáagawia (Sacagawea, Bird Woman), 23, 61, 221n40
Cambridge, Charles, 185–88, 190, 193–95, 205–6, 233n12, 235n48
Case, Rev. Harold, 31, 39, 44, 128, 142, 217n58, 217n1 (chap. 2), 220n31
Case, Ralph Hoyt, 107, 118, 121–22, 125
Casey, Edward, 12
Charging, Albert, 95
Charging, George, 107
Charging Eagle, 37, 42, 44, 107, 122–23, 131, 138, 163
Charlo, Victor, 196
Chase, Emmarine, 24, 38–39
Chase, Mrs. Frank, 150
Cherokees, 129, 185, 202, 234n21
Cheyennes, 20, 181
Chicago, Ill., 92, 167, 193, 199
Chippewas, 207, 234n21
Civilian Conservation Corps (CCC), 48, 63, 69, 131
Civil Rights Act of 1964, 205
Coalition of American Indian Citizens, 207

Cobb, Daniel, 1992, 197
Coffey, Pete, Sr., 79, 98–99, 226n41
Cohen, Felix, 73, 118, 137
Cohen, Lizabeth, 89
Collier, John, 48–50, 55–56, 64, 67–69, 92–94, 218n13
Colorado: Boulder, 186; and Department of Natural Resources, 205; Littleton, 198; and Native students, 234n21
Colorado Springs, Colo., 186–87
Congregationalist Church, 15, 31, 39, 44, 128, 135, 140, 185–87; and Board of Home Missions, 186
Conkling, James, 95
Cook, Lee, 205, 207
Coolidge, Calvin, 46
Corn Mother, 1
Court of Claims, 37, 69
Crees, 20, 205
Cross, Martin, 116–19, 122–27, 143–46, 148, 151, 166, 168, 174, 176
Cross, Phyllis, 166, 170
Cross, Raymond, 175, 209
Crossland, George, 206
Crow Flies High, 44, 65, 69, 123, 162, 165, 198, 220n27
Crow Flies High, George, 195, 198
Crow Flies High, Rosie, 165, 195, 196, 198
Crows, 20, 25, 58, 235n45
Crows Heart, 115
Custer, George Armstrong, 132, 136 196, 216n38
Cuthair, Brenda, 204

Dakotas/Sioux, 18, 61, 157, 202, 205, 207, 216n41, 234n21
Dancing Bear Creek, 27
Dancing Bull, Robert, 59, 222n51
Dartmouth College, 188
Daughters of Indian Uprisings,1492 Chapter, 191
Davies, Bruce, 184–85, 188–91, 199–202, 204–5, 210–12
Dawes Act (1887), 45–46, 48, 49, 73, 145, 221n43
Dawson, Anna, 2
Dean, William (Arikara), 147

Deane, Kenneth, 96
Deloria, Phillip Sam, 205
Deloria, Vine, Jr., 184, 189, 196, 233n12, 234n19
Deloria, Vine, Sr., 188
Dennison DeGroat, Eloise, 205
Denver, Colo., 167, 189, 193, 194, 195, 198, 200–201, 205, 207–8, 209
Denver Post, 188, 191–92, 201–4
Desert Land Act (1877), 111
Devils Lake, 60, 221n36
Diné, 202, 205–6
Drags Wolf, 59, 66–67, 162, 217n1, 222nn51–52
Dreadfulwater, Andrew, 196
Driver, James, 118–19, 130, 132, 138
Duckett, Mrs., 156
Dumont, Bob, 191, 194–96, 204–5

Eastman, Charles, 46
Ebeneezer Baptist Church, 211
Edna, Pearl, 165
Elbowoods, N.Dak., 27, 31, 37, 49, 54, 59, 66, 71, 91, 93, 107, 115, 121, 129, 131, 136, 142, 156, 163, 164, 170, 216n46, 217n54
Elbowoods Agency Council Hall, 120
Elbowoods Bridge Association, 42, 44
Elbowoods School, 70
Elk, Mary, 165–66
Ellis Island, N.Y., 199
Emerson, Gloria, 205
Enemy Hawk, 34
Episcopal Church, 187–88
Equal Employment Opportunity Act (1972), 205
Estes Park, Colo., 186
Evans, Wayne, 205
Everett, Clair, 59
Ex parte Crow Dog, 73

Farm Defense Program, 92
Farm Security Administration (FSA), 48
Federal Power Commission, 113
Federal Theater, Writers, and Arts projects, 48

Federal Housing Administration (FHA), 198
Federal Water Power Act (1920), 112
Felix, Louis, Jr., 95
First Creator, 1, 15
Flandreau Indian School, 109, 189
Flood Control Act (1936), 110
Flood Control Act (1944), 111, 116
Fort Berthold Action Anthropology Project, 128
Fort Berthold Americans, Inc., 69–70, 116
Fort Berthold Bulletin, 70–71, 90
Fort Berthold Indian Reservation (N.Dak.), 1, 8, 14, 30, 36, 42, 91, 106–7, 163, 169
Fort Berthold Reservation Civic Organization, 43
Fort Berthold Tribal Business Council, 55–56, 57–61, 67–68, 116, 120, 143, 146–47, 152
Fort Berthold Tribal Council, 56, 59, 73, 93, 113
Fort Berthold USO, 74–75, 83
Fort Clark, 25
Fort Laramie, Wyo., 2, 31, 107, 131
Fort Laramie Treaty (1851), 2, 29, 30, 138
Fort Lawton, Wash., 199
Fort Lewis College, 202
Fort Randall Dam, 227n7
Foucault, Michel, 4
Four Bears, 119
Four Bears Bridge, 44–45, 163, 217n1; dedication of, 42–43
Fox, Charles, 59, 67, 222nn51–52
Fox, Martin, 118, 122, 125, 138
Fox, Wanda, 210
Frazier, Lynn, 56

Garrison Reservoir, 113, 131–32, 146, 159, 162; Garrison Dam, 3
Gavins Point Dam, 227n7
Geboe, Charles, 205
General Allotment Act. *See* Dawes Act (1887)
Gill, Gerald, 204
Gill, John, 202, 204

Gillette, George, 2, 59, 106–8, 114, 119–20, 122–23, 129, 140
Good Bear, 33
Good Bear, Lawrence, 96
Goodbird, Ben, 59
Goodbird, Donald, 95
Goodbird, Ellen Blackhawk, 225n39
Goodbird, Emery, Sr., 225–6n39
Grandfather Snake, 43, 85
Grass, Martha, 196–7
Grease Creek, 15
Great Plains, 1, 16–17, 20, 33, 42, 111, 114
Great Plains Drought Area Committee (1936), 111–12
Great Northern Railroad, 22
Greenwich Village, N.Y., 202, 207
Grinnell, Allison, 42–43
Grinnell, David, 96
Grinnell, George, 59, 155
Grinnell, Mattie, 195
Gros Ventres, 20, 51, 149, 155
Guts and Tripe, 207–8

Hall, James, 107, 149
Hall, Rev. Charles, 15, 28
Hall, Susan Webb, 31
Hanley, Benjamin, 205
Harlem, Mont., 193
Haskell Indian Nations University, 109, 114, 185
Havre, Mont., 196
Hawk, Alfred John, 34
H.C.R. 108, 126
Heart, Ben, 148
Heart, Frank, 65, 173
Hidatsa Nuxpike shrine, 39
Hidatsas, 149, 157, 202, 235n45; and agriculture, 10, 17, 32; and Bird Woman, 61; and cultural values, 184; and Elbowoods, 54; and language, 12, 44, 51, 62, 77, 80, 96, 101, 114, 127, 139, 167, 182, 185, 226n46; and Mandan, 18–27, 30–34, 38, 42–43, 51, 57, 64–65, 130, 189, 193, 197, 210, 233n3; and Shell Creek, 37; and students, 234n21; and territories, 14–16, 29–30; and Three Tribes,